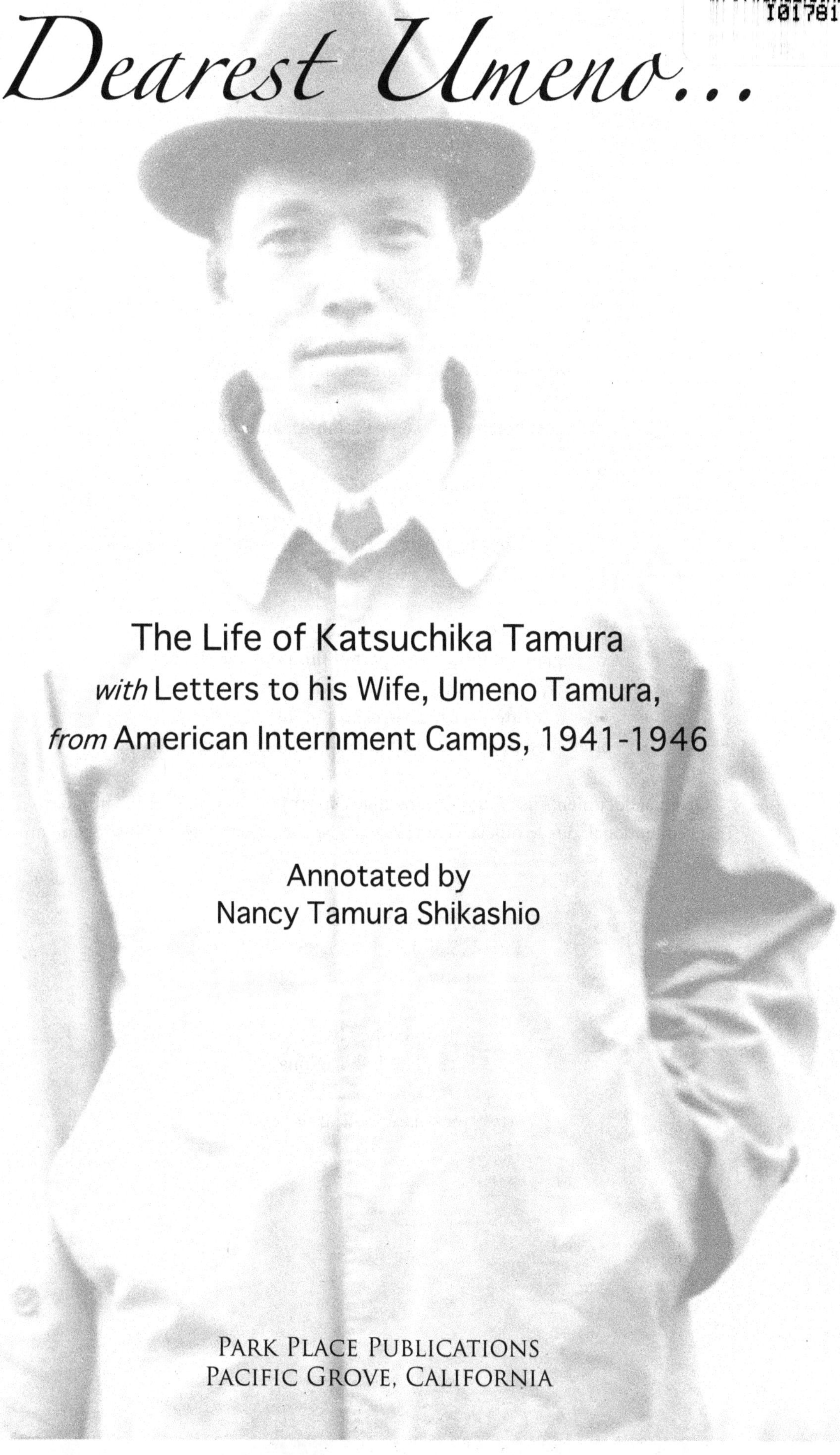

Dearest Umeno...

The Life of Katsuchika Tamura
with Letters to his Wife, Umeno Tamura,
from American Internment Camps, 1941-1946

Annotated by
Nancy Tamura Shikashio

PARK PLACE PUBLICATIONS
PACIFIC GROVE, CALIFORNIA

Dearest Umeno...
The Life of Katsuchika Tamura
with Letters to his Wife, Umeno Tamura,
from American Internment Camps, 1941-1946

Annotated by Nancy (Tamura) Shikashio

ISBN 978-1-935530-33-6

Original documents used in this book may appear faded, cut-off, or incomplete.
This is intentional, due to official censorship or the condition or age of the documents.

Printed in U.S.A.
First U.S. Edition: December 2010
Second Printing: July 2014

Published by
Park Place Publications
Pacific Grove, California
www.parkplacepublications.com

Dedication

This book is dedicated to my father and mother and to all those who were interned and survived to reinstate Japanese pride in America.

Acknowledgments

I would like to thank Shizuko Teshima Kamimoto, Umeno's sister-in-law, a Nisei, who, during their time together in the camps, translated Katsuchika's English letters into Japanese and read them to Umeno; Umeno dictated her replies in Japanese to Shizuko who wrote them in English for Katsuchika; Rose Ito Tsunekawa, for translating all the letters from Japanese to English; and Rokuryo Horiuchi and his wife, Chitose Horiuchi, of Chiba, Japan for the correct derivation of Katsuchika's name and research on his time in the Imperial Household Agency. Many thanks to my publisher, Patricia Hamilton, for her expertise and guidance.

CONTENTS

Katsuchika's mother, Yoshiko Ishii Tamura.

The Life of Katsuchika Tamura

1895, January 8
Born, third son of Katsusada and Yoshiko Ishii Tamura. Katsuchika was born into a samurai family whose ancestors were vassals of the Kujo family, Imperial court nobles. The Kujo family, originally of Kyoto, moved to Tokyo when the Japanese government relocated its capital there in 1868, as did the Tamura family. Katsuchika's father worked for the Japanese government and the family lived in the exclusive Aoyama area of Tokyo. Katsuchika attended elementary and private middle schools in Aoyama, then graduated from Meiji University Preparatory School in Tokyo.

1915, January 13 to 1920, March 23
Employed by the Imperial Household Agency. Assigned to the Board of Ceremonies where his duties were to accompany the envoys as an attendant on their official journeys to the various Shinto shrines. (He was probably employed by the Imperial Household Agency because of his family connections to the Kujo Imperial court nobles.)

1920, March 23
Resigned from the Imperial Household Agency.

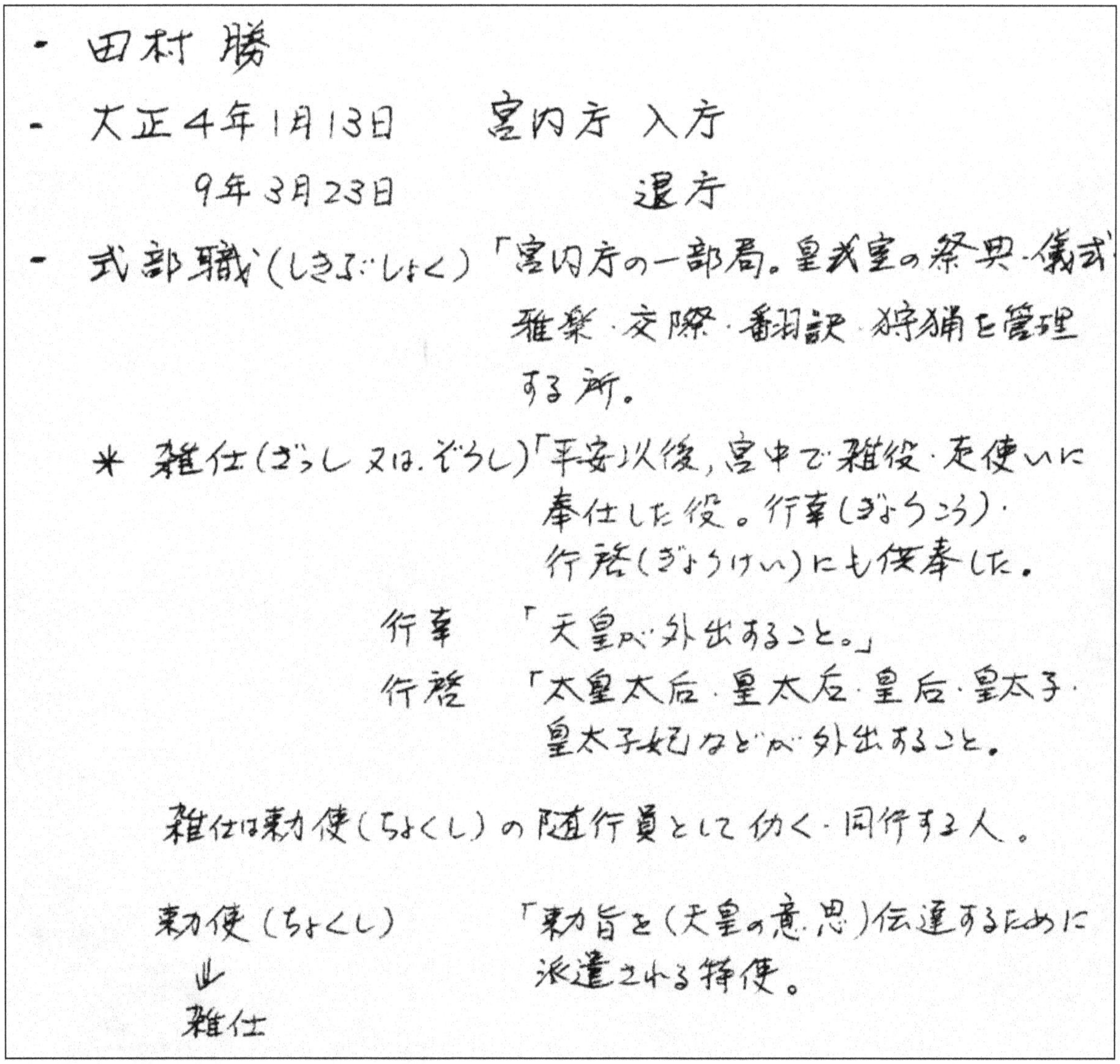
・田村 勝

・大正4年1月13日　宮内庁 入庁
9年3月23日　退庁

・式部職（しきぶしょく）「宮内庁の一部局。皇室の祭典・儀式・雅楽・交際・翻訳・狩猟を管理する所。

＊雑仕（ざっし又は、ぞうし）「平安以後，宮中で雑役・走使いに奉仕した役。行幸（ぎょうこう）・行啓（ぎょうけい）にも供奉した。

行幸　「天皇が外出すること。」

行啓　「太皇太后・皇太后・皇后・皇太子・皇太子妃などが外出すること。

雑仕は勅使（ちょくし）の随行員として働く・同行する人。

勅使（ちょくし）　「勅旨を（天皇の意思）伝達するために派遣される特使。
↓
雑仕

During the time Katsuchika was employed by the Imperial Household Agency, 1915 to 1920.

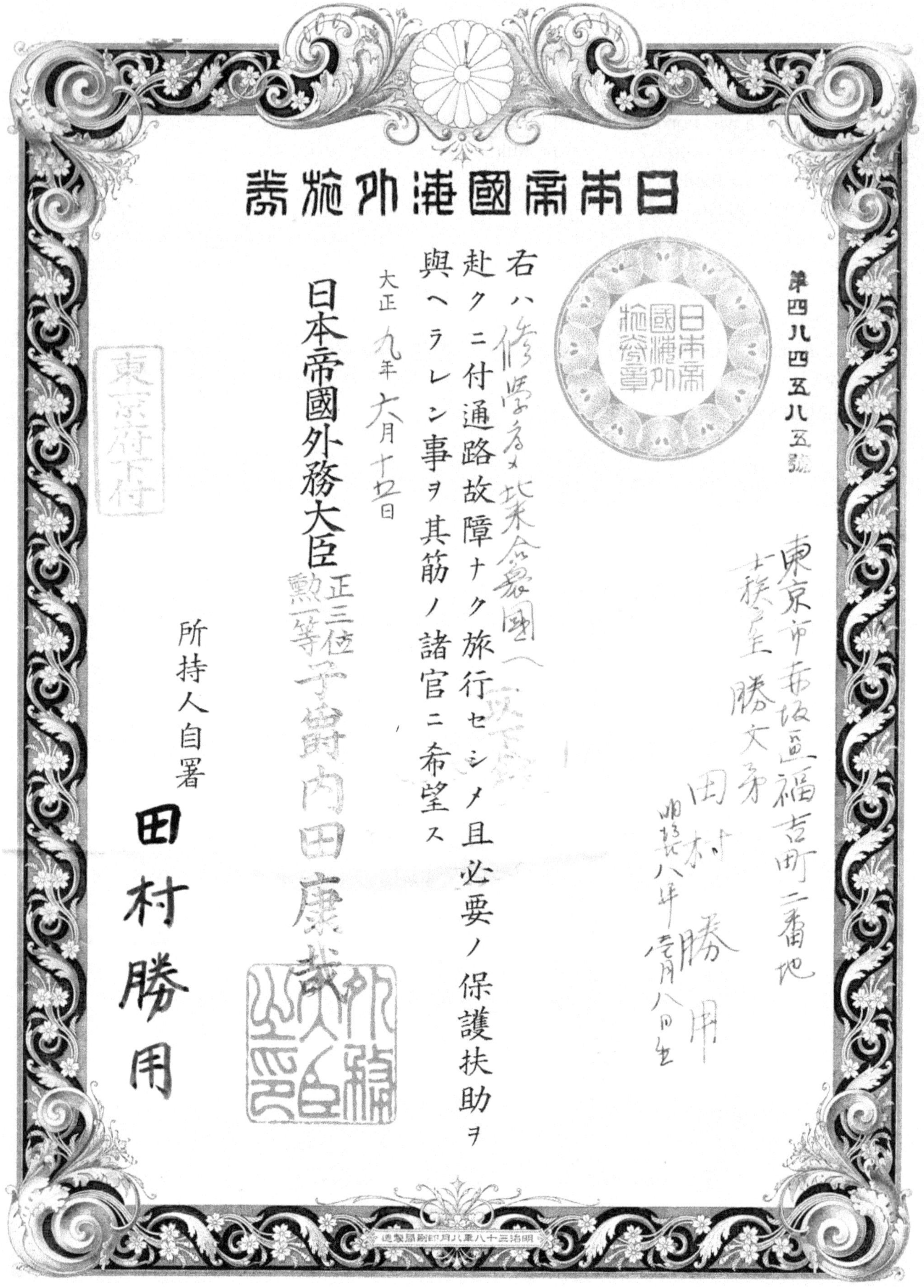

日本帝國海外旅券

第四八四五八五號

日本帝國海外旅券之章

東京市赤坂區福吉町二番地
士族戸主 勝文弟
田村勝用
明治廿八年壹月八日生

右ハ修學ノ為メ北米合衆國ヘ赴クニ付通路故障ナク旅行セシメ且必要ノ保護扶助ヲ與ヘラレン事ヲ其筋ノ諸官ニ希望ス

大正九年六月十四日

日本帝國外務大臣
正三位勲一等子爵内田康哉

外務大臣之印

東京府下付

所持人自署
田村勝用

明治三十八年八月印刷局製造

Tamura, Katsuchika's Japanese Passport, 1920.

（譯文）

該　氏名

任憑旅行無阻如有緊要事即請沿途各官加意照料善爲保佑

TRANSLATION.

IMPERIAL JAPANESE GOVERNMENT

PASSPORT.

No. 484585

Mr. Katsuchika Tamura.
Aged 25 years & 6 months

The competent Authorities and all whom it may concern are requested to allow the above named person proceeding to

The United States of America

to pass freely and without hindrance, and to give said person such protection and assistance as may be required.

The 15th *day of the* 6th *month of the* 9th *year of Taisho (19*20*).*

Viscount Yasuya Uchida.

His Imperial Japanese Majesty's Minister of State for Foreign Affairs.

Signature of the Bearer:

Katsuchika Tamura.

TRADUCTION.

LE GOUVERNEMENT IMPÉRIAL DU JAPON

PASSEPORT.

No. 484585

Les Autorités compétentes sont priées de laisser passer librement la personne ci-dessus mentionnée, allant :

et de lui donner aide et protection en cas de besoin.

Le jour du mois de la année de Taisho (19).

Ministre des Affaires Etrangeres de Sa Majesté l'Empereur du Japon.

Signature du porteur:

1920, June 25
Left Japan to study in the U.S. aboard the *Arabia Maru* and disembarked at Seattle, Washington on August 4. [It is interesting to note that the Japanese passports in those days stated "From a samurai family" by his name. You were either a "shizoku" (samurai family), "heimin" (commoner), or noble/aristocrat.]

1920, August to November, 1933
Worked as a school boy in Colorado and attended primary, middle and high school to learn English. He later attended the University of Colorado (unclear when and if he graduated). Also during this period, he worked as a seasonal farm laborer in the western U.S. He became concerned about his future and looked for a more stable job. Details of this 13-year period are unknown.

1933, December to March, 1934
Returned to Japan and was persuaded by a friend to go to the U.S. again and continue his studies (his friend supported him financially).

Katsuchika and a friend, T. Terada.

1935, June
Graduated from the University of California at Berkeley with a BA in English Literature. It is presumed that he started working for the Japanese Association (Nihonjin-kai) in Stockton as a manager after his graduation from UCB.

Katsuchika Tamura, far left, leaving Yokohama, bound for the United States, 1934.

THE REGENTS OF THE UNIVERSITY OF CALIFORNIA

ON THE NOMINATION OF THE FACULTY OF THE COLLEGE OF LETTERS AND SCIENCE
HAVE CONFERRED UPON

KATSUCHIKA TAMURA

THE DEGREE OF BACHELOR OF ARTS
WITH ALL THE RIGHTS AND PRIVILEGES THERETO PERTAINING

GIVEN AT BERKELEY THE SEAT OF THE UNIVERSITY THIS SIXTEENTH DAY OF MAY
IN THE YEAR NINETEEN HUNDRED AND THIRTY-FIVE

PRESIDENT OF THE UNIVERSITY

GOVERNOR OF CALIFORNIA AND PRESIDENT OF THE REGENTS

DEAN OF THE COLLEGE

Form SS-5
TREASURY DEPARTMENT
INTERNAL REVENUE SERVICE

U. S. SOCIAL SECURITY ACT
APPLICATION FOR ACCOUNT NUMBER

546 14 5641

PRINT NAME

1. Katsu (EMPLOYEE'S FIRST NAME) (MIDDLE NAME) Tamura 568 (LAST NAME)
(MARRIED WOMEN: GIVE MAIDEN FIRST NAME, MAIDEN LAST NAME, AND HUSBAND'S LAST NAME)

2. 140 St Anne St (STREET AND NUMBER) 3. San Francisco (POST OFFICE) California (STATE)

4. American Fruit Growers (BUSINESS NAME OF PRESENT EMPLOYER) Terminus Calif (BUSINESS ADDRESS OF PRESENT EMPLOYER)

6. 37 (AGE AT LAST BIRTHDAY) 7. Jan 8, 1900 (DATE OF BIRTH (MONTH) (DAY) (YEAR)) (SUBJECT TO LATER VERIFICATION) 8. Tokio Japan (PLACE OF BIRTH)

9. Katsusada Tamura (FATHER'S FULL NAME) 10. Yoshi Ishii (MOTHER'S FULL MAIDEN NAME)

11. SEX: MALE X FEMALE ___ (CHECK (✓) WHICH) 12. COLOR: WHITE ___ NEGRO ___ (CHECK (✓) WHICH) OTHER Japanese (SPECIFY)

1-5

13. IF REGISTERED WITH THE U. S. EMPLOYMENT SERVICE, GIVE NUMBER OF REGISTRATION CARD ___

14. IF YOU HAVE PREVIOUSLY FILLED OUT A CARD LIKE THIS, STATE no (PLACE) (DATE)

15. Oct 30, 1937 (DATE SIGNED) 16. Katsu Tamura (EMPLOYEE'S SIGNATURE, AS USUALLY WRITTEN)

DETACH ALONG THIS LINE

STATE OF CALIFORNIA — COUNTY OF SAN JOAQUIN

MARRIAGE LICENSE

These Presents are to Authorize and license any Justice of the Supreme Court, Justice of the District Courts of Appeal, Judge of the Superior Court, Judge of the Municipal Court, Justice of the Peace, Judge of any Police Court, City Recorder, Priest or Minister of the Gospel of any denomination, to solemnize within said County the Marriage of KATSUCHIKA TAMURA native of JAPAN aged 45 years race color Japanese resident of STOCKTON County of SAN JOAQUIN State of CALIFORNIA and UMENO KAMIMOTO native of HAWAII aged 28 years race color Japanese resident of STOCKTON County of SAN JOAQUIN State of CALIFORNIA

Said parties being of sufficient age to be capable of contracting marriage as appears by affidavit of record in my office.

In Witness Whereof, I have hereunto set my hand and affixed the Seal of the Superior Court of said County this 17th day of June A.D. 1940

EUGENE D. GRAHAM
COUNTY CLERK AND EX-OFFICIO CLERK OF THE SUPERIOR COURT IN AND FOR SAN JOAQUIN COUNTY
By Ben Scantlebury Deputy Clerk.

I HEREBY CERTIFY, That on the 20th day of June 1940 that by authority of a license to which this Certificate is attached at Stockton in the County of San Joaquin State of California I, joined in Marriage Katsuchika Tamura and Umeno Kamimoto in the presence of witnesses to wit: [illegible] resident of Stockton in the County of San Joaquin State of California and Ueichi Yamasaki a resident of Stockton in the County of San Joaquin State of California

In Witness Whereof, I have hereunto set my hand this 20th day of June A.D. 19[illegible]

Rev. Y. Ouchi
Signature of party performing ceremony

Minister of Buddhist Church
Official position or denomination of person performing ceremony

Witnesses:
[illegible]
U. Yamasaki

No. 31724

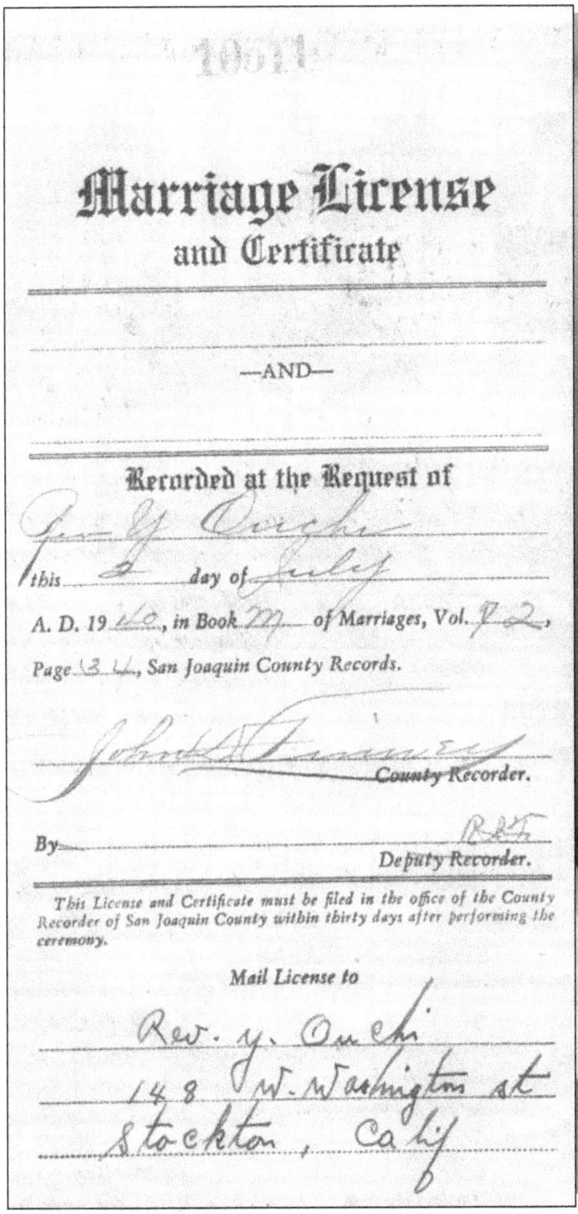

10511

Marriage License
and Certificate

—AND—

Recorded at the Request of

Gen. Y. Ouchi

this 2 day of July

A. D. 1940[?], in Book M of Marriages, Vol. 2,

Page 34, San Joaquin County Records.

John A. Finney
County Recorder.

By R.E.F.
Deputy Recorder.

This License and Certificate must be filed in the office of the County Recorder of San Joaquin County within thirty days after performing the ceremony.

Mail License to

Rev. Y. Ouchi
148 W. Washington st
Stockton, Calif

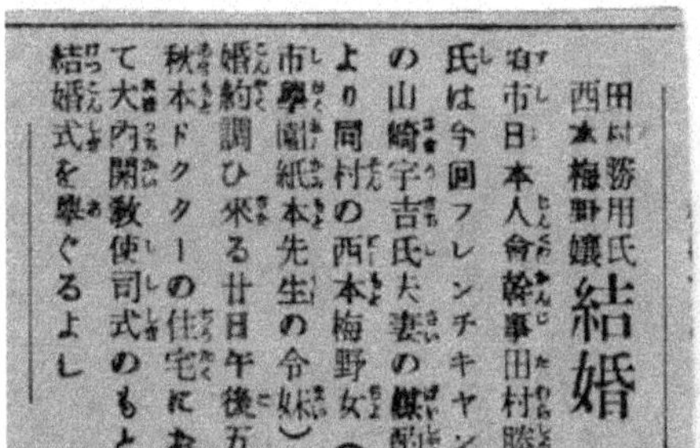

田村勝用氏 西本梅野孃 結婚

須市日本人會幹事田村勝用氏は今回フレンチキャンプの山崎宇吉氏夫妻の媒酌により同村の西本梅野女（須市學園紙本先生の令妹）と婚約調ひ來る廿日午後五時秋本ドクターの住宅において大内開教使司式のもとに結婚式を擧ぐるよし

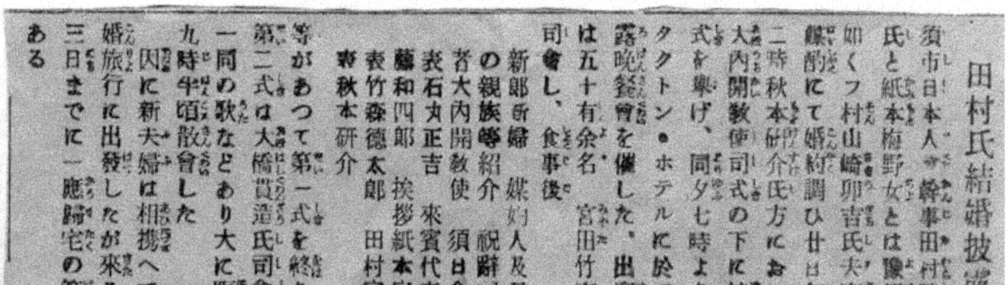

田村氏結婚披露

須市日本人會幹事田村勝用氏と紙本梅野女とは豫報の如くフ村山崎卯吉氏夫妻の媒酌にて婚約調ひ廿日午後二時秋本研介氏方において大内開教使司式の下に結婚式を擧げ、同夕七時よりスタクトン・ホテルに於て披露晩餐會を催した、出席者は五十有余名、宮田竹市氏司會し、食事後

新郎新婦媒妁人及双方の親族等紹介 祝辭司婚者大内開教使 須日會代表石丸正吉 來賓代表須藤和四郎 挨拶紙本家代表竹森德太郎 田村家代表秋本研介

等があつて第一式を終り、第二式は大橋貫造氏司會し一同の歌などあり大に賑ひ九時半頃散會した

因に新夫婦は相携へて新婚旅行に出發したが來る廿三日までに一應歸宅の筈である

1940, June

At age 45, married Umeno Nishimoto (DOB: 10/08/12), a lovely widow 17 years his junior, whose husband passed away in 1935 due to tuberculosis. Umeno had a son, Milton Yokichi (DOB: 11/15/32) and a daughter, Nancy Matsuko Nishimoto (DOB: 03/24/34). Katsuchika Tamura adopted Milton and Nancy and gave them his family name. Umeno had a 32-acre farm in French Camp near Stockton, and Katsuchika continued to work at the Japanese Association in Stockton.

1941, April 8

Son George Hiromu was born to Katsuchika and Umeno Tamura.

10,000 Aliens Prepare to Move by Tomorrow

548 Are Arrested by FBI in Raids Over Week-End in West Coast States

SAN FRANCISCO, Feb. 23 (UP)—More than 10,000 enemy aliens made last-minute preparations today to move from restricted coastal areas while the government drive against potential fifth columnists mushroomed along the coast and reached as far inland as Houston, Tex.

The Federal Bureau of Investigation will enforce the evacuation order before tomorrow's midnight deadline, but it was indicated the round-up and internment of aliens violating the decree will fall to military authorities under terms of a presidential proclamation which placed the West under limited martial law.

ROUND-UP CONTINUES

Agents of the FBI meanwhile continued their round-up of potentially dangerous enemy aliens. They arrested 218 in Northern California in week-end raids, more than 250 in Southern California and more than 100 in Washington and Oregon. Seventy-one were arrested at Houston, Tex.

FBI officers said aliens in custody were pro-Nazi, pro-Fascists and "highly nationalistic" Japanese. They reported some were members of an organization formerly directed by Japanese consulates.

For many, the evacuation order will force aliens only to seek other residences in the same city, although under terms of last week's presidential order even American-born Japanese, Germans and Italians may be removed from coastal states. They may be removed to interior states either to work in harvest fields or to live in remodeled CCC camps.

NO MASS EVACUATIONS

Lt. Gen. John L. DeWitt of the Western Defense Command today informed Representative John J. Tolan (Dem., Calif.), heading a special House committee studying migrant problems, that:

"Instructions under the presidential order have not been given in full yet. The public should not become disturbed.

"There will be no mass evacuations. The job will be done gradually, to take care of individual hardship cases."

About 90 zones in the vicinity of reservoirs, power plants and such strategic areas already have been evacuated by several hundred enemy aliens.

F. R. REPORT ON WAR TONIGHT, 7 O'CLOCK

WASHINGTON, Feb. 23 (AP)—President Roosevelt will report to the American people in plain language tonight on the progress of the titanic struggle which they must fight and how the ebb and flow of battles thousands of miles away affect even the remotest country towns here.

In his radio address at 7 p.m. Pacific war time he also is expected to outline in a general way American efforts to keep the enemy at bay until war production and trained fighting man power reach the proportions that will permit counter-offensives on many world fronts.

(World map on which the reader can follow more accurately the President's speech will be found on Page 21)

WORKS ON SPEECH

Mr. Roosevelt devoted much of his week-end to work on the speech, giving considerable time to analyses of the latest information.

Since the war's start, Japan has swept on from one spectacular triumph to another in the Pacific, until now the enemy has all but overrun the Dutch East Indies and is hammering at the backdoor to Australia.

AXIS SUCCESSES

On top of Japan's Pacific victories, the German submarine fleet has brought ruthless sea war to the coastal waters of the Western Hemisphere, playing havoc with shipping from Canada to South America. Three powerful Nazi warships have run the gauntlet of Dover Strait to sheltered home harbors from which they may sally for future attacks on Atlantic convoys. And grave concern exists lest the remains of the French fleet fall at last into Axis hands.

The battle score sheet of the United States and United Nations can show no such string of heartening successes.

JAPANESE ALIENS JAILED

Federal, city and county officers co-operated in a series of raids in the city and county over the week-end and rounded up 13 Japanese aliens, booking them at the county jail "en route to Federal immigration authorities."

13 Japanese Are Taken in Raid

Some Prominent in Business Circles

The week-end developed an unlucky 13 for that number of Stockton and San Joaquin County Japanese aliens rounded up in a series of raids conducted by federal, city and county officers.

Seized in the raids were several prominent leaders of the local Japanese communities, including officers of the only recently disbanded Stockton Japanese Association.

NINE JAILED SATURDAY

The nine jailed Saturday to add to four arrested earlier in the day, follow:

Seiji Yamagishi, 43, 138 South El Dorado Street.

Shakichi Ishimaru, 65, Garwood Road.

Takichi Miyata, 59, 113 South El Dorado Street.

Tadaki Murano, 47, 125 East Lafayette Street.

Taro George Masudo, 36, Lodi district farmer.

Jiichi Fujimori, 53, 147 South Center Street.

Tasaburo Masui, 58, 20 North Main Street, Lodi.

Yohichi Hatada, 47, Acampo.

Gosuke Sasaki, 60, Thornton.

TAKEN TO SAN FRANCISCO

After spending the night in the County Jail the 13 alien Japanese were loaded into an army truck yesterday morning and taken to San Francisco.

The aliens seized here were part of 218 arrested in Northern Cali-

FEAR GROWS IN LONDON NAVY TO SEIZE FRENCH

By WILLIAM B. DICKINSON
United Press Staff Correspondent

LONDON, Feb. 23 (UP)—The belief is growing today that Adolf Hitler is planning a major offensive and might even obtain temporary superiority over there, perhaps by taking over the French fleet.

Most observers have felt for a long time that Germany has awaited only a crucial moment in the war to seize the French battleships at Dakar, Casablanca and Toulon and would do it when it might upset the balance of naval power.

FACTS POINT TO IT

There are several indications that Hitler has decided that that moment is approaching. These include:

1. The escape of Germany's battleships Gneisenau and Scharnhorst and the cruiser Prinz Eugen, through the Dover Straits and the English Channel. They are now believed to be undergoing repairs either at Hamburg or at some Baltic dockyard.

2. Reports from Stockholm that the battleship Tirpitz and pocket battleship Admiral Scheer and the heavy cruiser Admiral Hipper have proceeded to Trondheim, on the west coast of Norway. British authorities do not doubt that Germany had constructed an important naval base there.

FRENCH BATTLESHIP

3. Reports from Vichy that the French battleship Dunkerque has arrived in French waters.

4. The major U-boat campaign that has been carried to the very shores of the United States.

1942, February 21
President's Executive Order 9066 was signed on Feb. 19 and Katsuchika was suddenly arrested on the night of February by the FBI (probably because he was working for the Japanese Association) and incarcerated at Bismarck, North Dakota. He was sent to camp under the Enemy Alien Act 1798.

A STATEMENT TO THE PUBLIC

by the

JAPANESE ASSOCAITION

OF STOCKTON

On behalf of all the Japanese and Japanese-American residents of Stockton we wish to express our deep sorrow over the conflict between the United States and Japan. We were as shocked as anyone to learn of the outbreak of war Sunday.

Now we must make our position as Japanese residents of this country clear.

We wish to pledge our sincere support of the United States of America, under which we enjoy all the precious privileges of freedom and democracy.

We pledge that we will do our part in the defense of this country—where our homes, our families, our businesses and all our interests lie.

We trust that the Government and People of the United States will treat us fairly and justly in a situation that is without parallel in our lives.

DR. K. AKIMOTO, Pres.
K. TAMURA, Secy.

Stockton Record, *December 9, 1941.*

Umeno and children Yokichi, Mutsuko and Hiromu, April or May 1942. Many families had photographs taken before leaving for the assembly centers.

Umeno and the children on the family porch. Mother made the "V" for Victory patch on Yokichi's jacket, so he would be known as an American citizen.

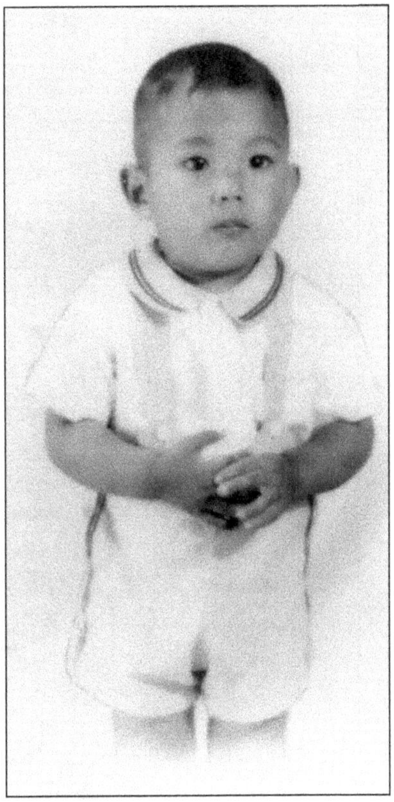

Hiromu (George) Tamura, photo taken at Gila River, Arizona.

1942, June to July
Incarcerated at Camp McCoy, Wisconsin while wife Umeno and three children were still in Turlock Assembly Center, California.

1942, July to June, 1943
Incarcerated at Camp Livingston, Louisiana. Family was at Turlock Assembly Center from May 3, 1942, and transferred to Gila River Relocation Center, Arizona, August 12, 1942.

1943, June to May, 1944
Incarcerated at Santa Fe Detention Center, New Mexico while family was interned at Gila River, Arizona. Family transferred to Tule Lake on May 23, 1944.

1944, May to November, 1945
Family finally reunited in Tule Lake, California after two years and three months of separation. Umeno and the four children left Tule Lake October 1, 1945 and settled temporarily and worked at the Chugoku Hotel in Lodi run by her relatives, the Okazaki family. Chugoku Hotel was a 56-room hotel mainly for the many unwed Issei men (they were barred from bringing picture brides here from Japan due to legislation passed in approximately1928 that prohibited it) working as day farm laborers in the area. (Cost of lodging was $1 a night, and meals cost $.50.) Katsuchika left Tule Lake in March 1946 and also worked at the Chugoku Hotel, mainly tending bar until 1946.

1945, April 20
Son Sam Osumu was born while family was interned at Tule Lake, California.

WWII Internment Camps & Detention Centers
[Partial listing]

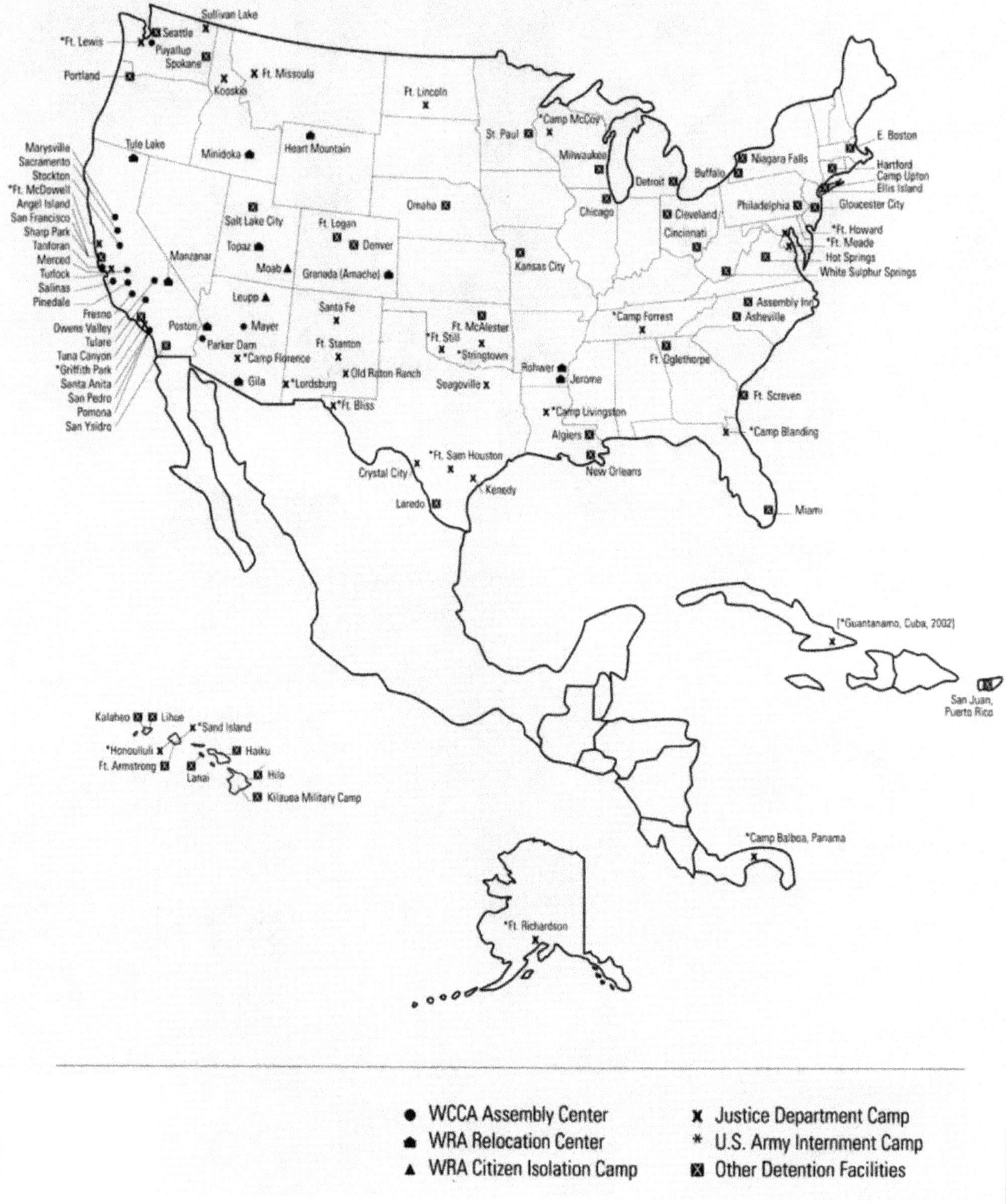
Sullivan Lake
*Ft. Lewis
Seattle
Puyallup
Spokane
Portland
Ft. Missoula
Kooskia
Ft. Lincoln
Tule Lake
Minidoka
Heart Mountain
Marysville
Sacramento
Stockton
*Ft. McDowell
Angel Island
San Francisco
Sharp Park
Tanforan
Merced
Turlock
Salinas
Pinedale
Fresno
Owens Valley
Tulare
Tuna Canyon
*Griffith Park
Santa Anita
San Pedro
Pomona
San Ysidro
Manzanar
Salt Lake City
Topaz
Moab
Ft. Logan
Denver
Granada (Amache)
Leupp
Santa Fe
Ft. Stanton
Poston
Mayer
Parker Dam
*Camp Florence
Gila
*Lordsburg
Old Raton Ranch
*Ft. Bliss
Crystal City
Laredo
*Ft. Sam Houston
Kenedy
St. Paul
*Camp McCoy
Milwaukee
Chicago
Detroit
Omaha
Kansas City
Ft. McAlester
*Ft. Still
*Stringtown
Seagoville
Rohwer
Jerome
*Camp Livingston
Algiers
New Orleans
Cleveland
Cincinnati
Buffalo
Niagara Falls
*Camp Forrest
Ft. Oglethorpe
Assembly Inn
Asheville
Ft. Screven
*Camp Blanding
Miami
E. Boston
Hartford
Camp Upton
Ellis Island
Philadelphia
Gloucester City
*Ft. Howard
*Ft. Meade
Hot Springs
White Sulphur Springs
[*Guantanamo, Cuba, 2002]
San Juan, Puerto Rico
Kalaheo
Lihue
*Sand Island
*Honouliuli
Ft. Armstrong
Lanai
Haiku
Hilo
Kilauea Military Camp
*Camp Balboa, Panama
*Ft. Richardson
WCCA Assembly Center
WRA Relocation Center
WRA Citizen Isolation Camp
Justice Department Camp
* U.S. Army Internment Camp
Other Detention Facilities

Stockton area men. Katsuchika Tamura, center, back row; Dr. K. Akimoto, second from left, front row, Santa Fe Detention Center, New Mexico, August 25, 1943.

Nancy Tamura, left, 1944. The children were moved from the farm to a confined area with many noted professionals: dancers, artists, writers, musicians, and other craftspeople. Everyone was exposed to the cultural arts and learned many fine things.

Sam Tamura, right, 1945 or 1946. Taken in Lodi.

THE UNITED STATES OF AMERICA

ORIGINAL
TO BE GIVEN TO
THE PERSON NATURALIZED

No. 7301162

CERTIFICATE OF NATURALIZATION

Petition No. 24787

Personal description of holder as of date of naturalization: Date of birth January 8, 1895 sex male complexion sallow color of eyes brown color of hair black height 5 feet 6 inches weight 115 pounds; visible distinctive marks a small mole on left side of nose
Marital status married former nationality Japanese
I certify that the description above given is true, and that the photograph affixed hereto is a likeness of me.

Katsuchika Tamura
(Complete and true signature of holder)

STATE OF CALIFORNIA
COUNTY OF ALAMEDA } ss:

Be it known, that at a term of the Superior Court of the State of California in and for the County of Alameda held pursuant to law at Oakland, California on November 18, 1955 the Court having found that KATSUCHIKA TAMURA then residing at 3125 Boston Avenue, Oakland, California intends to reside permanently in the United States (when so required by the Naturalization Laws of the United States), had in all other respects complied with the applicable provisions of such naturalization laws, and was entitled to be admitted to citizenship, thereupon ordered that such person be and (s)he was admitted as a citizen of the United States of America.
In testimony whereof the seal of the court is hereunto affixed this 18th day of November in the year of our Lord nineteen hundred and fifty-five and of our Independence the one hundred and eightieth

Clerk of the Superior Court

By ______ Deputy Clerk.

Seal

It is a violation of the U.S. Code (and punishable as such) to copy, print, photograph, or otherwise illegally use this certificate.

DEPARTMENT OF JUSTICE

Naturalization papers, 1955.

1946 to 1947 *circa*
Worked as a gardener on a nine-acre estate in Tiburon. He was given a cottage to live in with his family on the estate.

1948 *circa*
Started business in partnership with the Takemoris in Berkeley but later pulled out.

1949 *circa*
Worked in janitorial service for Hotel Claremont in Berkeley. On the side, he worked for Mr. Katayama who had a dry cleaning business in Berkeley and later got a license and owned his own dry cleaning business in Oakland until his retirement. His wife Umeno helped in the shop doing alterations, etc.

1991 January
Moved with wife Umeno who was suffering from Alzheimer's Disease to Marina, California to live with widowed stepdaughter, Nancy Shikashio. Nancy had lost her husband Ned in January 1989 to cancer. Nancy provided care at home to both her mother and stepfather until their deaths.

1992, September 9
Umeno passed away at age 79.

1996, January 12
Katsuchika passed away four days after his 101st birthday.

Katsuchika and Umeno.
taken in Lodi, 1946,
shortly after he returned home.

Katsuchika Tamura was almost 51 years old when released after being incarcerated for 45 months in internment camps. So although he was fluently bilingual in both Japanese and English, he never had the opportunity to work in an occupation where he could fully utilize and be compensated for his high education, skill and talents. It was a tragedy, although he never seemed to harbor any bitterness regarding this matter. He was a very dignified, quiet mannered gentleman.

He loved classical music and opera (he and a friend went to see Caruso perform when he was an impoverished student in the U.S. and fell in love with the opera) and later in his retired life, he enjoyed watching video tapes of operas daily. He was also an avid sports fan, especially baseball, football, tennis and golf. He was playing golf on that fateful Sunday, December 7, 1941 when Japan attacked Pearl Harbor.

Katsuchika, Nancy and Umeno.
Marina, Monterey County,
California, 1991.

Father and His Love of Sports

Though Father was a cerebral father, he had a certain love of sports. Living through the era of Jack Dempsey, Bobby Jones, Bill Tilden, Babe Ruth and the Yankees, you can well imagine he developed an interest in all their sports.

Growing up in his household, Dad had this uncanny knowledge of all sports and this from a guy who emigrated from feudal Japan. He played golf, loved baseball, followed the San Francisco 49ers and showed us how to play pool. It made you wonder what kind of upbringing he had!

The one bit of history that I have of my father and sports is a small window into the games he followed; it was not about his love of sports, but rather the emotion he showed in this one particular case. You have to understand my father showed very little emotion when it came to expressing joy for the victors, or expressing anguish for the defeated. He just didn't show his emotions one way or the other. A chip off the old block, I too show few emotions outwardly—the old saying just might be true: an acorn does not fall far from the oak tree.

I remember a particular Sunday, late in the afternoon, my father came through the front door in a very agitated state. In a strong voice, and you have to know my father was a very soft-spoken man, he stated that he had just come from an Oakland Raiders football game at Youell Field, in downtown Oakland. Youell Field is the football field that the Laney College Eagles and the Oakland Junior College Thunderbirds had played their football games on. It consisted of two bleachers and the sidelines—that was it!

Father never ventured out to see a baseball game, or go to the opera (and he loved opera), he simply did not go out. So we were very surprised when he announced he had gone, on his own, to an Oakland Raiders football game.

The 1960 Oakland Raiders were the eighth charter member of the American Football league and in those early years they played like the eighth charter member. But it was the big surprise that he went to a Raiders game and second that he went by himself unbeknownst to the rest of the family. To top it off his greatest outburst was his proclamation that the Raiders were the lousiest football team he had ever seen and that he would never go back! He never did go back, or venture out of the house again for any other sporting event.

Dad did mellow as the Raiders became a better team; he even became a Raiders fan—from afar!

Hiromu Tamura

Little Vignettes of Dad

Like the day he took me to kindergarten or first grade, I don't know because it was such a long time ago and all I remember was the first day. Nothing about the second day or the next month or the next grade or year. Just nothing about going to school in Berkeley. All I remember was Dad taking me by the hand and handing me off to the school teacher. I don't remember crying or if I made a big fuss or anything like that. You're right about Dad keeping his feelings to himself whether he agreed or disagreed with anything. He was always on an even keel. I remember one time at the Dwight Way house, I was with a group of maybe three or four other youngsters. I couldn't have been much older than five years and probably the youngest in the group when Dad chases us out from under the crawl space of the house. We had started a fire in what was probably a 5 lb. coffee can right under the flooring. What seemed like innocent play could have been a real disaster. But Dad never scolded us or at least me. I never had a repercussion because of it. I knew when he chased us out that it wasn't something to do again. I don't remember if George was there, just Dad chasing us out, overturning the can to put out the fire and tamping it out. There were many times when many a father would have been critical of a decision or act but not Dad. He always kept his calm and hid his personal feelings to himself. I remember when I joined the Marine Corps, you could see his concern in his eyes but he was not judgmental or openly emotional. He just asked if I would be "OK."

Dad had many hidden talents and interests that we would see snippets of or learn of years later, like George's story of Dad going to a Raiders' game or the story of his love of opera that I only learned of when Celeste and I saw him enjoying an opera on TV in Italian or German. I remember seeing his golf clubs but never made the connection until the day he took me to the driving range and watched him hit a bucket of balls then going home. I'm sure he felt this was luxury, to buy a bucket of balls; he only bought one. One day while visiting the Okazaki's in Lodi we decided to go fishing. Uncle had set George and I up with fishing gear and off we went with Aki to somewhere in the delta. Well, Dad being inventive, found a grape stake somewhere where we were fishing, rigged up a string, hook and bait. Well, you guessed it. Dad had the biggest bite and biggest fish if he could have landed it. The fish broke the grape stake and got away. There are many other stories I could tell.

Sam Tamura

Dear Ann: Could you reprint a prayers by Cardinal Cushing on how to deal with the tough times in life. It helped me pull myself together when you first ran it several years ago. I need it more than ever now. Please try to find it and run it again. Thank you. — Woodland Hills, Calif.

Dear Woody: Here it is, a favorite of mine, too. Thank you for asking. Prayer for Bad Times

Dear God: Help me be a good sport in this game of life. I don't ask for an easy place in the lineup. Put me anywhere you need me. I only ask that I can give you 100 percent of everything I have. If all the hard drives seem to come my way, I thank you for the compliment. Help me remember that you never send a player more trouble than he can handle.

And, help me, Lord, to accept the bad breaks as part of the game. May I always play on the square, no matter what the others do. Help me study the Book so I'll know the rules.

Finally, God, if the natural turn of events goes against me and I'm benched for sickness or old age, help me to accept that as part of the game, too. Keep me from whimpering that I was framed or that I got a raw deal. And when I finish the final inning, I ask for no laurels. All I want is to believe in my heart that I played as well as I could and that I didn't let you down. — Richard Cardinal Cushing

■ ■ ■

Ecclesiastes
or,The preacher
Chapter 3

1. To every thing there is a season,and a time to every purpose under the heaven.
2. Atime to be born,and a time to die: a time to plant,and a time to pluck up that which is planted:
3. Atime to kill,and a time to heal: a time ~~a time~~ to break down,and a time to build up:
4. A time to weep, a time to laugh: a time to mourn,and a time to dance:
5. A time to cast away stones, and a time to gather stones together: a time to embrace,and a time to refrain from embracing:
6. A time to get,and a time to lose: a time to keep and a time cast away:
7. A time to rend,and a time to sew: a time to keep silence,and a time to speak:
8. A time to love,and atime to hate: a time of war, and a time of peace.

Some papers found in Katsuchika's belongings.

William Shakesepeare
(1564-1616)

Winter

When icicles hang by the wall
And Dick the shepherd blows his nail,
And Tom bears logs into the hall,
And milk comes frozen home in pail;
When blood is nipt,and ways be foul,
Then nightly sings the staring owl
Tu-whoo!
To-whit,Tu-whoo! Amerry note!
While greasy Joan doth keel the pot.

When all about the wind doth blow,
And coughing drowns the parson's saw,
And birds sit brooding in the snow,
And Marian's nose looks red and raw;
When roasted crabs hiss in the bowl--
Then nightly sings the staring owl
Tu-whoo!
To-whit,Tu-whoo! A merry note!.
While greasy Joan doth keel the pot.

Where The Bee Sucks

Where the bee sucks,there suck I:
In a cowslip's bell L lie;
There I couch when owls do cry.
On the bat's back I do fly.
After summer merrily:
Merrily,merrily,shall I live now
Under the blossom that hangs on the bough.

Katsuchika at home.

Katsuchika reading a partial book. If heavy books were received as gifts, Katsu would carefully cut them into three, four or five sections, so the book would not be so cumbersome to read.

Katsuchika Tamura, celebrating his 100th birthday, January 8, 1995, at home in Marina, California.

Shizuko Teshima Kamimoto, Umeno's sister-in-law, with her son, Hideo, 1942. She translated Katsuchika's letters to Umeno and preaddressed envelopes to use.

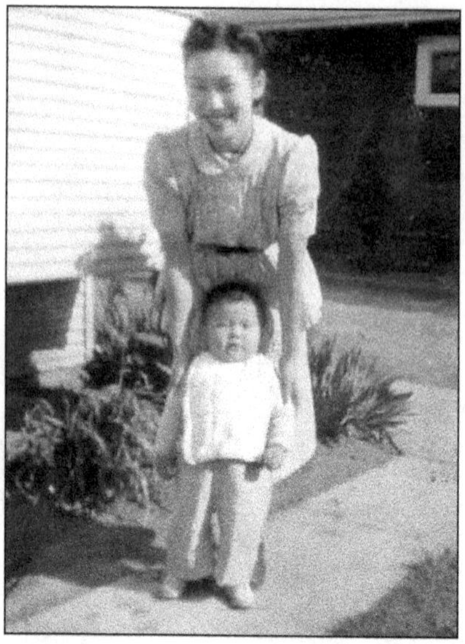

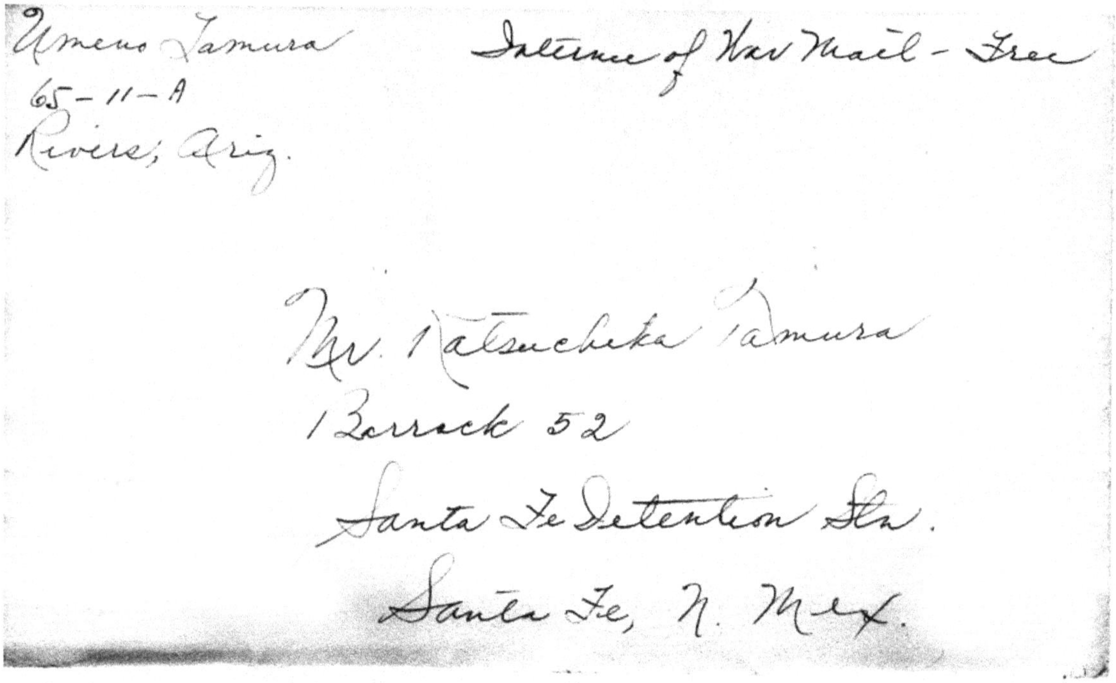

Umeno Tamura
65-11-A
Rivers, Ariz.

Internee of War Mail - Free

Mr. Katsuchika Tamura
Barrack 52
Santa Fe Detention Sta.
Santa Fe, N. Mex.

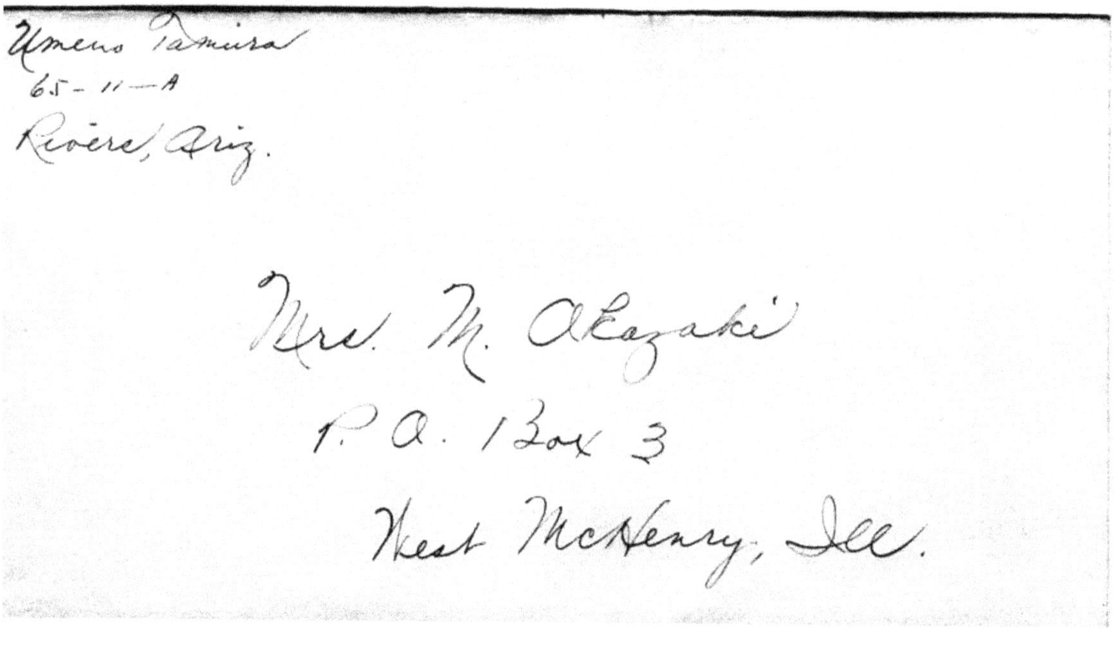

Umeno Tamura
65-11-A
Rivers, Ariz.

Mrs. M. Okazaki
P.O. Box 3
West McHenry, Ill.

BISMARCK, NORTH DAKOTA

February–June 1942

The following letters are from Katsuchika Tamura while incarcerated at Bismarck, North Dakota, to his wife, Umeno Tamura, at Rt 6 Box 305, Stockton, California, and at the Turlock Assembly Center, Turlock, California.

The few letters written in English are shown in their original wording. All the letters are censored and some portions cut out with the following stamp, a poignant reminder of the times.

Most of the letters are written in beautiful, neat, meticulous Japanese penmanship reflecting his high education and character.

His original letters written in English begin on page 105 and his original letters written in Japanese begin on page 139.

DETAINED
ALIEN
ENEMY MAIL
EXAMINED
BY............
U.S.I&N.S.

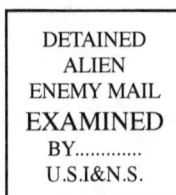

All of the letters are jammed into one paragraph to maximize use of space as he was allowed to write only one page letters twice weekly.

The first letter to Umeno from Katsuchika, February 27, 1942.

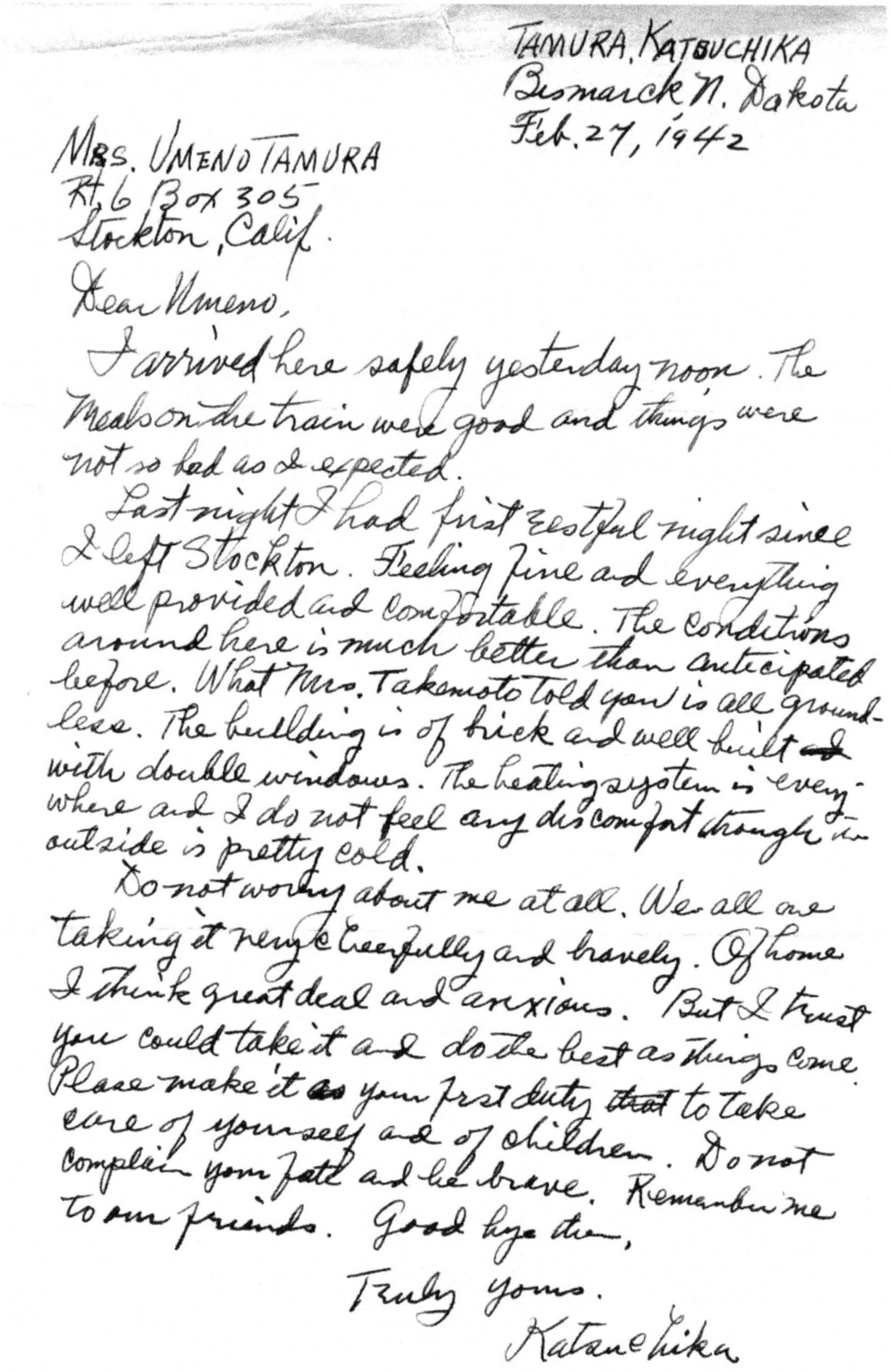

TAMURA, KATSUCHIKA
Bismarck N. Dakota
Feb. 27, 1942

MRS. UMENO TAMURA
Rt. 6 Box 305
Stockton, Calif.

Dear Umeno,

I arrived here safely yesterday noon. The meals on the train were good and things were not so bad as I expected.

Last night I had first restful night since I left Stockton. Feeling fine and everything well provided and comfortable. The conditions around here is much better than anticipated before. What Mrs. Takemoto told you is all groundless. The building is of brick and well built ~~and~~ with double windows. The heating system is everywhere and I do not feel any discomfort though the outside is pretty cold.

Do not worry about me at all. We all are taking it very cheerfully and bravely. Of home I think great deal and anxious. But I trust you could take it and do the best as things come. Please make it ~~as~~ your first duty ~~that~~ to take care of yourself and of children. Do not complain your fate and be brave. Remember me to our friends. Good bye then,

Truly yours.
Katsuchika

March 1, 1942 *(original in Japanese)*
Dearest Umeno,

Like I told you in my previous English letter, our daily life is much better than anticipated so there is nothing for you to worry about. The meals on the train were very good and compared to that, the meals here are not as good, but we do not feel any hunger at all.

The mealtimes are 7:30 a.m., 12 noon, and 6:00 p.m. The building is of brick; the rooms are spacious and the windows are double-paned so it is not cold. Right now, I am not experiencing any inconveniences so please do not worry. So you do not have to worry about me, but I am worried about how you are managing in my absence. The others have worries, but most do not have to worry financially. But we are not prepared (financially) and since you have Hiromu, I'm anxious as to how you are getting by. Please try not to worry too much and don't exert yourself more than you have to. If possible, it might be good to find somebody to live with you so you won't feel so lonely. At any rate, worrying is the worst thing so please take care.

As for the children's lifestyle, if at all possible, please continue as you did up to now. For their sake, I don't think it's a good idea to cut down too drastically.

I am allowed to write two letters weekly, only one page in Japanese and one in English. There is only one person doing the censorship so the Japanese letters will probably take a little longer getting to you.

Well, I will close for today. Please try not to worry about things. My best regards to Yoshimis, Tanakas, Takemotos, Takemoris, Nii-san *(older brother)* and Okazakis.
Affectionately, Katsuchika

No Date *(original in Japanese)*
Dearest Umeno,

How are you doing? Is everything going along all right? There's worry about evacuation, but as far as we can tell, French Camp is not in the evacuation area. Are Yot-chan, Mut-chan and Hiromu-chan well? In another month, it will be Hiromu's birthday. Did you get somebody to come and stay with you? It's better to not get lonely.

I don't think there are any restrictions in getting letters from the outside. It is okay to write in Japanese so please write occasionally to let me know how things are. There are some people who airmail the letters, but it doesn't seem to make too much of a difference so just use 3 cents postage.

I received the package you sent me the other day. I'm wearing the underwear now. The other things look very warm and I appreciate it very much.

How are things around Stockton? Read a little about the Uedas and others in the paper, but do not know where or what they are doing now. Here, we are not allowed to work yet. Of course there is kitchen work, barber, etc., that is voluntary and with no pay.

Yesterday was Sunday so for breakfast we had an apple, two boiled eggs, cornflakes, milk, bread, butter, jam, coffee and tea. For lunch, we had hamburger steak, salad, rice, soup, etc. I don't like the morning coffee because it already has sugar and cream in it.

If you think it is better to sell the car, please do so. I think it is better than just leaving it around for a long time.
Affectionately, Katsuchika

March 15, 1942 *(original in Japanese)*
Dearest Umeno,

How are you? Are the children all healthy? Today is Sunday. It snowed all night, so everything is covered with white snow. Indoors is kept at 70 degrees so it is just right. We have not been given any jobs yet so we all pass the time cleaning our rooms. Since I last wrote to you, I have received two letters and walnuts from you. I really appreciate your thoughtfulness. Please relay my regards and appreciation to Kanegaeda-san and others. At this time, I think it is better that I refrain from writing to them directly. As for the books, since I am living with many others, I don't know if I can truly enjoy reading the books that are sent to me, so please wait until I ask you to.

As you said in your previous letter, you and the children's good health is most important. Please do not fret too much about the future and try to have peace in your heart. Encourage good habits in the children and try to get them to remedy bad habits. Have you found someone to live with you yet? You must be lonely by yourself. Regarding the car, please talk to someone and if possible, sell it. I have talked to Miyata-san about money from the Japanese Association, so if they give it to you, I think it's okay to accept it.

If it's once weekly, I think the letters would be okay written in Japanese. You don't have to spend your busy time writing detailed letters… just send me a short letter telling me that you are all well. I am afraid that I didn't get one of your letters. Do you think Hiromu will be walking pretty soon? Please tell Yot-chan and Mut-chan thank you for their letters.

Affectionately, Katsuchika

March 17, 1942 *(original in Japanese)*
Dearest Umeno,

I first received your letter in English, then three letters in Japanese and one letter from the children. The first letter was postmarked the 12th and I received it on Monday, the 16th. As for your inquiry into the weather here, we are told that we are experiencing a 30-year record breaking warm weather… I can hardly see any sign of snow from the window here. Our rooms are kept at a constant 70 degrees so it is quite comfortable. The Stockton people are receiving many warm clothes that are too heavy so some people are sending them back. I know that you are thinking about me, but until I request it, please do not send anything. Just your kind thoughts are enough. For everyday things, there is a store here and someone comes once a week and opens a store and they take orders so I do not lack for anything. I'm thinking about quitting smoking, but since they give us a bag of tobacco, it's hard to stop.

I am so happy to hear that everyone is very kind towards you. Please relay my appreciation to them. As I have repeatedly told you, please do not worry too much about the future and live each day cheerfully.

Looks like you are going to have to give the strawberries a lot of fertilizer this year. Please tell Yot-chan and Mut-chan to be good and study hard. It pains me very much to be so far away from my family, but when I look at the people around me, I shouldn't complain. I look so forward to your letters. Until next time, please take care of yourself.

Affectionately, Katsuchika

March 24, 1942 *(original in Japanese)*

Dearest Umeno,

Received your letter dated March 17th on Monday, March 23rd. Our future here is not very clear, so for the past month we have been leading a monotonous life without much to do. On nice days, we go outside and exercise but other than that, we have to listen to rambling conversations. People like me that have no interest in that sort of conversation spend the time thinking about the past. I think about Monterey, Gilroy and Santa Cruz. And although it was expected, I cannot forget what happened on the eve of February 21.

I'm sure Hiromu's fever will go away. The other day, they gave us vaccinations here, but I think it would be a good idea to get Hiromu to a public health clinic for shots as soon as possible. Can't you ask Takemori-san or Nii-san?

As for the money from the Japanese Association, I don't think there is much hope at this time. It's due to their thoughtlessness and nothing we can do about it. I am really worried about your living expenses. Please do not exert yourself and if you encounter hardships, please let me know. Please give those who are extending their kindness towards you my heartfelt appreciation. There is no limit on incoming mail, but I can only write twice weekly so I cannot write to the kind individuals.

You asked me about sending coffee, etc., but we are treated very well here and I do not lack for anything so please do not worry about me and only send me things that I request. The people here from Stockton are receiving many unnecessary items from home and they don't know what to do with it. People back home hear all these rumors that are groundless. My biggest problem is that I am so far away from you. Please tell Yot-chan and Mut-chan to do as much as possible by themselves.

Affectionately, Katsuchika

No Date *(original in Japanese)*

Dearest Umeno,

Received your letters dated March 21 and 23. Am glad to hear that everything seems to be going well. We had four days of heavy lightning and thunderstorm··· experienced real North Dakota weather. I appreciated the heavy underwear that you had sent me. In every letter, you mention the kindness from everybody, but I cannot respond to each of them so please relay my heartfelt appreciation. I heard that new regulations are restricting the movements of even those Japanese Americans with citizenship. We'll just have to do the best we can under the current situation.

As for the car, I only stated my thoughts that I thought might be helpful to you, so you should go ahead and do what you think is best. I do not need any money now, but may need it next month but please do not send any until you hear from me.

Am so happy to hear that the children are well. That is the best news. Looks like Hiromu will be walking soon. Perhaps around his birthday? There is no limit on the number of mail I can receive, but I can only write one letter in Japanese and one in English weekly. So from here on, I will write you in Japanese and the children in English every week.

The evacuation may be happening soon, but until then, I sincerely pray that you will live each day cheerfully. Will close for today.

Affectionately, Katsuchika

April 14, 1942

Dearest Umeno,

Received your letter of April 7. I have to write this letter in English because I wrote one letter already in Japanese this week.

As you say the time the Stockton Japanese people have to move out seems approaching and it worrys me a great deal since I am helpless in the time of need. Takemori and your brother would help you but they have their family to look after and I doubt how much they can assist ~~you~~ in moving out. However try not to worry too much. Actuality of a feared thing is not as bad as you first anticipated it. I realized this fact many times in my past experiences. So keep your chin up and face the problem bravely.

Of your ranch, do not worry too much. Do your best and take the result philosophically. Think of less fortunate ones than you are.

I have no important or valuable possessions there. Whether they may be kept or not does not matter much.

In getting ready for evacuation, take only things absolutely necessary. I saw a list of things should be taken along to the Camp in the Japanese American News. That may help you too. Or you might make a list of your own. It simplifys ~~the~~ preparation for moving out. With a baby and two small children it is not easy task, but look at the brighter sides of thing and you will do nicely. With Love

Affectionately
Katsu Tamura

April 4, 1942 *(original in Japanese)*
Dearest Umeno,

Today is April 4th. It's April and Hiromu's birthday is soon. If I could, I would fly to you. Are you and the children living happily? I imagine you are worried hearing all these various rumors. Looks like evacuation is near. I am not around to do anything so there is no use in saying anything. I know it is a heavy burden on you but you must do what you think is the best way. It cannot be helped. As for the land, please talk to WCCA and National Farm Loan's Stockton office. As for the evacuation, I don't think you have to worry. Please trust the authorities and act calmly. Many stores are having bargain sales but don't buy any needless stuff. I know we don't have much money, but it's better to have it in cash. I am healthy so please do not worry about me. Atsumi-san sleeps beneath me. I do not lack for anything at all so please do not worry about me. But can you send me a $20 bank check?

How are the people in the neighborhood? Please give the Yoshimis my best regards. How is Nii-san? Is he at the islands? How about the Takemoris? Did he close his shop? Do you read the Japanese American newspaper? This week I cannot write any more letters in Japanese. Seems such a long wait. Until I write again, please take good care of yourself.
Affectionately, Katsuchika

April 18, 1942 *(original in Japanese)*
Dearest Umeno,

Hope you are well. I am fine as usual. I received a letter and $20 from Hiroshi-san. I wrote him a thank you letter but please thank him from you too. I am so glad to hear that there is someone to lease the farm. There is nothing among my possessions that are of importance so just put them away in a box. Please use all the trunks and suitcases. I think my brown suitcase is still usable. As I mentioned in my letter, what is happening to the money? Please go talk to Tadao miyata, Kenzo Fujimori or Tsutomu Okamoto and try to get as much money as possible before evacuation. The bank is saying it is okay to take the money out, so don't just leave it up to them. I am given most everyday necessities, but I still do need some money. So when the money comes in, or if you sell the car, I would feel secure if you could send me about $50 before evacuation. Knowing our circumstances (financial), it pains me to have to ask you this, but not knowing what the future holds for me, I must ask you.

Sounds like Hiromu is a handful. I can just picture him playing and crawling all over the floor. Is Yot-chan and Mut-chan being good?

Today it is raining here. It is becoming warmer and the lawns are gradually becoming greener. Please keep cheerful and try not to worry too much. Until my next letter, I pray for your health.
Affectionately, Katsuchika

April 23, 1942 *(original in Japanese)*
Dearest Umeno,

Received your letter dated April 15th. When the draft of the lease paper is ready, please send it to me. There is no problem. But if there is no time, then trust Hiroshi-san and sign the papers. This is a short note of only urgent matter.
Affectionately, Katsuchika

April 26, 1942 *(original in Japanese)*
Dearest Umeno,

I received your letter of April 20, and am glad and relieved to know that you are well. Am happy that the children are all healthy too. Read the Nichibei dated April 22nd and looks like the evacuation date has been set. It is happening so quickly that I'm sure there is going to be a lot of confusion. Please act calmly, putting the welfare of the children above all else. As for me, what you have done for me is enough so please do not worry about me. I'm relieved to hear that you received $100. Please ask those people before evacuation to send you $100 in May to the relocation address.

If you receive this letter before evacuation and you still have time, and you haven't yet sent me my summer clothes, then put them in a cardboard box and ship it to me. Please put a summer suit in there. I will buy a suitcase here. Regarding my previous letter about sending money to me, I probably won't need as much. I'll leave the amount up to you.

I will probably be writing my next letter to you at your evacuation address. Until then, please try to be cheerful in whatever you do.

Affectionately, Katsuchika

P.S. In your last letter, you mentioned that you sent the children's pictures, but there were none enclosed in the letter. Do you suppose the pictures got lost?

May 5, 1942 *(original in Japanese)*
Dearest Umeno,

I was in bed as it was already 10:45 p.m. and past lights-out time but Yagi-san came in and told me I had a letter. It must have fallen out of the batch that is handed out in the evening. So I got up and took it to the hallway and read it in the dim hall light.

Leasing the land, preparing and registering for the evacuation, dealing with the bank, etc; how busy you must have been. I have been worried about you having to go through these things that only you can do. I can only imagine the extreme hardships you must be going through with small children and trying to get rides··· my heart goes out to you. If all goes well, this letter should get to your evacuation address.

I received the pictures. The pictures came out well. The children seem happy so I am relieved. Hiromu is still chubby like I remember him. On May 2, I received a letter and a check for $50 from Rit-chan Kaneda. Please tell her how much I appreciate her kindness and all she is doing to help you. I did write to her. I received a box of summer clothes. That is plenty. I do not need anything more. Really appreciate your thoughtfulness. I imagine you are now living at the evacuation place. I'm sure it is very inconvenient and I feel for you. Although you are encountering many hardships, I pray that you will gradually adjust to the conditions there. Please be brave and persevere and try to be cheerful. Will write you again.

Affectionately, Katsuchika

May 10, 1942 *(original in Japanese)*
Dearest Umeno,

Received your letter dated May 5 on the 9th. I had been worried, but looks like you have safely settled in so I am relieved. There are so many things that you are not familiar with and so you must be distressed, but I pray that you will do your best for the sake of the children and remember there are others in less fortunate situations than you are. When I think about the uncertain future I get depressed, but we must be brave and overcome everything.

Even in our all men's dining hall, it is quite noisy during mealtime, so I can imagine what it must be like for you with children. I feel for you.

Yesterday, I received a letter from Setsuyo Yoshimi-san. I understand she returned home the other day. She said she visited our home and wrote about Yot-chan, Mut-chan and Hiromu.

I wrote a thank you letter to Rit-chan Kaneda the other day. The best news from you is that you and the children are all fine and well. So please be extra careful in everything you do and try not to get sick.

Please give my regards to Kamimoto Nii-san, Shizuko-san and Takemori-san and his wife. Please let me know who your new neighbors are.

Affectionately, Katsuchika

May 16, 1942 *(original in Japanese)*

Dearest Umeno,

Today, I received your letter dated May 12th. Last night it looked like it would rain today, but this morning I woke up to a heavy snowfall. Of course I don't have to work outdoors and this is a very fine, well built brick building so I do not feel the cold. I can imagine how inconvenient the daily life must be at the evacuation center. I myself have experienced having to walk to the dining hall for meals so I sympathize with you. It is our fate to have lived in these times so we must endure and solve the problems. I'm sure Hiromu is at an age when he needs a lot of constant care. He's not just lying down any more and it's too dangerous to let him play by himself now, but he is probably at a most "kawaii" (adorable) age. Nothing better than to hear that Yot-chan and Mut-chan are healthy. Get lots of milk and have them drink it.

Unlike the life you had before, you probably have to act and talk with constraint, always conscious of people around you. I really feel for you. Meals, laundry, bathing, etc., are especially a problem I'm sure.

The other day, a man from our room left here, but we don't know the reason. Some people are optimistic and others are pessimistic. As for me, I believe that I will be able to go home. I want to go home even if I have to sacrifice everything. Whether it is an assembly center or a relocation center, the daily life is probably not much different. But I still would like to return home and live together with you. Please give my very best regards to Mr. and Mrs. Takemori, Yoshimi-san and Mr. and Mrs. Kamimoto.

Affectionately, Katsuchika

P.S. Received the suit from Lodi. Please let them know that I received it and thank them for me.

May 26, 1942 *(original in Japanese)*

Dearest Umeno,

The terrible wind that plagued us for two days has died down and today is a very nice day. After breakfast, when I stood and looked out the window, the scenery had changed drastically from what I saw three months ago when I arrived here. The vast desolate landscape I saw then has changed into a stretch of green lawn surrounded by beautiful green trees and has turned into a lovely park. Yellow dandelions and poppies that I saw in California are blooming everywhere. On top of the cotton tree in front of our building, a robin has built its nest.

I am fortunately blessed with good health and although the daily life here is monotonous, I have nothing to complain about. My biggest wish above all else is to return home to you.

So glad to know that you are well. It must be very hard to live where you have to always be conscious of the people around you. My heart goes out to you. Please endure everything and do your best. Until I write again··· Please give my best regards to the neighbors.
Affectionately, Katsuchika

May 30, 1942 *(original in Japanese)*
Dearest Umeno,

I received your letter dated May 25th together with the letter from the children. I was relieved to know that you are all well. The days certainly go by fast and it's already been three months since we parted. Everyone is praying for a quick peace, but there is nothing we can do. Has the camp gradually become somewhat organized? How is the food? The letters from the Stockton people complain that vegetables are in short supply. How are you doing with Hiromu's food? Do you have to buy your own cans of baby food? How is the camp store? Is Takemori-san and Kamimoto-san working?

Fortunately, I am quite healthy. The weather here changes a lot··· one day it's a lovely spring day and the next day is cold and seems like winter. This morning the sky was dark again and it rained and the temperature was down so I again turned on the heater. I spend my days reading and doing nothing. Lately, people are going around picking up rocks. They are collecting pretty and unusually shaped rocks and polishing them. But I don't feel like doing it. Day before yesterday afternoon, I worked at spading the yard for about three hours and yesterday I worked in the kitchen. All of us must take turns and work. Atsumi-san worked as a cook and Ichiho-san (owner of Osaka-ya) went to the bakery. Setsuyo Yoshimi-san wrote me a letter. She tells me she returned home for about five days before being evacuated. Please take extra care with sanitation and stay healthy.
Affectionately, Katsuchika

CAMP MCCOY, WISCONSIN

June–July 1942

The following letters are from Camp McCoy, Wisconsin to Umeno at Block B, Barrack 37, Unit 2, Assembly Center, Turlock, California. Some words or parts of the letter are cut out due to censorship and therefore difficult to translate.

June 13. 1942 *(original in Japanese)*
Dearest Umeno,

Received your letter of May 5th. Always so happy to receive your much awaited (natsukashii) letters. It was decided that I would not return (to Japan) during the duration of the war and was moved to another camp. There are some people returning and I know that you are worrying about many things, but under these trying times, it cannot be helped so please stay strong and don't despair. Among my colleagues here, there are people that are in more pitiable situations than we are, but we must bear and resign ourselves to our fate.

My heart aches thinking about you all and I have been praying day and night, but right now there is nothing we can do until everything (war?) is over. As for me, as long as you stay determined and devote yourself to raising/educating the children, I have nothing more to say. Whenever I look at your (smiling) picture, I am hoping that you are smiling happily inside your heart too. Some people are saying that there may still be a chance to return to Japan with our families. Of course, we would be returning with only what we have on our backs. Please let me know of your feelings (regarding this matter) in your next letter.

The place (camp) has changed, but our daily life is the same and we are treated well. We left Bismarck on the afternoon of the 11th and headed east, east, east... from St. Paul, Minnesota, we turned south and got here. This place is called Camp McCoy in Wisconsin and is in the mountains and the scenery is beautiful. 1'm doing fine so please do not worry.

There are so many things I want to tell you, and so many things come to mind but I cannot write it. Please try to understand.
Affectionately, Katsuchika

June 16, 1942 *(original in Japanese)*
Dearest Umeno,

Hope all is well with you. I am fine. I heard you will be moving soon. I pray that it is to a place with nice weather. I am extremely worried that it will be another difficult move for you with the children. Please rely on Nii-san and Takemori-san and do your best. Just like the weather that finally clears up after you think it is never going to end, the day will surely come when we can happily meet again.

Please do not worry at all about me. Life at this new camp is not bad. It's in a mountainous area near Chicago and right now the weather is good and I have no complaints as far as the food and the treatment we are receiving. The only thing that darkens my mind is being away from you. There has been talk that we may be united with our families but not very reliable. How is Nii-san and Takemori-san? Please give them my best regards. Right now there are (cut out). I am the only one from Stockton. Perhaps some will be coming later. I don't know. Please take care of yourself and say hello to the children.

Affectionately, Katsuchika

June 24, 1942 *(original in Japanese)*

Dearest Umeno,

How have you been since? I haven't received a letter from you for ten days now so I am rather concerned as to how you are doing. I am guessing that you are probably busy since you will be relocating inland soon. Are the children all well? I was harboring faint hopes that by now, I could be with you and helping you but under these circumstances it is regrettable. I'm thinking about brothers Urano and Yasui and realize it can't be helped. As I have said many times, please keep cheerful thoughts inside and do your best. In one's lifetime, things that seem so unbearable now will some day become spiritually valuable experiences later.

I am fortunately quite well. The staff are all very nice so we are fortunate. We are between mountains, surrounded by oak and pine trees and on clear mornings like today, it feels quite refreshing. The days before and after moving here, I thought and I worried about you and the children and I was quite distressed. But now I try to take care of my health so that I can look forward to happily seeing you again and I try to be careful about my personal daily hygiene. Please, please take care of yourself. I'm anxiously awaiting your letters.

Affectionately, Katsuchika

June 30, 1942 *(original in English)*

Mrs. Umeno Tamura
BLKB BRK 37 Assembly Center
Turlock, California

My dear Umeno,

Since I sent you a letter last week, I've received two letters dated the 20th and a letter dated the 23rd from you. I'm so glad to know that you are doing fine. I am also fine too.

Yesterday we had a terrible thunderstorm and heavy rain. I heard that this area has this kind of storm quite often during summertime. Today is a nice day after the heavy storm.

I heard that Dr. Akimoto is coming here but he has not arrived yet; probably because he may still have some business in Bismarck. As you mentioned in your letter, you would be lucky if you can go to Tule Lake. People tell me that the place is a dried lake with sandy soil and it may be hot, but it is still within California. Therefore you may feel better than going to other states. I'm sure Mr. Takemori will be helping you out a lot for which I feel ever so grateful. Please thank him from me.

Is the Okazaki family in Stockton? Please give them my best regards. I am so sorry to hear about Hirano-san. Please convey my deep sympathy to the family. Also give my best regards to your neighbors and the people of French Camp.

Katsuchika

June 30, 1942 *(original in Japanese)*
Dearest Umeno,

Since I wrote to you last week, I have received three letters from you, two dated June 20th and one letter dated June 23rd. I am so glad to hear that you are doing okay. I am fortunately quite well. Day before yesterday, we had a terrible thunderstorm and heavy rain. We are told that this happens quite often in the summertime in this area. But today is a very beautiful day, like the "quiet after a storm". I heard Dr. Akimoto will be coming here, but has not arrived yet... probably has some work to still do at Bismarck. It would be nice if you (we) could go to Tule Lake like you mentioned in your letter. From what people tell me, the lake is dried up so it may be sandy and hot, but it is still within California so at least, emotionally it might be better than going to another state.
I'm sure Takemori-san will be helping you out a lot and you will be quite indebted to him. Please convey how grateful I am to him. Is the Okazaki family in Stockton? Please give them my best regards. I feel very badly for Hirano-san. Please convey my deep condolences to the family. Please give my best regards to the neighbors and friends from French Camp.
Affectionately, Katsuchika

July 2, 1942 *(original letter in English)*
Dear Milton & Nancy,

How are you? Hope you are well. What kind game do you have there? At our place we have softball, table tennis and horseshoe pitching. I can't play golf anymore so I play table tennis very often, but I am not very good at it yet. Nancy do you eat plenty of vegetables and drink lots of milk. They are most important food for you. Too much sweet things are not good.

Say "hellow" for me to Henry, Fred, George, Masako, Sachiko, Tayeko, Barbara, Marion, Takeo, Johnny, his brother Jimmy, Yukiko and Misako. Be nice boy and girl. Goodbye.
Affectionately yours, Father

July 9, 1942 *(original in Japanese)*
Dearest Umeno,

How have you been since?. Is Hiromu walking quite a bit now? Has he started to talk? Is Yot-chan and Mut-chan being good kids? Are they going to school? Have you adjusted to the camp life? Who is living in our house now? Heard the onion prices are rather low. Is everything well with Yoshimi-san, Tanaka-san and Takemoto-san? Please give them my best regards. Is Nii-san doing some kind of work? Hideo-san must be getting quite big. How about Shizuko-san? What is Takemori-san doing? Whatever happened to the story about going to Tule Lake? Heard that the people who went to Arizona are suffering from heat. Have you gained any weight? How many pounds is Hiromu now? This area is experiencing an unusual cool summer so we are having it easy. The food is good and the camp commander is kind so except for being apart from you and the children, I have no complaints.

I have not applied to return to Japan yet. What does Takemori-san and Nii-san think about this matter? Since I am one of the earlier internees in this camp, I am helping the more recent arrivals settle in here. Like in my former job, I encounter many troublesome problems, but rendering help to others is not an undesirable thing. Until I write again....
Affectionately, Katsuchika

July 21, 1942 *(original in Japanese)*

Dearest Umeno,

There were a couple of hot days, followed by few days of cool weather and this morning it's quite chilly here. From your letter and from the newspaper article that Setsuyo Yoshimi-san sent me, I understand you will soon be relocating to a place called Gila River in Arizona. I'm sure it is a hot place but I don't think it is a bad place for your health. Please be careful in everything you do and take care of your health. This will probably be the last letter you will be receiving from me at Turlock so when you get to the new camp, please send me your new address right away. By the way, Setsuyo-san sent me a box of cigarettes. Please write to her at the "yama" (sanitarium'?) and inquire as to her health and thank her from me. I think of how difficult it must be for you having to move with small children in tow. Please ask Nii-san and Takemori-san for their help. No one is here yet from the Stockton area so I feel lonesome. I will be praying that you will all safely arrive at your new location.

Affectionately, Katsuchika

CAMP LIVINGSTON, LOUISIANA

July 1942–May 1943

The following three letters are from Katsuchika Tamura at Camp Livingston, Louisiana to his wife Umeno at Turlock, California Assembly Center. Some parts of the letters are cut out due to censorship.

July 30, 1942 *(letter in original English)*
My dearest wife,

How is everything with you? Have you already moved out? If you have, how hot is it down there? Are children all right? We were transferred to a new place again. This place is away down in the south. It is pretty (cut out) than the place we have been. Trees around here are mostly pines. Their. needles are much longer than those in California. I am doing fine and you have nothing to worry about me. From now on until I let you know, I wish you write letter to me in English. Japanese letters are permissible but it takes too much time to reach me. Don't forget to let me know where you are, how you are getting along. You know how anxious I am to know what kind? you had to move and how you all are.
Affectionately yours, Katsuchika

August 3, 1942 *(letter in original English)*
Darling,

How is everything? Are children all right? How was train travel? Did you have very hard time? I wish I were with you. What kind of place is it down there? Guess it is very hot, is it not? Did Takemori and your brother take their dwellings near you? I feel very helpless. When you needed me most, I was away from you, and you had to carry all burdens alone. Why? Why? Why? Forever I ask and get no satisfactory answer. Only thing I can do is to keep my chin up and take our fate with fortitude. I miss you though (rest of sentence cut out). We get shower often in summer season and sure it helps to keep (cut out). Pine trees around barracks are lovely to look at but they make poor shade. I met only one friend from (cut out). Well, I must bid you good-bye now dear. Take good care of your health.
Yours ever, Katsuchika

August 6, 1942 *(letter in original English)*
Dear Umeno

I just received your letter dated August 1. Am very glad to hear you all are in good health and

spirits. It was indeed fortunate you were still there to receive my letter. Otherwise it would have taken a long time before I hear from you. I am becoming more accustomed to new surroundings and getting along very fine. Last week we had an exhibition of internees hand works. There were curious stones, tree roots carved as flower vases, water color painting, wooden sculptures and many other things. Two letters you mailed on July 29 and 30 respectively I have not received yet. No doubt they will forward them to me from McCoy but if they are in Japanese, it will take a little time before they reach me. Well I must say goodbye now until next time meanwhile take good care of yourself.
Yours ever, Katsuchika

The following letters are from Katsuchika Tamura at Camp Livingston, Louisiana to his wife Umeno at Rivers, Arizona. Some parts of the letters are cut out due to censorship.

August 18, 1942 *(original in English)*
Dear Umeno,

I have just received your first letter since you arrived at Gila River Relocation Center. It makes me very happy to hear that everything went well on the train and the trip was a very pleasant one. Children must have had a wonderful time. The heat in Arizona must be very hot. Take good care of yourself and children. Until you get used to the new climate and adjust yourself to the new surroundings, go easy and don't be over ambitious to do too much work. I think it is fortunate to share the room with your brother. It is nicer this way than you take one alone. I have received all your letters except two which were written in Japanese and reached at McCoy right after I left. I am sure they will come by and by. I feel I can't express my thanks enough to the Kamimotos, Takemoris and Teshimas who so kindly looked after you. Give my best regards and extend my sincere gratitude to them. Until next time...
Always yours, Katsuchika

August 21, 1942 *(original in English)*
Dear Umeno,

How is everything down there? Hope you and children are in good health. Have you become used to the new place? Is the heat very hot yet? I hear you get sand storms too. Is it pretty bad? Can the children take the heat? Write me soon. I am waiting to hear from you.

I am doing fine as usual. The weather is changeable but it is cool in the morning and evening. It may sound awfully selfish but sometime ask Mr. Takemori if he can spare a few golf balls and one or two iron clubs for me. It is not regular course, but a sort of miniature course we made. I think it would be nice if I can have them here. You did not take mine with you, did you? Oh well, it is ridiculous question to make. However I am sure Mr. Takemori has a few extra ones beside his regular sets. If I am asking too much at this time, don't bother it now. Take good care of yourself. So long.
Yours ever, Katsuchika

August 24, 1942 *(original in English)*
Dear Umeno,

Hello. How are you? This is eight o'clock in the morning. It must be seven in Arizona. Is the heat very hot yet? It is much cooler here and I wish your place too. The day before yesterday, I received your letter written July 27 in Japanese. I wonder what has happened to the other you said you mailed a few days before this one. It seems you wanted something to tell me in that letter. As I haven't received it I wish you would write me again telling me what you wanted. In this letter which is lying before me, you seem worrying about our children who are picking up bad manners and becoming unmanageable. It is pretty bad. Though we can't do much to correct them under the current conditions do your best. It's one good thing that they are in good health. Tomorrow I will write to them telling to mind you. Well, let me hear from you soon. Until then I am..

Yours ever, Katsuchika

August 26, 1942 *(original in English)*
My dear Umeno,

Your letter and Masaru-san's written July 26 and 25 respectively, have finally reached me yesterday and I came to understand what you wanted to tell me. Well, about repatriation I'm doing my best, but it is unlikely we get our turn this time, for there are too many applicants ahead of us. However, don't be discouraged by this disappointment. In the present conditions we must forbear many trials and afflictions. In a few days I will write you in Japanese. Though it may not reach you as quick as English one, I can express myself better in it. Wish you do the same besides English ones, as to hear from you is my happiest expectation here. Will you extend my cordial thanks to your brother for his kind letter.

Yours ever, Katsuchika

August 30, 1942 *(original in English)*
My dearest Umeno,

A few days ago I received your letter of August 23 telling me that you were going to move to Camp #2 from Camp #1. It made me very happy as always to hear from you. I wanted to reply immediately but as I had used up my two letters a week allowance in writing you that *(the rest of the letter is censored and cut out)*

September 1, 1942 *(original in Japanese)*
My dear Umeno,

I hope you are all well. When it was decided at Bismarck that I would be interned, it was recommended that I immediately apply to return to Japan: but since I could not make such a decision just by myself, I was transferred to Camp McCoy (Wisconsin) so I just let the matter sit. Since then, I have learned how you feel regarding this matter, but there are many things to consider after we return (to Japan) and also there is talk that families might be reunited again, so I thought I would wait and see what happens. Even if I had applied earlier, unless I had applied real early, I've heard that the applicants are twice as many so we probably would not have made the second ship anyway. Recently, especially after reading your letter dated July 26 and letter from Nii-san, among other things, I am concerned about the children's education so I have applied to return. Of course we can always change this, so if you change your feelings regarding this matter, please let me know.

Half a year has gone by since we parted after 15 months (of marriage) and I am anxiously yearning to see you again. But even though the government is planning on reuniting the families, we don't know when or how this will happen. I hear that Arizona is terribly hot and there are sand storms so you must be enduring very difficult situations. I'm concerned about your problems in disciplining/ raising the children. Don't know what to think of Hiromu too giving you problems. If everything goes well, we should be able to get on the next ship so please be patient and persevere.

I will not be writing Nii-san at this time so please give him my best regards. Also, Takemori-san and Teshima-san too. Please take care of yourself.

Affectionately, Katsuchika

September 6, 1942 *(original in English)*

My dearest Umeno,

This is Sunday morning and we had our breakfast at 7:45, an hour later than weekdays. It consisted of fresh peaches, dry cereals, fresh milk, bacon and an egg, bread and butter and coffee. We get plenty of sugar too. Our barracks being next to the mess hall, we always know what we are going to have for the next meal in advance. Roast chicken and apple pie a la mode for this noon. Doesn't it sound good?

Your letter of September 2 was handed to me yesterday and it made me very happy as always to hear from you and to know everything is fine and well with you all. I have nothing to complain about, but miss you terribly. How are our children behaving these days? Is Hiromu getting bad and mischievous as you said he is? Don't be too ambitious about obtaining a job. Your health is the most important thing for all of us, and you should take good care of it. As for golf clubs, if you haven't written for them yet, do not bother anymore. I might be able to obtain them here.

Yours ever, Katsuchika

September 14. 1942 *(original in Japanese)*

Dearest Umeno,

Received your letter dated Sept. 9th. I understand you couldn't read my English letter very well since some of it was cut out. I didn't think I wrote anything that would be a problem. You said that you also applied (?) there. I think that is good. As for money: we can send as much as we wish, but at the present time I have no need for it. I have about $50 that I deposited with the military. I only bought a small trunk, a large bag to hang my clothes in and rubber shoes so I have the rest of the money. You can hold the money if we return, so there is no need for you to send it to me. We are allowed 32 square foot and I'm sure we can carry on small bags. In any case, we don't know what will be happening so don't worry about it too much. If I think of something, I will let you know. I want to unite with you as soon as possible. Otherwise, I am worried about the train ride. As I have repeatedly said, please do not needlessly worry about the future. Please take extra care of your health and wait for the day to come. From here on, except for the urgent matters (in English), you can write me in Japanese and they will reach me in time. I hate to ask you to write the letters in English when you are busy. I can purchase the golf clubs here. If it is already there, send me number 7 & 8, putter and golf balls. Well, I will close for today.

September 16, 1942 *(letter in original English)*
Dear Umeno,

Glad to hear all of you are fine. So am I. So they had cut off so much from my letter of August 30 that you could not make out head or tail of it. Well as long as you learned what I wanted to say from my Japanese letter, it didn't matter much. You surely did the right thing by taking out the application there. Though I neglected until now, I wanted to suggest you to do it. At present you have nothing else to do. Just sit tight and wait till the time comes. You could send me any amount of money, but do not do it until I ask you to. I still have fifty dollars deposited in the hand of military authorities. When I was at Bismarck I bought a small trunk and a pair of overshoes. Then I ordered a cloth cover and a few small items at Camp McCoy.

Well, dear Umeno, this is all for today. Goodbye and good luck.
Always yours, Katsuchika

September 21, 1942 *(original in English)*
Dear Umeno,

Hello! How is everything with you? The weather here has changed since yesterday. It became very cool so many of us started wearing a sweater. I rather like this kind of the weather as it is invigorating. A few days ago I received a very kind letter from Matsuo-san and Satsuno-san, urging us to go back to Japan. I wrote them a letter immediately thanking them for their sympathetic considerations for our situation. I think you know, dear Umeno, that they are soon going to move out to Arkansas, an adjacent state to Louisiana; a quite long way from California, isn't it? Thank you for the first edition of the Gila News Courier. I enjoyed it every bit; it is so interesting and informing about the camp life and its activities that I feel I know pretty well the relative aspects of your new home. Remember me to the Kamimotos, Takemoris and Teshimas and tell the children that I am always thinking of them. Wishing you all the luck.
Yours ever, Katsuchika

September 28, 1942 *(original in English)*
Dear Umeno,

How is everything with you? Received your letter of Sept. 22, but not yet the Japanese one. Heard that they send them to an eastern office for censoring. This is likely the reason for their delay. After I mailed my last letter to you I've got two more camp newspapers. I enjoy them very much. Now I think I know much about your camp. By the way, did you hear that they caught a rattlesnake at the Canal Camp the other night. Well you have to look out, as there is no assurance that there is none at the Butte Camp. Last night it rained cats and dogs out here, and this morning the air is so fresh and clean; but before the sun was up it dropped to 43 degrees F. and we felt cold. Hurriedly, we set up the stove in our barracks and started a fire. Otherwise everything is all right with me. This is all for today. Meanwhile let us all take good care of ourselves. As usual, please remember me to all our dear friends.
Yours ever, Katsuchika

October 7, 1942 *(original in English)*
Dear Umeno,

This is a rare fine morning. Yesterday I worked in the kitchen and stayed in bed later than usual this morning. This job comes every fortnight and everyone has to work. I hope you are feeling fine. How are the children? Has school started already? You know you must let them do what they can do themselves. I received the camp papers no. 4 and 5. Some people seem to be worrying about the table manners in the mess hall. The youngsters are apt to acquire bad habits very easily; so you must see to it that they would not run away from your reins. The outlook of our situation is just about the same as before. I am in the best of health. Remember me to the Kamimotos, Takemoris and Teshimas. I am waiting your Japanese letter but up to date I've not received it yet. Well, I must say goodbye now. Take care of yourself.

Always yours, Katsuchika

October 8, 1942 *(original in English)*
Dearest Umeno,

How have you been? Are the children well too? They must have grown quite a bit. I worry about many things but cannot do anything about it. The ship has not departed yet so I don't know when our turn will come. Under the current circumstances, we must stay calm and wait for the time to come.

Have you gotten a little used to the camp life there? According to the camp newspaper that you sent me the other day, it states that eight months out of the year is good weather there. I'm sure you are anxious about many things, but please live each day taking care of your health above all else. As for working, do not exert yourself since you have the children. These days, the weather is nice here and I do not lack for anything, but it saddens me to be away from you all. There are sports and activities so I try to participate to keep my mind off my worries but because of my personality, this kind of life is very distressful for me. I received a very kind letter from Matsuo-san. When you find out the Arkansas address, please let me know. I've been meaning to write to Nii-san but I haven't gotten around to it yet so please give him my best regards. Are you having Shizuko-san write your English letters? Please thank her for me. My regards also to Takemoris and Teshimas. Until I write again···

Affectionately, Katsuchika

October 12,1942 *(original in English)*
Dear Umeno,

This Monday morning, I have just finished listening to radio news after our breakfast. The weather has been fine for a week. As the temperature is mild now, I gave up my reading and do more outside exercises. Yesterday we had two representatives from the International Young Men's Christian Association. They promised more athletic equipments.

Well, how is everything with you? I suppose Yokichi and Mutsuko are going to school now. How is Hiromu? Does he talk much now? Well, take very good care of yourself and children and keep your chin up··· I am always thinking of you and waiting patiently for the day when we shall be reunited again. My kindest regards to the Kamimotos, the Takemoris and the Teshimas. So long until the next time.

With love, Katsuchika

October 16. 1942 *(original in English)*
Dear Umeno,

I have already written you one English letter this week and intended to write this one in Japanese, but I received two letters from you (Japanese one of Sept. 9 and English one of Oct. 12) after I had mailed mine. I decided to write this one also in English. You know, it is much quicker to reach you than Japanese letter. You can hardly imagine how happy your letters make me. Every time I receive them, I read them again and again. Under the present conditions, this is only means by which we feel nearness to each other. Will you tell Milton and Nancy that I am delighted with their nice letters. I am sure they made a great improvement in letter writing. I am glad to know that you have made a satisfactory adjustment and have settled everything concerning our French Camp property. As usual I am in good health. Please give my best regards to all our friends. Take good care of yourself. So long···
Yours ever, Katsuchika

October 19,1942 *(original in Japanese)*
Dear Umeno,

Today is October 19th. The days sure go by fast. I worry about you day and night. Right now, it's like we are being swept by a big current, and there is nothing we can do but flow with the current and wait for the right time to come. Let's just be cheerful and pray that we can meet again soon. Although our life together at French Camp was short, they were memorable, happy times. And I have high hopes of my future because I have you and the children. If our return to Japan becomes possible, I heard the cost is $300 per person, but as far as I know, I think this fee is for adults over age 21 so do not worry too much about the future and wait calmly. What I am worried about is your travel (train ride). It would be so nice if we can be together before that. They say the allowed luggage is 32 sq. ft. per adult. Of course, I think the adults and children can each carry a suitcase beside this.

This week I wrote the Japanese letter first. I'm sure this will take time reaching you, but I didn't want to put it off. Have you adjusted somewhat to the life there? I know that kind of life does not suit people like you, but please take care of yourself and try to live each day cheerfully.
Affectionately, Katsuchika

October 24, 1942 *(postcard original in English)*
Dear Umeno,

How are you? Hope everything is all right with you. I am fine and dandy. I have written one letter in Japanese to you and another to children. So this card is the last mail I can send out this week. Take good care of yourself. So long.
Always yours, Katsuchika

October 27, 1942 *(original in Japanese)*
Dearest Umeno,

Today is October 27th. It hadn't rained for about a month but several days ago it rained all day followed by a clear day and has become cold since. It feels like early December in California. It is not unbearable and the air is refreshingly clear.

I'm sure you know already, but the second ship to Japan has not departed yet so I don't think our turn to return to Japan will be coming up anytime soon. I spend the days in peace as I believe you are all in good health and although you may be inconvenienced and lacking in some things, you are living a secure life.

The other day there was a golf tournament and luckily I won first prize. Of course, it wasn't my skill··· I was just lucky. Now that school has begun, I'm sure the two of them spend most part of the day at school, so I think it is better than playing around all day like they have been doing. How is Hiromu? He must have grown quite a bit. Does he get up quite often during the night? Here, most of the people are in pretty good health and hardly anybody is getting sick. I too have not even had a cold. Under these trying times, we all have to bear our burdens and must put our health first and please try to live cheerfully. I pray day and night that all is well with you. I thought I was near you, but I woke up from my dreams and realized that I was still far away from you and was so distressed and lonesome. Until I write again··· Affectionately, Katsuchika

October 29, 1942 *(original in English)*
Dear Umeno,

How are you and children? I am doing fine. The weather here is very unsteady these days. One day it's cold and the next day warm. An autumn weather I guess. Oak trees are mostly bare now, but pine trees are as pretty as ever. Zinnias which we sowed after we arrived here are now profusely blooming. I hope you are as contended as I am here. I wonder if you could get two pairs of everyday pants for me. I mean work pants of denim jeans. Didn't I have one at home? My waist size is 30. Could you cut it to my length? Khaki color is prohibited for us to wear. When you send them I wish you would send me a small scissors too. Today, I received a letter from Milton and Nancy, written last Sunday. Take good care of yourself and don't catch cold. Then until next time... so long.
Yours ever, Katsuchika

The following letter written in English is from Katsuchika Tamura to his son Milton and daughter Nancy in its original English.
October 22, 1942
Dear Milton and Nancy,

Thank you. I am fine. I am glad that your school has started. You should study hard and be good pupils. I see Miss Sato teaches Nancy's class. Who is Milton's teacher? I am proud of you both for writing such nice letters. They surely make my heart warm.
Will you, Milton, thank Akira or me for his giving Hiromu a tractor. You are lucky to have Akira and Hitoshi to play with you all this time. Nancy, dear, you have quite many subjects to carry this year. 1 bet you like music best. I long to hear you sing.

Please give my love to Mom and tell her to take good care of herself. I did not forget her birthday, but I could not send her a birthday cake this year. So long, both of you, and be good children.
With love, Father

November 6, 1942 *(original in Japanese)*
Dearest Umeno,

It's cloudy this morning but it is warm and it is just right without a sweater. Your letters in Japanese take quite some time to reach me but I'm sure they will eventually get here. There is no change in our daily living here··· it's a repetition of what I've told you in my letters. I'm sure you and children are all well and fine so I am happy. You are probably faced with many inconveniences and the life there does not suit you, but we are faced with having to live in these times and we cannot escape the burden of our fate so please persevere.

By the way, did the Okazaki family go to Arkansas? In the newspapers that you sent me, it stated that people arrived from Stockton so I thought maybe they may have asked to come there.
I am filled with thoughts of you day and night. Looking at your picture, I'm sure the three of you haven't changed much since, but Hiromu must have grown quite a bit. Since school started, I'm sure things are much better for Yot-chan and Mut-chan these days. How is the weather there these days? Mornings must be cold.
I pray that peace will come soon. Will close for today. Please give my best regards to all.
Affectionately, Katsuchika

November 12, 1942 *(original in Japanese)*
My dearest wife,

Yesterday I wrote you in English acknowledging the receipt of the pants you sent me. It's a very good quality pants and it fits me well so I am very happy. The weather is good and I am fine physically and emotionally so please do not worry. Right now, I lack nothing except the sadness of separation. When I repeatedly pondered over things I've kept inside of me, I think I have more things to be thankful for than not. First of all I am very healthy and I have the mental strength to endure these conditions. Our life here is not one of hardship. The food is good, water/hot water is plentiful, the buildings and bathrooms are clean··· so for those of us who have to live in this insecure world, I think we are the most fortunate among the fortunate.

Our biggest anxiety is the education of the children, but there is nothing we can do but to do our best. I hope both you and the children are well. Hiromu must have gotten quite big by now. He seems like a mischievous little boy. I don't know when the exchange ship (to Japan) will be leaving. At any rate, please take good care of yourself and let's pray that we can get together real soon.
Please give my best regards to Nii-san, Shizuko-san, the Takemoris and the Teshima family. Are you together with the French Camp people? Until I write again···
Affectionately, Katsuchika

November 14, 1942 *(postcard in original English)*
Dear Umeno,

In my last letter, I asked you for my golf clubs, but that same afternoon, I got them through the canteen. So, please forget all about my golf clubs. I hate to change my mind so often but we are never certain whether I can get a certain thing through our canteen or not. I am fine and I hope you are the same. So long and good luck.
Always, Katsuchika

November 20, 1942 *(original in Japanese)*
Dearest Umeno,

I think of you constantly. It was my biggest hope to do everything together with you, but under some strange fate, I am distressed that we have had to live apart for so long. Time goes by so quickly and pretty soon it will be a year (since we parted). When I reminisce about those days, my heart aches. Although I don't have an ounce of guilt in my heart, in these times of unrest, whether you are guilty or not, we have fallen prey to fate and no matter how much we struggle emotionally, it is futile and nothing can be done about it. Every now and then, I hear of a rumor that gives me a glimmer of hope, but like the white snowflakes that fall on the water, it quickly disappears. So my biggest hope is that until this international situation clears up, you and the children will be happy and healthy and will wait and endure patiently.

Have you become adjusted to the life there? How are the children these days? Are things better now that school has started? When people are relegated to live in conditions like you are in, we tend to complain, but it all depends on how we look at things. Take care of yourself.
Affectionately, Katsuchika

November 23, 1942 *(letter in original English)*
Dear Umeno,

How is everything? Maybe you have been wondering why you haven't received any letters from me for sometime. Well, the fact is I haven't received any letters from you for a week. The reason is that they have changed the manner of handling our letters and they send all our letters, either English or Japanese, to an Eastern Office for censoring. So do not worry though you haven't heard from me for a while as I am in good health and spirits. How are the children? Are they behaving all right? I hope by this time they installed the stove in your barracks. What became of the water situation? Do you get enough water all the day?

This is all for today. Take good care of yourself and watch out that the children don't catch cold this time of the year. So long and good luck.
Always, Katsuchika

November 27,1942 *(original in Japanese)*
Dearest Umeno,

As I wrote you the other day, even the English letters are now sent to an eastern office or censorship so I haven't received any letters from you for two weeks now and I am sure the situation is the same with you. But I take it you are all well. I am getting along in good health too: so let's not worry about each other. Recently, the mornings are rather cold but it is warm during the day··· this weather feels very good. Lately there is talk that they would unite us with our families so I am praying day and night for this to happen. I don't know if we get to join you or if they are going to build another camp and put us together. Of course, this might just be another one of those rumors, so I can't really pin my hopes on it too much. Did Okazaki-san go to Arkansas? Do you hear from him? What is Nii-san doing? Is he still the block vice manager? Takemori-san does not have a golf course there to play at, does he? Have the children become a little better since school started? Children tend to mimic others so it must be difficult. Please take good care of yourself.
Affectionately, Katsuchika

December 9, 1942 *(original in Japanese)*
Dearest Umeno,

Lately your letters haven't reached me so I was feeling very lonely, but yesterday I received your letter dated October 21 and today, the 26th. Both were written in Japanese and I was so happy to read it. Guess Hiromu is at a most adorable age. Wish I could meet him soon. I know you are lonely without friends, but to live through these times we all must endure many things, so please try to be cheerful. I never dreamed that things would turn out this way... I always believed that we would live happily together, but many unexpected things can occur in one's lifetime. Although I do not lack for anything in my daily life here, I do worry constantly about you and the children. Christmas is fast approaching and I'm sure the children are expecting presents, but this year I cannot do anything for them so please buy them something there.

It had been rather warm here until about a week ago, but the last few days has been rather chilly in the mornings. Still, this is in the south so this is nothing compared to North Dakota. This building is not as well built so we probably feel the heat and cold more. Will close for now. Please give my regards to everyone.
Affectionately, Katsuchika

December 11, 1942 *(original in English)*
Dear Umeno,

This is rainy morning and still dark at 8 o'clock. How is everything with you? Yesterday I received your Japanese letter dated Oct. 22. By that letter you seemed enjoying a nice mild weather, but it is pretty cold in the mornings now, is it not? Do you get frost there these days? No, we don't get much frost here yet. I think you are wondering why you haven't heard from me lately. As a matter of fact I am writing you every week but our letters take much more time than before to reach either way. The letter I mentioned took almost fifty days to reach me. However, do not worry because I am treated well and in the best of health and spirits, and keep on writing whether you get mine or not. Otherwise, you know I shall be very lonely without hearing from you at all. Will you give them my best regards. How are the Takemoris, the Kamimotos and Teshimas?
Yours always, Katsuchika

December 16, 1942 *(original in Japanese)*
Dearest Umeno,

Lately, both the English and Japanese letters are late in arriving and it troubles me. My letters to you came back to me for minor things so you must be worried. I am writing this letter like this, but I don't know when it will get to you.. it is so disheartening. At any rate, I am well so please do not worry. I received three Japanese letters. The recent one is dated November 10. So happy to know that the weather is good and you are all living in good health. That is the best news. I received the scissor and pants. It fits me well so I wear it every day; I wrote to you at that time that I received them but that letter came back to me so I am letting you know again that I received them. Like I've told you, they censor and cut out things that common sense can not comprehend, so I can't write anything. Why they *(words cut out)* I don't understand their reasoning.

Yesterday, I sent four getas, tablets, pencils and candies. I'll be so happy if they get to you okay. Will close for now. Please take care in everything you do and lead a happy life.
Affectionately, Katsuchika

December 18, 1942 *(original in Japanese)*
Dearest Umeno,

The Japanese and English letters both take the same amount of time reaching its destination so I will write in Japanese. I don't know when this letter will get to you since things are so vague and unreliable, but I imagine that you are okay and living peacefully and I try not to worry. I'm sure you too are worried about me since the letters are so slow in reaching you, but I am quite well as usual so please do not worry. There are rumors that we may be reunited, so I'm praying day and night that it will happen.

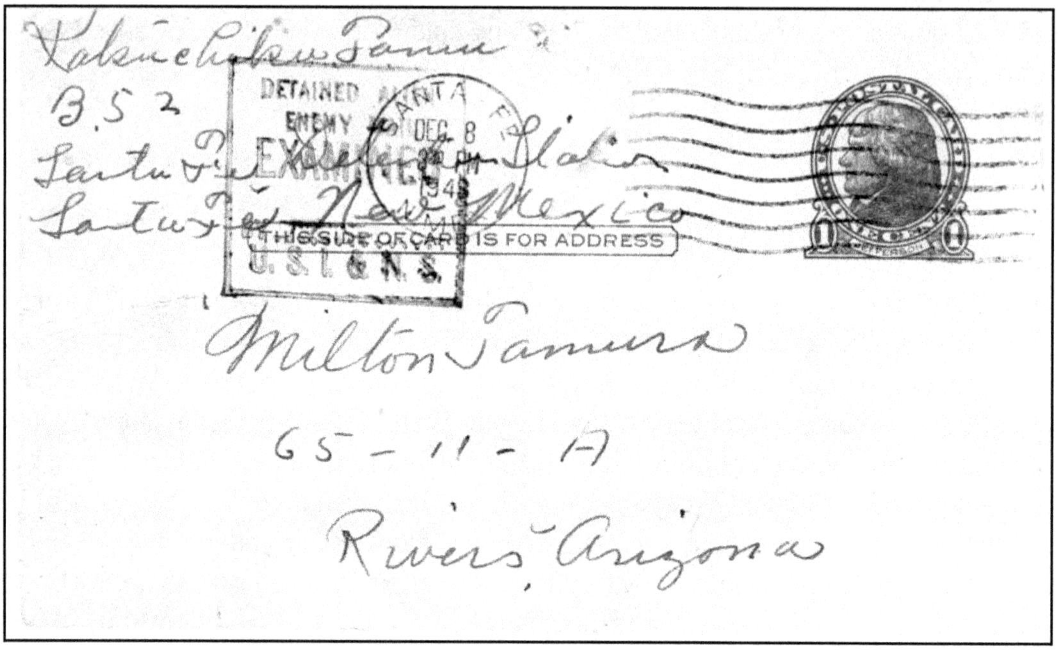

Front and back of a Christmas postcard to Milton, 1942, perhaps hand drawn.

Here, the climate is still nice and we're having good weather, so during the day I play golf and try to divert myself from this helpless, uneasy feeling, but my desire to be with you again never escapes my mind, even for a moment. I should involve myself in reading books, but in this kind of environment, it is difficult to settle down and do any serious reading, so I just pick up something light to read to while away the time.

Generally speaking, I don't have any complaints about the life here, but as I have repeatedly said, I feel a deep, unspeakable sadness in having to live apart from my family. Well, until I write again...

Affectionately, Katsuchika

December 22, 1942 *(original in Japanese)*

Dearest Umeno,

Last night, I went to bed listening to the rain pounding the roofs, but this morning it is unusually beautiful ... the air is clear, the sky is blue and the pine forest is so green and lush. How great it would be if we could enjoy this together.

Yesterday, I received your letter dated Nov. 16. The letters take so long in getting to me so I'm not learning the recent happenings and therefore have been somewhat anxious, but I'm relieved to know that you are all well. I'm so sorry that I caused you so much trouble regarding the golf clubs. As I wrote previously, I have been able to get two clubs here, but it would be nice if I could get one more club. Also golf balls are hard to obtain, so I'm hoping you could send me about six balls. My golf is not getting any better though.

Regarding the insurance, I think you did the right thing. Under the present circumstances, I think it is best to leave it like that. Keep in mind that it doesn't make any difference whether you write in Japanese or English. I am satisfied as long as you do what you think is the best way. Please take care of yourself and live happily.

Affectionately, Katsuchika

December 24, 1942 *(original in Japanese)*

Dearest Umeno,

Tomorrow is Christmas. People are individually making preparations here. The children's school must be out now. Oshogatsu (New Year) is only several days away. I reminisce about our last oshogatsu and feel very sad and lonely. Although it is already 9 o'clock, this morning it is cloudy and dark so it depresses me more. Of course, we've been apart for almost a year so it can't be helped (that I feel this way). This past year has been an unforgettable year. Although this is the tragedy that war brings, to have to be torn apart from my family when I have no dark background whatsoever... no matter how hard I try to forget and resign myself to this, I cannot. There is talk that they might unite us with our families but we won't really know until it happens. I just fervently pray that this will happen. I don't think this letter will get to you before year-end, but as I write this, I am praying that you will all have a happy oshogatsu.

Affectionately, Katsuchika

December 31, 1942 *(original in Japanese)*
Dearest Umeno,

Today is the last day of the year. This was such an unforgettable year. I am thankful that I can greet the new year in good health. I hope you too will all have a happy and healthy new year. Thank you for sending me the Christmas present the other day. They were all articles that I can use right away so I was very happy to receive it. Please let the children know my gratitude too. Packages reach here rather quickly. The insurance papers came yesterday so I signed it immediately and mailed it out. I did ask them to hasten the mailing, but I'm afraid it will take a month or so. It can't be helped. I am in a hurry so I will close for now. Please take good care of yourself. Recently, I've begun teaching English.
Affectionately, Katsuchika

January 7, 1943 *(original in Japanese)*
Dearest Umeno,

I am happy that we were all able to greet the new year in good health. Last year was an unforgettable year for us, filled with great sadness. I'm praying day and night that this year, no matter what hardships we may encounter, that we will be able to live together. New Year's Day was a nice day and we celebrated, and on the 2nd there was a stage performance. It was an unexpectedly good performance for a place like this. Please rest assured that I am well. Thank you for the Christmas present. The socks came in very handy. Mut-chan, I am using the toothpaste. Tobacco is something I like and I had run out of it. That was a pretty nice calendar. The (camp) newspapers are arriving steadily so I can picture your daily life there. Received your Japanese letter dated Nov. 26 and English letter dated Nov. 28. Since I hadn't heard from you for a while, it was a much awaited, yearned for letter. It is very troubling that the letters take so long in reaching our destinations. I always write twice weekly so I'm sure that eventually you will receive them. I did receive the scissors. I also mailed out the insurance papers, but I regret that there was no quicker way to send them. Well, please take good care of yourself and live happily.
Affectionately, Katsuchika

January 8, 1943 *(original in Japanese)*
Dearest Umeno,

How are you? Have the children started back to school? Recently there was a man whose family member was ill, so he hastily left here to go see them. This worries me. Please take extra care of yourselves. It has been raining here for a few days so it has become cold, but I'm sure it will warm up as soon as it stops raining. I did receive the mail from Okazaki-san. Because of the communication delay, I've not written to anybody. Have you heard from him lately? I hope that they are all well. Recently, I am teaching English. Today, I have a class at 1:00pm so I must prepare. I don't have any reference books so it is difficult. Activities that we had outside until recently have now been moved indoors. The room is small so it is divided into two or three sessions. I went last night, but it is not enjoyable by myself. I keep praying that we will be reunited. That is all I think about. The other day, one of the men received good news, but I did not get anything. I don't know why, and it bothers me. I feel so badly that I am putting you through this hardship. I am well so at least do not worry about me. I will close for today.
Affectionately, Katsuchika

January 11, 1943 *(original in Japanese)*
Dearest Umeno,
I imagine you are all well. How is the weather there? Are you using the stove now? According to the paper, it seems quite cold in the mornings. Do you get frost? Here, after a week of cold weather, yesterday it started to warm up. It has been almost a year since we parted... what a long year this has been. I encountered so much and experienced so many sad things. Imagine it is the same for you too. After leaving French Camp where you lived for many years, you had to go to hot Turlock and then to Arizona. I can imagine how hard it must have been for you with small children in tow. A person that visited this camp recently told us that the families of the internees were very concerned about us. But such worries are unnecessary since except for the loneliness of being separated from our families, we are not experiencing any difficulties in our everyday life here. This is something I have repeatedly told you, but since this recent camp visitor voiced the concerns of the families, I must reiterate it again... please be at peace and do not worry about my life here.
Will close for today.
Affectionately, Katsuchika

January 14, 1943 *(original in Japanese)*
Dearest Umeno,

This is already the middle of January. This morning it is overcast and gloomy weather. It looks like the inside of my heart since I left you last year. But I keep telling myself that someday it will clear up and I patiently wait for the day.

Hope you are well. Are the children healthy and going to school? I'm sure they have really grown big. Please let me know their weight and height. Is Hiromu going to the clinic every week? Does Mut-chan eat everything now instead of being picky? Hope you have plenty of green vegetables. How is your teeth? I hope you are seeing the dentist. Is Yot-chan coming home, not forgetting the time. Does he still catch colds? Please take good care of yourselves. I am well as usual but as the days go by, the loneliness becomes increasingly unbearable.

I teach English four days a week. For exercise, I play golf but I keep losing balls. If I am still here when you receive this letter, please send me a few golf balls. Please extend my regards to everybody. I will close now praying that you all will take care of yourselves.
Affectionately, Katsuchika

January 28, 1943 *(original in Japanese)*
Dearest Umeno,

For three days, the north winds made the weather cold. This morning the wind has subsided and looks like it is going to warm up. Some people have already begun their laundry.
The communication (mail) is so irregular that I have this unsatisfied feeling, but I pray and believe that you are all well and happy. I wrote Yot-chan and Mut-chan a letter last week. Hiromu must have grown big. Is he healthy? Has he stopped calling you "papa"? They say they are putting us together with our families, so I am praying that this will happen very soon. I keep telling myself that I will accept my fate bravely, but I worry day and night about you and I have no desires or ambitions beyond being together with my family.

How is the weather lately? You have children so you mustn't exert yourself and feel like you have to work. The camp paper gets here quicker if it is put in an unsealed envelope. I must close for now as they have come to inspect the rooms. Please take care.

Affectionately, Katsuchika

January 29, 1943 *(original in Japanese)*

Dearest Umeno,

Is everybody well? Fortunately, I am getting along fine. Last night, after I got into bed, I heard the rain, but this morning it is clear and the cold has eased and probably will warm up during the day. I get up at 6:30 and breakfast is at 6:45. Right now, it is still dark at breakfast, but the days will gradually become longer and more time to play.

I don't think there are people like that there, but I've heard that at some camps, there are some internees that have been swindled out of money. As you know, I have absolutely no guilt in my background and there is no reason for me to be incarcerated in this place but there is nothing anybody can do about my situation. So being reunited is our only hope so don't let people talk you into anything.

Did you receive the insurance papers that I sent you? If you received it, please process it as soon as possible. This afternoon I have an English class. I also tutor individuals privately. For exercise, I still play golf which hasn't gotten much better. Until I write again....

Affectionately, Katsuchika

February 4, 1943 *(original in Japanese)*

To my dear wife,

Yesterday I received two letters from you. One was from last year-end and another from first part of this year. It was a long awaited letter so I was very happy to read it. I am so glad to know that you and the children are all well. I think the childrens' "S" grade is satisfactory. When I hear of the family members of the internees here being ill, I worry so about your health. When you have three children, accidents/illnesses are apt to happen. In three weeks, it will be a year since we parted. I feel like I've been away from you for a much longer time. This past year, you must have been burdened with concerns to have to leave your home and move to Turlock and then to Arizona with the children and live an inconvenient camp life.

I received the scissor and pants quite a while ago so please do not be concerned. I am getting along fine. The weather is very nice so lately we have activities outdoor at night. Please give my regards to everybody and take care of yourself.

Affectionately, Katsuchika

February 9, 1943 *(original in Japanese)*

To my dear wife,

For us, receiving letters are the most happiest, eagerly awaited thing, so yesterday was an especially happy day for me since I received three letters. As you are aware, due to the censorship, I am getting letters in bunches. Each letter was so special expressing your feeling at the time. As I read your letters, I can picture the goings on there, and I am so grateful that you are all getting along safely. When I think about the family camp, I am somewhat concerned about the children losing their school and friends there.

Although I sent out my package to reach you by Christmas, it must have been delayed because of the busy season. At any rate, I'm glad you finally received it. I am receiving the Gila News steadily. The other day, we were happy to receive some artificial flowers from Gila. I don't know why but the mochi has not arrived.

We too are having very nice weather these last several days. I am writing this letter under a spring like lovely day. When I gaze through the window at the sky without a speck of cloud and the refreshingly green pine trees, my heart becomes enlightened. I wish the peaceful day would come that we could all enjoy this beautiful natural scenery together. Please tell Yot-chan and Mut-chan that I received their letter and for them to write often. Please give Nii-san and others my best regards.
Affectionately, Katsuchika

February 11, 1943 *(original in Japanese)*
To my dear wife,

I received two letters together. The letters are getting here more quickly and this letter was one you had written recently, so I really enjoyed it and read it over and over again. I am so happy that the children are growing up innocently, but I am worried that you are concerned about things and are unhappy. Of course it is understandable that being in our kind of situation, we can't help but be anxious about our current and future life. But under the upheaval like we are experiencing now, there is not one person that is not affected one way or another. In the past, during challenging, difficult times like we are experiencing now, it was the people who were strong mentally and physically that survived. Therefore, we must be strong and persevere this ordeal and overcome it for the sake of our children. Of course, it is an indescribable mental anguish to be stripped of our freedom, but we can soften it somewhat by our mental outlook.

According to the Gila News, it looks like an unfortunate incident took place in the neighborhood. I too am surprised. I can understand why you are feeling gloomy. Like a poet once said, "human beings are weak.'

By the way, yesterday I received a box of cigarettes. Thank you. I guess you know that I still can't quit smoking. I am not smoking much these days though. A carton will last me about a month. Well, take care of yourself, dear wife.
Affectionately, Katsuchika

February 16, 1943 *(original in Japanese)*
To my dear wife,

I was so happy to receive the letter you wrote earlier this month. It is wonderful to know that you are all well. Is Hiromu well now? I received Yot-chan and Mut-chan's letters. We all so look forward to receiving letters so please ask them to write me soon. I am receiving the twice weekly Gila news in sequence. Thank you so much. The papers tell me what is going on there. The other day we received many artificial flowers and we decorated the mess hall with it. The mochi finally arrived but since it took so long in getting here, it was covered with green mold and none was edible. I troubled you so much regarding the clubs, but I think we should just forget about it. Please send me the string balls that you have. I wonder why the French Camp people will not send me my clubs. Except for the shoes that I have been given at camp, I only have the one pair that I wore when I left home. I should have bought one sooner. If you have the chance, I would be very happy if you would buy me a pair. You don't have to go out of your way though. Size 7 wide width would be good. I don't know how you are looking at the situation, but except for the sorrow of being apart, I am living a peaceful life so please do not concern yourself about me.
Affectionately, Katsuchika

February 22, 1943 *(original in Japanese)*
My dearest wife,

I received your letter that you wrote about ten days ago. So happy that the letters are getting here quicker. Today is Sunday. The last few days have been quite warm and last night, it became cloudy and this morning it is raining. If the weather was nice, we would be having a baseball game in the afternoon, but looks like we are going to have to spend all day indoors. Fortunately, we have the radio and there are books to read so we are not bored. It is regrettable, as you wrote, that if we were in French Camp now, we would be enjoying all the various flowers in bloom. I've taken out the pictures and gazing at it and reminiscing... it was a happy life that I will never ever forget. For two, or three nights in a row, I have dreamt about you. It wasn't necessarily a bad dream but I guess I dream about you all because I am so concerned about you. Hiromu looked like he was being strapped on your back. [He looks like me.] I was surprised at how big Yot-chan and Mut-chan were. I guess they have really grown, huh.

Today is the 21st. I can still vividly picture that night. I didn't sleep a wink that night. Several people have been reunited with their families. But there are still a small number of us who must still live like this. I feel very sad but please persevere and wait a little while longer. They tell us that they will reunite us with our families soon. Until I write again...

Affectionately, Katsuchika

February 25, 1943 *(original in Japanese)*
My dearest Umeno,

Received your letter dated February 10th. More than anything else, I am glad to know that you are all well. I can just picture Yot-chan and Mut-chan happily going to school. It is good to hear that various vegetables are growing okay there. We are not able to pluck the vegetables from the fields and put it on the tables here. There is talk about starting a vegetable garden, but I doubt if we can get good crops out of it. They say we will soon be able to live with our families, but we have been disappointed so many times in the past so we can't rely too much on it. But I pray day and night that it will become a reality some day soon. Although there are no worries regarding our daily life, there are various mental anxieties apt to arise. Let us both try to be mentally strong and try not to let things needlessly bother us and let's look towards our children's future.

Please give my regards to everybody. I did receive Yot-chan and Mut-chan's letters. Please tell them to take good care of themselves and study hard. Until I write again.

Affectionately, Katsuchika

March 3, 1943 *(original in Japanese)*
My dearest Umeno,

Lately, the postal communication has become so good that I received your letter of several days ago today. So glad and relieved to hear that everyone is well. I am doing fine as usual too. It rained for a few days, but yesterday it turned into a north wind and this morning it is somewhat chilly but I think it will warm up in the afternoon. I know you are worrying about many things but, as I have repeatedly told you, our living condition here is quite satisfactory and if fortunately we get to go to an internees' family camp, I'm sure this will not change, so please do not believe all the rumors you hear.

I did receive the package of golf balls and cigarettes. I was happy to receive it and do appreciate your thoughtfulness, but it must be quite troublesome for you so you do not have to send me anymore cigarettes. And please keep in mind that you can send me packages direct to my camp address. I am getting the Gila News in sequence too. Some of the families interned in Arkansas are coming here to

see their husbands/fathers. But there is good and bad in this, since the small children do not understand and some beg their fathers to go home with them. The fathers tell me this is so painful.
Some people are getting notices to go to family camp and so I am getting restless, but we mustn't rejoice prematurely until we are finally really together. I pray day and night that this will happen. Until I write again.... take care of yourselves.
Affectionately, Katsuchika

April 7, 1943 *(original in Japanese)*
My dearest wife,

Received your letter of March 26th and was happy and relieved to know that you are all well. I am well, too and try to live each day happily so don't be concerned. Some people have already moved out to the family camp so I keep anticipating that my turn will come next and waiting eagerly for the day.

Tomorrow is Hiromu's birthday. I reminisce about those days two years ago and the many things that happened then. The weather has warmed up quite a bit here. We will be taking out the stove this week. There is a difference of day and night from the place we were in last year this time. It's too bad that the chicken pox is going around. It can't be helped if they get it although you have been careful. Seems like children have to get these various diseases once. And you shouldn't worry yourself too much about the children's grades. Boys tend to be like that so unless it is really bad, you shouldn't scold him too much.

I did tell you previously that I received the golf balls. I used one of them last Sunday. It's a very good ball. I don't know when I'll be able to get more so I am using it with care. I have nothing else I need now so please don't worry. You talked about pictures, but unfortunately, this camp does not have such conveniences. Will close for today. Please take care of yourself and live cheerfully.
Affectionately, Katsuchika

April 14, 1943 *(original in Japanese)*
My dearest Umeno,

Received your letter of April 1st and was very happy to know that you are all well. Hiromu is learning naughty things so you must be troubled. I picture the scene from your letter and I am amused and burst out laughing.

Received a letter the other day from Set-chan Yoshimi. She is still in California so I think it is better for her. I am well too. It has been hot for several days and hasn't felt good, but today is an unusually nice clear day with a little breeze.

Tokunaga-san who owned the Kashu Laundry sent me a box of candy through people who come to visit the camp. I am filled with gratitude that there are people who have not forgotten me. When the golf clubs get there, please send me just the #7 iron. I am praying that the day will arrive soon when we can all go to the family camp, but the preparations are taking time and it will not happen real soon.

Please give my best wishes to the children. Until I write again, take care of yourselves.
Affectionately, Katsuchika

April 21, 1943
To: Mrs. Umeno Tamura 6 5- 3- D Rivers, Arizona
From: Katsuchika Tamura ISN-23-4-J-1 01 2-C1 Camp Livingston Int. Camp Box 2O,
General Post Office New York, New York
My dear wife,

Hope you are all well. I imagine it is getting quite hot there. I am in good health so please do not worry. It had been quite warm for several days so I put the stove away, but it suddenly turned cool again and being cold blooded, I am not bearing it too well. When the weather clears up, I'm sure it will warm up again.

Have not heard anything more about reuniting us. I'm sure it will eventually come about.. probably taking time to make proper preparations. Last Sunday, we were supposed to have a golf tournament but it was rained out. I spent the day reading and listening to the radio. When I hear the raindrops hitting the roof, I become very lonesome and think about you and the children and my heart becomes very heavy.

Yot-chan and Mut-chan are at an important age and I'm sure you have many concerns and worries. But living during this era, we must resign ourselves to the fact that we couldn't avoid this fate and so I think it would be better to not be too stern with them. No matter how trying the circumstances may be, I live everyday trying to be cheerful (in my heart) and not be bitter. I hear people are having to conserve food items on the outside, but here everything is plentiful and I have no complaints. Well, I will close for now. Please take care of yourself.
Affectionately, Katsuchika

April 24, 1943
To: Mrs. Umeno Tamura 65-3-D Rivers, Arizona
From: Katsuchika Tamura ISN-23-4-J- 1 01 2-C1 Camp Livingston Intern. Camp Box 20,
General Post Office New York, New York
My dear Umeno,

I read your natsukashii (yearned for) letter. I am glad to hear that you are all in good health. I'm sure that the children are enjoying Easter and school vacation. Did they hunt for colorful Easter eggs? Today is a rare, beautiful morning and it feels real good.

As usual under these current situations, many things are happening and at times I become very concerned, but fortunately it ends peacefully than I thought. I often think about learning something practical, but nothing comes of it and I end up passing the time reading and playing golf.

There is work that I must do, but it is not that difficult and everything is going well. I asked for a golf club... has it arrived yet? The club that you were able to get... is it from French Camp or did you have to buy it? I am familiar with life there from the newspapers you continually send me, but the daily life must have become rather boring after such a long time. The preparation for the family camp seems to be taking time. Is Hiromu still giving you a bad time? Well, I will close f o r today. Please stay well.
Affectionately, Katsuchika

May 19, 1943
To: Mrs. Umeno Tamura 65-3-D Rivers, Arizona
From: Katsuchika Tamura ISN-23-4-J- 1 01 2-C 3rd Internment Co. 1902 Camp Livingston Inter. Camp Box 20, General Post Office New York, New York
My dear Umeno,

It has become quite hot here. I am sure it is quite hot there too. According to the letter that my roommate has received, it is very hot there and at night, cannot fall asleep until past midnight. I feel for you. I've heard that many people have installed air-conditioners there.

Have you put one in? Things are about the same here for me. It is hard to read in the room so I spend the day practicing golf in the mornings and evenings, avoiding the mid-day. The other day, the young people put on a play and tomorrow is the weekly movie night. Currently, I don't do physical labor due to my job, but I don't have much time for it either. Right now, our biggest hope is that we would be reunited with our families. The process is slow. Are the children out of school now? How is Hiromu? Is he getting more bad? He must have learned a lot of words by now.

Please take care o f yourself and try to live cheerfully everyday.

Please say "hello" to the children.

Affectionately, Katsuchika

May 25, 1943 *(original in Japanese)*

My dear Umeno,

It started getting cloudy around 3:00pm and looked like it might start raining but it didn't even after dark. But as I am writing this letter, lightning and big drops of rain are hitting the roof. The rain will hold down the dust and cool down the heat so it's good. It must be awfully hot and hard for you to bear the heat there. I heard many people installed air coolers... did you?

I am quite well. I hope you and the children are all well, too. I received the beautiful picture that Mut-chan sent me yesterday. I was so very happy to receive it. Please convey my thank-you to her. When will school be out? I'm sure the family camp will be opening some day, but it is sure taking time. Sometimes I begin to doubt if there is any hope. It is a helpless situation. Well, so long for tonight... please take care.

Affectionately, Katsuchika

June 2, 1943 To: Mrs. Umeno Tamura

6 5- 3- D Rivers, Arizona

From: Katsuchika Tamura ISN-23-4-J-1 01 2-C1 Camp Livingston Intern.

Camp Box 20, General Post Office New York, New York

My dear Umeno,

Read your letter with nostalgia. I am happy to hear that you are all well. Is everyone well at Nii-san's family and the Takemori family? It must've gotten very hot there by now. It's become quite hot here too, but not unbearable. Fortunately, I am healthy and busily living each day so please do not worry. I yearn to see you again, but they keep us waiting.

I understand school will be out the middle of this month. The children must have grown quite big by now. Please see that he doesn't get hurt practicing judo. Overdoing sports is sometimes harmful.

Perhaps my next letter will show a different return address, but it is nothing to worry about. I am waiting for Hiromu's picture. The little devil must be giving you a hard time.

I put away my golf clubs so I can't play anymore but I am kept busy so I am not too bored. At night I pass the time reading magazines.

Well, I will close for today. Please take care of yourself and keep happy thoughts in your heart.

Affectionately, Katsuchika

KATSUCHIKA TAMURA
BRK 52
S.F. DETENTION STATION
SANTA FE, N.M.
INTERNEE OF WAR
POSTAGE FREE
SANTA FE
SEP 15
2 30 PM
1943
N.MEX.
MRS. UMENO TAMURA
65-3-D
J
RIVERS, ARIZONA

SANTA FE, NEW MEXICO

June 1943–May 1944

The following letters are from Katsuchika Tamura at Santa Fe Detention Station, Santa Fe, New Mexico, to his wife Umeno interned at Rivers, Arizona.

June 8, I 943 *(original in Japanese)*
My dearest wife,

Arrived here last night. It is rather chilly, the weather is good and the scenery is very nice. Since I just got here, I am not settled in yet, but I wanted to let you know of my move and my new address.

I am closer to you now and the letters should arrive more quickly so I am very happy about that. I don't know if this means that we will be reunited with our families soon or not, but I am praying that it will.

Hope everybody is well. Please give everyone my best regards. Will close for now. Take care.
Affectionately, Katsuchika

June 10, 1943 *(original in Japanese)*
Dearest Umeno,

Please rest assured that everything is well and I am fine. Mornings and evenings are quite cool and especially since it is cloudy today, I need a sweater. If you can, please send me about $20 since my money has not yet arrived from Camp Livingston.

Hope you are all well. How are the children? It must be very hot there. Has school let out?

From a high place, I can see the city very well. The scenery is nice and the air is clean... it is somewhat like Denver. We are surrounded on three sides by mountains and reminds me of Kyoto. The soil is sandy and pebbles get in our low shoes. Will close for now. Please take care.
Affectionately, Katsuchika

June 15, 1943 *(original in Japanese)*
Dearest Umeno,

Received your later dated May 27th today by way of Livingston. Your letter was long awaited for and I was happy to know that you are all well.
Everything is going along well here. We are at a 7,000 ft. elevation so mornings and nights are very cool... I must admit we are very lucky when you are all living in heat.

Last night, some new people arrived here and I met some people I hadn't seen in a long time.
Take care.
Affectionately, Katsuchika

June 18, 1943 *(original in Japanese)*
Dearest Umeno,

I read your much awaited letter, and looked at Hiromu's picture. He sure has grown. He must be a handful. I met a person from Gila who told me that Hiromu looks like me, but I think he looks more like you than me. Either way, more than anything else, he looks very healthy and quite chubby and that makes me very happy. Yot-chan and Mut-chan must have grown too. It would be nice if you can send me pictures of them too.

Many people came here from Stockton. There are some that went back. I don't have any idea what's happening to our future. At this point, if we could only go to family camp together, that would be the best. I met people that I hadn't seen in a long time and the talk was endless. It was sure good to hear about the people around Gila. Looks like many things are happening one after another there. I'm sure you are very concerned about the children.

Will close for today.

Please take care in everything you do. Tell Yot-chan I received his painting.
Affectionately, Katsuchika

June 21, 1943 *(original in Japanese)*
My dear Umeno,

Read your letter with nostalgia. I am happy to hear that you are all well. Is everyone well at Nii-san's family and the Takemori family? It must've gotten very hot there by now. It's become quite hot here too, but not unbearable. Fortunately, I am healthy and busily living each day so please do not worry. I yearn to see you again, but they keep us waiting.

I understand school will be out the middle of this month. The children must have grown quite big by now. Please see that Yot-chan doesn't get hurt practicing judo. Overdoing sports is sometimes harmful.

Perhaps my next letter will show a different return address, but it is nothing to worry about. I am waiting for Hiromu's picture. The little devil must be giving you a hard time.

I put away my golf clubs so I can't play anymore, but I am kept busy so I am not too bored. At night I pass the time reading magazines.
Well, I will close for today. Please take care of yourself and keep happy thoughts in your heart.
Affectionately, Katsuchika

July 2, 1943 *(original in Japanese)*

My dearest wife, I received your letter this afternoon, but as I was somewhat busy with things, I couldn't take my time reading it. After dinner, it rained and things quieted down, so I was able to read your longed for letter over again. I am glad to know that the children are well in spite of the heat. Here it is cool and I can sleep very comfortably at night for which I am quite grateful.

I want you to know that I did receive the $20 that you sent me. The office did not notify me of the remittance until recently and that is the reason for the delay in acknowledging receipt. I'm just hoping that I did not put a strain on you (financially) with my request.

This spring, I met a person who lived there (Gila) and he told me of the various incidents and occurrences. It saddened me deeply to learn of the frailty of human nature in these disgraceful conducts.

Some of the people here are gradually returning, but no one knows who is going to be next, and the family camp seems slow in coming about, so it is a repeat of an unsettling feeling. Well, until I write again, please stay well and be happy.
Affectionately, Katsuchika

July 6, 1943 *(original in Japanese)*
My dearest wife,

It has been a month since I arrived here. The last three days have been quite hot, but this afternoon due to the light clouds, it is getting cool. I am quite well so please do not be concerned. The carpenters are daily pounding away, building a new dining hall. I think we will be sitting around a new dining table to eat next week. Right now, it is like a picnic every day and it is fun.

We laughed as we were told that the other day, when a friend's family came to visit him here, a child about Hiromu's age said "Bye bye Oji-san" (Uncle, mister) to his father as he left.

I hope the children are healthy. Have Yot-chan and Mut-chan started summer school yet? As long as the children grow up with an obedient disposition, we shouldn't be too concerned. Hideo-san must have grown a lot too.

Lately, a golf course was completed so I go to play once in a while. By the way, is there any way I can get ahold of my golf clubs that I left at French Camp? Well, take care of yourselves in this heat.
Affectionately, Katsuchika

July 9, 1943 *(original in Japanese)*
My dearest wife,

I read your letter of July 2nd. I am so happy to know that you are all well in spite of the severe heat. How difficult it must be to get to sleep when you are sweating even after you are in bed. Fortunately, we are in a high elevation here so when the sun goes down it is cool. We even need a sweater when we have outdoor movies at night. Some men are returning to the centers, but most of us are still here and do not know what is going to happen and we pass the days with unsettling feelings.

I imagine vegetables and melons are plentiful there. Vegetables grow here but there are no melons. For breakfast, we are given oranges and canned fruits. Well, I will close for now. Please take care of yourselves.
Affectionately, Katsuchika

July 14, 1943 *(original in Japanese)*
My dearest wife,

I received and read your yearned for letter of July 7th. Was relieved to hear that you are all well in spite of the severe heat... I am grateful to Buddha for his divine protection. I am as usual quite well so please do not be concerned. I understand it rained a little the other day, but I'm sure the coolness did not last very long. Since so many people are using the water supply, I'm sure it is not enough.

According to the Spain consular, he said families should be reunited by the end of October. We've been led on for so long that I don't know if we can believe his story or not, but I would like to believe it. I don't have any complaints of the life here, but I just can't stand living apart from my family. There are some men who left here and perhaps you have talked to some who were here, but it looks like I don't have much of a chance of leaving here. I don't see any difference between me and the ones that are leaving here, but I guess that is life. At any rate, let's take care of ourselves and look forward happily to the day we can be reunited again. Will close for now.
Affectionately, Katsuchika

July 22, 1943 *(original in Japanese)*
My dearest wife,

I received your letter and am getting the Gila News in sequence one after another so I am relieved that everything seems to be going well for you. Fortunately, I too am quite well and am busy everyday with my own things and doing things for others.
At this time of year, California's skies were beautiful, and here too the scenery is very beautiful, with clear skies and lush green mountains surrounding us on three sides so I spend much of my time outdoors.

Yesterday, a lady brought a child to visit an internee here and I imagined that Hiromu probably has grown and looks about like him. As is normal in times like this, both tragic and comic things happen, but we must be strong and face and overcome everything.

I have heard from people who have left here, and all the news seems pretty good. I don't think there is anything to be pessimistic about. I asked the man who left here for Camp Rohwer to give my best regards to your younger sister.

Are Yot-chan and Mut-chan well and enjoying going to summer school? They must have grown quite a bit. Are photos pretty expensive? I have pictures of them from French Camp, but I sure would like to see their recent pictures. Well, I'll close for today. Take care.
Affectionately, Katsuchika

July 24, 1943 *(original in Japanese)*
Dearest Umeno,

The days go by quickly.. in another week, I will have been here two months. Compared to the heat there, I have much to be thankful for here, but I just spend the days with unsettled, unfulfilled feelings because I am away from you. I've been asked to teach school again but I declined this time. I go to play golf sometimes, but I'm not getting better and I'm not able to do as much reading as I anticipated since the library here doesn't have much and the lighting is poor. And we don't have picnics anymore since the new dining hall was completed. Last night, we had a movie and tonight we are supposed to have a play.

Hope you and children are well. Are you still having a water shortage? It must be a hardship in this hot weather. Do you have a cooler or fan? According to the Ikeda's daughter, most barracks have one or the other. Please give my best regards to everybody.
Affectionately, Katsuchika

Translator's notes: From around these letters, I've noticed that Mr. Tamura's neat, meticulous penmanship and the tone of his nihongo has gradually changed, reflecting his deep mental anguish, irritation and impatience. It is difficult to translate these letters without shedding tears.

July 28, 1943 *(original in Japanese)*
My dearest wife,

This morning is a beautifully clear highland scenery. During the day, the sun is hot so I take a walk in the mornings. Surrounded by mountains on three sides, one side is this town. Sometimes I hear the voices of children chasing sheep and it is hard to imagine that the world around us is in a state of unrest... it seems so peaceful here. In days past, in peaceful times I used to get up early and hurry down to the golf course, but I don't know if I will ever be able to walk down that road feeling the same again.

Probably better to think that I never will.

Everything seems to be going well. I really haven't heard any good news though. Before moving here, I anticipated that after the move things would move along more quickly, but that has not happened and I feel betrayed. Eventually I guess it will come about, but I don't have any idea when it will happen.

The severe heat must be continuing so it must be hard for you to cope. Are the children healthy and going to school? They must have grown so much that I probably won't recognize them. I wish I could see them.

Well, this will be all for today. Please take good care of yourselves.

Affectionately, Katsuchika

July 29, 1943 *(original in Japanese)*

Dearest Umeno,

I take it you are all well. I was very happy to receive a Father's Day gift from the children last week. It must be very hot there these days. I feel for you. Many things happened here but everything went well and I am living happily.

I was surprised yesterday that although the sun was out, lots of water flowed down. It was the water from the evening rain on the mountain range that thundered downhill. It was a strange phenomenon.

I met some people from Stockton. Some of them are leaving, but my turn does not seem to be coming up. Will close for now. Take care.

Affectionately, Katsuchika

August 4, 1943 *(original in Japanese)*

My dearest wife,

I received your much awaited letter dated July 22nd and was happy to hear beyond anything else, that in spite of the terrible heat that you are all well. There are men that are gradually leaving here to go to your camp so you must feel very forlorn, but I am sure the reunification that has been put off or so long will take place in another few months, so please be patient for a little while longer. According to a letter from a man who left here and went to Rohwer, the families of the internees are very worried about our conditions... I feel very badly about worrying you and appreciate your concerns very much.

As I have repeatedly said, in unusual times like this, not only us, but many, many people are facing various difficult situations. We must be strong emotionally and pray that peace will come about soon.

I heard that the heat in Poston is terrible too, but here, fortunately, although the sun is pretty hot during the day, the mornings and evenings are cool... we even needed a coat for the outdoor performance (play) the other evening.

The doctor I met after one year has not changed at all. I don't think I have changed either. Will close for now. Until I write again. Sayonara.

Affectionately, Katsuchika

August 9, 1943 *(original in Japanese)*

My dearest Umeno,

Since we entered August, it is raining more here, but it is a refreshing rain... it does not rain very

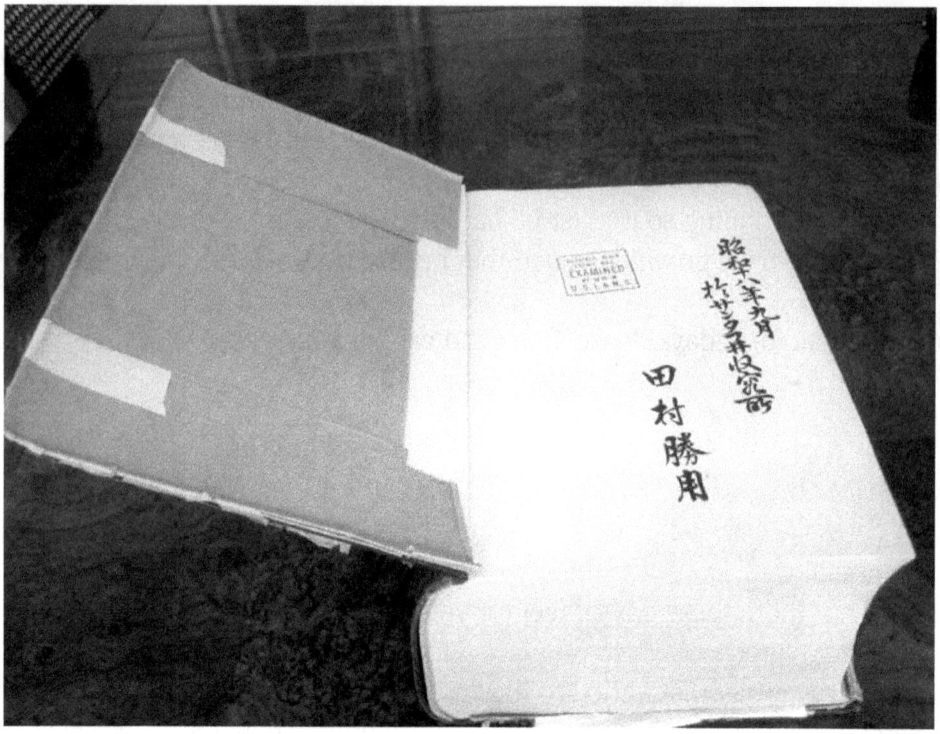

Two dictionaries, pictured below, ordered by Katsuchika in August 1943.
The inscription, above, reads: September 18, 1943. Santa Fe Internment Camp, Tamura, Katsuchika.

long, just a short time, and after that the clouds part and we can see the blue skies again. I guess that is how it is in the high elevations. I am quite well as usual and while the days away with no good news and no change in our lives. Compared to the daily lives of the people living in the camps, our lives may seem awfully carefree, but no matter how much we worry, there is nothing we can do, so we are resigned to our fate and just waiting for the day to come.

Are the children healthy and going to school? I can almost imagine your daily life by reading the Gila News that you send me and from the conversations with visitors from there. Looks like vegetables grow well there. It must be because there are a 1ot of experienced people from around the French Camp area. How about the melons? Are they sweet? We get melons every once in a while. Colorado's Rockyford? is noted for its melons but I don't know whether that is where it comes from or not. It wasn't of very good quality though.

Please give everybody my best regards, and apologize to them for my not writing them.
Affectionately, Katsuchika

August 13, 1943 *(original in Japanese)*
My dearest wife,

We had a play performance last night and the result was something that you don't expect in a place like this. The actors who played the leading female roles, Shizuka-gozen and Oyone, were so good that there was a big commotion among the all male audience. It was performed outdoors, but after 9 o'clock, it got quite chilly and we donned our overcoats. It must still be terribly hot there and the children must be bothered by heat rash. I'm glad to hear that you at least have ample supply of water.

I'm sure you have heard from the men that left here, that our life here is nothing for you to be concerned about. Since last year June, I too have applied to be reunited with my family and for the past year, that hope is what has kept me going and just as you have been distressed, I sometimes feel quite irritated that nothing has happened, but it's no use agonizing over it so I wait, resigning myself to this fate.

The rationing of items is nothing to be concerned about. I have more things than I really need and I don't wish to add to my belongings. But the other day, I did order two dictionaries and so my pocket money is getting kind of low. There is no hurry, but if you can send me about $30, I would appreciate it. I'm only writing this because you had inquired about the rationing... you don't need to send the money right away. Such a request from me may be a hardship since we don't have any income. Will close for now.
Affectionately, Katsuchika

August 17, 1943 *(original in Japanese)*
My dearest Umeno,

It rained quite heavily last night, and as I had left the window open by my bedside, I had to get up in the middle of the night to close it. But this morning it is very clear and a quite refreshing day. The men are going out to play golf or baseball but I have a meeting to attend today. I've had enough of meetings but even here, I am still asked to do things and it is hard to refuse and I am troubled.

Compared to the cool weather here, I hear it's unbearably hot there... I feel for you there. Are you all getting along well? By the way, whatever happened to the Sumitomo thing? Is it left the way it was? If it is, I think for the time being, we can just leave it as. I got a letter about it the other day so I thought I would ask. Well, I will close for today. Take care.
Affectionately, Katsuchika

Lady Shizuka, in a book illustration by Kikuchi Yōsai.

Shizuka Gozen (1165--1211), or Lady Shizuka, one of the most famous women in Japanese history and literature, was a shirabyoshi (court dancer) of the 12th century, and a mistress of Minamoto no Yoshitsune. Since she, like many others, are featured largely in the Heike Monogatari (Tale of Heike), Gikeiki (Chronicle of Yoshitsune), and a number of plays of various traditions, her story is quite well-known, but it is difficult to separate fact from fiction within it.

Her mother, Iso no Zenji, was a shirabyoshi as well. According to the Gikeiki, Shizuka was invited at one point by Retired Emperor Go-Shirakawa, along with ninety-nine other dancers, to dance for rain after the chanting of one hundred Buddhist monks failed to bring that same result. Though ninety-nine dancers likewise failed to bring rain, Shizuka's arrival brought the desired effect. She was then praised by the Emperor, and it was at this time that she met Yoshitsune.

When Yoshitsune fled Kyoto in 1185, after the end of the Genpei War, and following a disagreement with his brother, Yoritomo, the first Kamakura shogun, Shizuka was left behind in Yoshino. The exact details of how far she traveled with Yoshitsune before being sent back, or whether she traveled further than Yoshino at all, differ from one literary work to the next, as do many of the other finer details of her tale. In any case, she was captured by Hojo Tokimasa and forces loyal to Yoritomo, and, according to some versions of the story, forced to dance for the new shogun at Tsurugaoka Hachiman-go. There, she sang songs of her longing for Yoshitsune, which angered Yoritomo; but Yoritomo's wife Hojo Masako was sympathetic, and helped to have her released. However, she was by this point pregnant with Yoshitsune's child; Yoritomo declared that if it were a daughter she could live on peacefully, but if it were a son, he would have the child killed. A short time later, when Shizuka was 19, she gave birth to a son; Adachi Kiyotsune tried to take the child, who was instead given to Shizuka's mother. She then traveled back to Kyoto, where she became a Buddhist nun. Shizuka was later killed, however, along with her and Yoshitsune's child, by the order of Yoritomo.

According to some versions of the story, she did not become a nun upon her return, nor was she killed. Alternatively, she returned to Kyoto and was welcomed by Hojo Masako back into court life, where she remained for a time. She then left the capital once more, committing suicide by drowning herself in a river, though versions differ on where this occurred.

Shizuka features prominently in the Noh play "Funa Benkei" and the bunraku play "Yoshitsune Senbon Zakura", both of which were later adapted by kabuki, and in a number of other works of literature and drama, both traditional and modern. She is also celebrated throughout the country in various festivals; many towns across Japan claim to be the location for her religious exile, her death, or other significant events of her life. *(Text, Wikipedia; PD-Japan, old photo)*

August 26, 1943 *(original in Japanese)*
My dearest Umeno,

I'm glad to hear that in spite of the heat you are all doing well. I am well as usual. Have you also heard there that some people are moving to Tule Lake around the end of October? Wonder what is going to happen to Nii-san and Takemori-san? After the repatriation ship leaves, I'm sure some families will be going to Family Camp and I'm praying that we will be among them. Yesterday, I took pictures with some Stockton people. When it's done, I will send you a photo. Please take care.

Affectionately, Katsuchika

August 30, 1943 *(original in Japanese)*
My dearest Umeno,

Received your much yearned for letter dated August 21. I am glad to know that you are all well. I am quite healthy so please do not be concerned. Tonight we are having an unusual rainfall and the sound of the rain hitting the roof makes me sorrowful. The man next door returned to Japan so I feel all the more forlornly.

I did receive the money and the club. I was happy to hear from men that visited your camp that you are all well and safe. Soon we may be moved to the Family Camp. Of course I have no way of knowing whether I will be selected or not, but I am praying that the day will come soon. Please take care.

Affectionately, Katsuchika

September 3, 1943 *(original in Japanese)*
My dearest Umeno,

I woke up early this morning and went for a walk before breakfast, but already there were early risers walking and doing exercises. There is a mountain on the east side so the sunrise is later than the flatlands, but it is a really beautiful scenery when the sun peeks from the mountain edge.

I heard the repatriation ship has finally left port so our friends are on the seas embarking on a long journey. Are our children healthy and growing up correctly? I am well as usual. I was told that I can only write one letter next week, but don't be concerned. Will close for now.

Affectionately, Katsuchika

September 10, 1943 *(original in Japanese)*
My dearest Umeno,

It wouldn't be an exaggeration if I said that the mornings and evenings are cold. The events outdoors are cold now. I guess you are still bothered by heat. When does it start cooling off? I am very well. Heard five families from there received notices to go to Family Camp. Has our turn come up yet? I am patiently waiting as that would be the best news ever. Am sending you the photos. The sun was strong so my eyes look funny, but I am doing well here. I am sure that you are all well. Please take extra care of yourselves.

Affectionately, Katsuchika

September 16, 1943 *(original in Japanese)*
My dearest wife,

Are you all healthy and doing all right? Although individually, we haven't committed any crime, having to live during these tragic times and not being able to avoid this terrible fate, you must be very bored with the monotonous daily life there. I feel for you. I am very sorry to hear that your father in Japan passed away. Needless to say, when I think about how concerned he must have been about you all, I am lost for words. I am sure that your mother is quite distressed, but I pray that she stays well until peace comes and everyone can happily meet again. Please convey my heartfelt condolences to Nii-san.

Fortunately, I am living each day in good health so please do not be concerned. Are the children growing up obediently? Well, until I write again, please take care.
Affectionately, Katsuchika

September 23, 1943 *(original in Japanese)*
My dearest Umeno,

I believe you are all safe and healthy. Yesterday, I had a physical exam and I am very healthy so please do not be concerned. Lately, the good news seems to be coming from the families. Have you received any good news? From the conversation with a person from there the other day, he said that we were among the ten families going to Crystal City. If that is true, how wonderful that would be. I can only pray day and night that this will happen real soon so I can see your safe and healthy faces again. I am sure you received the pictures I sent you. Until I write again.
Affectionately, Katsuchika

October 2, 1943 *(original in Japanese)*
My dearest wife,

Received your letter of September 27 and was happy and relieved to know that you are all well. Glad to hear that Yot-chan and Mut-chan started back to school. No matter what happens, schooling is very important. How is Hiromu these days? Is he naughty and giving you a bad time? It sounds like it has cooled down quite a bit there. Here, the mornings and evenings are cold, but we have wonderful fall weather during the day and the mountain scenery is just beautiful.
It is already October but I have not received any good news. I don't know what happened, but the pictures I sent you went to Gila and came back to me so I sent it out again. I am sure you have received it by now. Do you hear from the Okazakis? Was the baby they had since a boy? Until I write again.
Affectionately, Katsuchika
October 9, 1943 *(original in Japanese)*
My dearest Umeno,

Received your letter informing me of the receipt of the pictures and I was happy to know that you are all well. I am very well too so please do not concern yourself about me. The peak of the mountains were covered with snow, but yesterday's warm weather melted it away. It is fall and the leaves are turning yellow and reminds me of desolate winter. I am praying that before winter arrives, we can finally live together as a family. From what I am hearing, there is no good news and I am just whiling away the days. Will close for today.
Affectionately, Katsuchika

October 12, 1943 *(original in Japanese)*
My dearest wife,

I am sure that you are well. After move after move, you must be emotionally unnerved, but I am sure that you are persevering and doing your best.

By the way, the Liquidation Committee of Sumitomo Bank is badgering us... what should we do? With the interest, I think it is about $270. If they will return us the certificates, and we put it away, it

Umeno's father's funeral. Seated in front, from the left: Mrs. Kohara, Umeno's aunt; another aunt; Mutsu, Umeno's mother; unidentified man; child, Yoshimi, with her mother, Umeno's sister.

may be of use some day.

In the evenings, sometimes we have short rainfalls, but the next morning, it is nice and clear and a refreshing day. There are so many people around that I really can't settle down and read, but I pass the days playing golf and other games outdoors. Well, until I write again.
Affectionately, Katsuchika

October 20, 1943 *(original in Japanese)*
My dearest Umeno,

Received your letter acknowledging receipt of the package and was happy to hear that the children were happy with what I sent them. (A southwestern piece of clay pottery. It was a pretty little pitcher, perhaps made by local Indians. It was lost or broken over the family's many moves.) Some mornings are quite cold now and this morning the water in front of the barracks was covered with a thin film of ice. The trees in the distant view that were lush green have changed their colors to yellow and reminds us of autumn's arrival. A second autumn is here since we parted and not knowing exactly when we might see each other again, I sometimes become depressed and melancholy and can't help but feel the stir of fall. I am sure you too are distressed with the same feelings. But for the sake of the children, please try to live cheerfully. How dark and healthy Hiromu looks in the picture. Will close for today.
Affectionately, Katsuchika

October 22, 1943 *(original in Japanese)*
My dearest wife,

Hope you are all well. I am very well so please do not be concerned. Three days ago, it was very cold and my hands became dry and chapped, but today the north wind has died down and the sky is clear without a speck of cloud, so it will probably become warm during the day. Lately, we have been growing quite a few vegetables here and some are of good quality. The daikons are pretty large and we make tsukemono and daikon oroshi (grated daikon) and eat it. According to a man that visited Topaz recently, he says the living conditions at the camp have improved, so I'm sure it is the same with your camp. I remember that last winter you didn't have a stove and you said that Hideo and Hiromu's hands were cold as ice, but I don't think that will be the condition this year. Please give my best regards to the Takemoris and Nii-san's families.

Affectionately, Katsuchika

October 24, 1943 *(original in Japanese)*
My dearest wife,

I received your airmail letter of October 19th and I agree with everything. There are many people here that temporarily visit the camps, and I too have considered applying but, number one, it is quite an expense, and number two, I've heard that the transportation system is quite congested and it is not an easy trip, and number three, what worries me most is that we would only see each other for a short time and would have to part again.

Since I parted with you that night in French Camp, you have not left my thoughts day and night. I pray constantly that we would be reunited again, but unfortunately that has not happened. I feel so sad that the time that we have been separated is now longer than the days that we lived together. But memories should not be measured by the length of time, and I think about the happy, wonderful times we shared together and believe that if we are patient and persevere, those days will come again. Hopefully, when we again meet each other, we will not be separated again, for I cannot bear the thought of a temporary visit and having to part with you again.

In regards to the bank (Sumitomo), if we can come up with the money, I will inquire whether they will definitely return us the certificate. Of course I don't expect you to have that amount of money, but I thought I would talk this over with you. If there is nothing we can do about it at this time, we will just have to leave things as it is for now.

For your information, when the temporary visit application gets approved, I can't just leave immediately; I must wait my turn. So, please be patient and persevere and wait for the day.

Affectionately, Katsuchika

November 1, 1943 *(original in Japanese)*
My dearest Umeno,

There is frost on the ground lately and we need our overcoats to go to the dining hall, but it is still warm during the day and we can exercise outdoors. It's already November, so I have cut away the October calendar and there are only two more months left. My heart is filled with thoughts that are hard to describe.

According to Yot-chan and Mut-chan's letters, you've moved to a new barracks so you must've been very busy. Ever since you had to leave French Camp, I realize that you must've encountered various mental anguishes and worries that you could not describe in letters to me. At times like this, I think of the story about Basho (famous Japanese Haiku poet). One autumn, Basho embarked on a trip down the Tokaido Trail accompanied by his apprentice, Senri. And the two looked forward more than anything else to viewing the majestic Mt. Fuji. But that day, unfortunately it had rained and blurred the scenery, dashing their hopes. Senri was very disappointed and he blamed the rain. But Basho read a haiku saying "misty rainy day that prevents viewing Fuji is also interesting". He didn't let the bad weather bother him, but instead immersed himself in enjoying things just as it is. Of course, it would be difficult for us ordinary, simple human beings to think like Basho, but we should try our best not to aimlessly blame our current circumstances, and take a philosophical view that this is one of life's ordeals and a valuable opportunity. I don't know the reason, but the visits to the camps have been temporarily discontinued.

Please give my regards to the Takemoris and Nii-san. Do you hear from the Okazakis?
Affectionately, Katsuchika

November 10, 1943 *(original in Japanese)*
My dearest Umeno,

We are having moderate weather for a few days here so I am spending an enjoyable time. How is the weather there? From your letter, I understood your decision so I wrote a letter to Sumitomo Bank. I'm sure I will hear back from them.

By the way, do you have a dentist there? Are you having any trouble with your teeth since? I feel bad that although we should have had it taken care of, we didn't get around to it. When I was in Bismarck, my wisdom tooth started to crack and the work I had done on it was not very good so since I got here, only the root was left. I got it pulled day before yesterday. Of course, I was given a shot before extraction so I wasn't in pain then, but I didn't feel too good after the shots wore off. My jaws still hurt, but I feel good that I got it done. I remember having trouble with my teeth when I was a child, but it concerned me to have to finally have one of my 32 teeth pulled for the first time. I pray that you and the children won't experience much dental problems. Are the children growing up obediently? Well, take care now.
Affectionately, Katsuchika

November 18, 1943 *(original in Japanese)*
My dearest wife,

How are you? Have you settled into your new place? Are the children healthy? It's getting cold so please take care that they don't catch cold. Probably due to the change in the weather, there are many men with colds and recently three were taken to the hospital from our barracks. Fortunately, I am well, but I try to take extra care in not getting ill. We've had good weather for the last ten days or so and I am spending almost every day outdoors. Yesterday, I went to a real golf course in Santa Fe. In spite of the amount of practice that I am getting, my golf is not improving much but I continue as it is good exercise. I really would like to spend my time doing more worthwhile things like reading, etc. but it is difficult to settle in and do anything in this type of environment. I just feel that I am whiling away my time doing useless things and have this concern that is hard to describe. Sorry that I have not written to Nii-san and Takemori-san, but please give them my best regards.
Well, I will close for now.
Affectionately, Katsuchika

November 23, 1943 *(original in Japanese)*
My dearest Umeno,

How are you all? Good weather is continuing, and there are many men with mild colds, but I am very healthy. I got the enclosed letter from Sumitomo Bank so please have Shizuko-san read it and if possible write a letter in my behalf from you and send the money ($269.92 plus $0.04 cents per day interest if not remitted by Nov. 30, 1943) directly to the bank. And please ask them to mail the two Yen Certificates of Deposit (collateral security on a loan) directly to you at Gila, I will also write to the Bank and request them to please send the Yen Certificates of Deposit to you. Will close for today.
Affectionately, Katsuchika

November 30, 1943 *(original in Japanese)*
Dear Umeno,

Hello! How are you? I am getting along fine. The weather here is still nice and we can exercise a lot outdoors yet. Did you have a nice dinner on Thanksgiving Day? We are fortunate in having an excellent cook in our kitchen. He used to work in Chicago and has had a long experience in gastronomical art and cooked us everything in perfection from mock turtle soup to mince pie.
Yesterday, I received your two Japanese letters, one of Oct. 14 and another of Oct. 16. They made me very, very happy as I did not hear from you in Japanese for long while. I suppose you haven't received my (rest of the letter is missing)

November 30, 1943 *(original in Japanese)*
My dearest wife,

I read your longed-for letter that you wrote to me on Thanksgiving Day. When New Year comes.. when Easter comes..when Thanksgiving comes.. maybe by Christmas.. all my anticipations and hopes have been shattered and here it is this time of year. I see no difference between me and the men leaving here, but I guess under these unusual times, I must patiently persevere and wait for the day to come. If you have sent the money and you receive the Yen Certificate of Deposit from the bank, please let me know.

I think it is best to leave our belongings at French Camp for a little while longer. It doesn't look like any more Japanese families will be going to the Crystal Family Camp. Therefore, it will probably be Tule Lake or another new camp so I think we should wait until things are more definite. For me, moving to Tule Lake is not a problem, but I can't help but be concerned about the long trip for you with the children. I already have too many things and I don't need any more winter clothing. I have enough money for now. I will ask you for it when I need it. Writing in response to your letter.
Affectionately, Katsuchika

December 4, 1943 *(original in Japanese)*
My dearest Umeno,

Day before yesterday, we had a big snowfall and the mountains and fields surrounding us has turned into a vast silvery scene. But today it is a nice day, and walking to the dining hall for breakfast in the morning twilight, the stars twinkling in the cobalt blue sky and the dark shadow of the mountains was a most beautiful sight, I am quite healthy as usual. I received the Christmas cards from Yot-chan and Mut-chan.

The Sumitomo Bank sent me documents to sign for the receipt of the Certificates, which I did yesterday and sent back. They said they would send you the Certificates as soon as they receive the

BEN C. CORLETT
SUPERINTENDENT OF BANKS
OF THE STATE OF CALIFORNIA

GEORGE H. MILL[illegible]
SPECIAL DEPUTY

THE SUMITOMO BANK OF CALIFORNIA

IN LIQUIDATION
400 L STREET
SACRAMENTO, CALIFORNIA

November 19, 1943

Mr. Katsuchika Tamura,
Barrack 52,
Santa Fe Detention Station,
Santa Fe, New Mexico.

Dear Sir: Re; Loan #5113.

In reply to your letter of November 9, 1943 regarding the return of the Yen Certificates of Deposit which were pledged by you as collateral security on the above mentioned loan:

Please be advised that if you send your check in the amount of $269.92 to take care of the principal and interest in full on or before November 30, 1943; the Yen Certificates will be returned to you.

Amount due on Principal - - - - - - -	$240.00
Interest from November 2, 1941 to November 30, 1943 @ the rate of 6% per annum - - - - - - - - - - - - -	29.92
	$269.92

You will notice that I have figured the interest to November 30, 1943; should you not be able to get your payment here by November 30th., 1943, add $0.04 cents for each day thereafter when making your remittance.

Yours very truly,

The Sumitomo Bank of California,
in liquidation

By George H. Mills
George H. Mills,
Special Deputy.

P. S. Always sign your letters with the signature that compares with the one on file with this bank.

Mills.

DETAINED ALIEN
ENEMY MAIL
EXAMINED
BY 25-4
U. S. I. & N. S.

signed documents.

As far as going to Tule Lake, at this point, it is only a possibility and I have not heard anything further. When I think about spending another Christmas and New Years apart from you, I feel this indescribable loneliness. Perhaps I erred in accepting everything too passively as fate. I pray for your health from the bottom of my heart.

Affectionately, Katsuchika

December 8, 1943 *(original in Japanese)*

My dearest wife,

It has become colder, but are you okay? Are the children well? I am as usual quite well. There are cold days here, but the weather has been usually good up to now and yesterday afternoon, I went to play golf. In regards to the family reunification, I've been told that by next spring, something should materialize. I heard that all the men here whose families are interned at Tule Lake will soon be going there. If you move to Tule Lake, it's possible that our reunification might occur sooner, but I am concerned about you leaving your friends and I don't know if this would be in the best interest of the children. What do you hear there?

Yesterday, we received some green tea from the repatriation ship (from Japan). Did you also get some too? For about a month, a mild cold was going around the barracks, but it has waned down··· fortunately, I was spared. I hope I will not catch a cold this winter. I hope you and the children will take extra care, too.

Affectionately, Katsuchika

December 10, 1943 *(original in Japanese)*

My dearest Umeno,

Yesterday, it snowed all day, but today it is clear and the sun is shining brightly on the vast silvery scene. If these sunny days continue for several days, then the snow will melt away and we can exercise outdoors again, but for now we can only take short walks and spend most of the day indoors.

Received the Christmas package that you sent me··· you sent me all these unexpected things and I truly appreciate your thoughtfulness. I was like a kid not able to wait opening the gifts··· I rejoiced at holding Mut- chan's yarn dog, the warm sweater, the golf balls, etc. in my hands. But I decided to not open the long, narrow box until Christmas. Please tell that to Yot-chan and Mut-chan. I was only able to send you all token little gifts. I did order a book for Yot-chan but they were out of it, so I could only send him something I had here. Please tell him that if I get a chance, I will get him something to make up for it.

Sumitomo Bank sent me a copy of the Certificate and letter they sent you so it looks like everything is settled okay. Will close for today.

Affectionately, Katsuchika

December 24, 1943 *(original in Japanese)*

My dearest wife,

Hope you are all well. I am quite well. It has been snowing heavily since day before yesterday, and it is ome vast snowy scene. The mornings are terribly cold, but today the sun is out and it makes me feel good. Received letters from Yot-chan and Mut-chan. I'm so glad to know that they are both well. I've heard that at some camps, there are not enough doctors. So, please take extra care of your health.

269^92
44
20
56
270^56

65-11-A
Gila River Reloc. Center
Rivers, Ariz.
Nov. 26, 1943

The Sumitomo Bank
400 L Street
Sacramento, Calif.

Attention of Mr. George H. Mills, Special Deputy,

Dear Sir:

This is in regard to the loan #5113 and the return of the Yen Certificates of Deposit of Katsuchika Tamura.

I have just received a letter from my husband, Katsuchika Tamura, [who is at Santa Fe, N. Mex.] directing me to pay you the ~~money~~ [loan].

I enclose a Postal Money Order for the amount of $269.92 which will [cover] in full the principal and interest.

Please be very sure ~~that~~ [to return two] Yen Certificates of Deposit, to me at the address shown above in the heading. I am sure my husband, from Santa Fe, N. Mex., has [al]written you already [clearly specifying] ~~in Yen certificates~~ that the Yen Certificates are ~~to be~~ [not to be] sent to him but to me here at Gila Riv. Rel. Center ~~sent to me here instead of~~ ~~him~~ [to his place].

Yours truly,

Umeno Tamura, wife

I received a Christmas card from Okazaki-san. I will write to him. I'm sure it is awfully cold where he is, too. There are quite a few men leaving here, so people with families are getting very nervous, I am sure it is the same with their families in the camps. I don't think reunification (with the families) will become definite until next spring. As I have repeatedly said, please keep happy thoughts in your heart··· instead of thinking only about our miseries, let's think about the tragic global situation and pray that peace will come about soon. The majority of the Stockton people have reunited with their families, so I sometimes become very saddened asking myself why I am still left here, but then when I think of the people who are in more unfortunate situations than me, I try to resign myself to the fact that there is nothing I can do but wait calmly, instead of futilely worrying about it. I will close for now praying that you will all be all right.
Affectionately, Katsuchika

December 29, 1943 *(original in Japanese)*
My dearest Umeno,

Hope you are all well. Please rest assured that I nm quite fine as usual. It just didn't seem right to open the presents before Christmas, so on Christmas Day I opened it, and rejoiced at each gift like a child. The sweater is very warm and fits me just fine, I looked inside but I couldn't find the store's label, and after looking at it more closely, I realized that you must have knitted it. It feels real good when I put it on and I wear it everyday filled with gratitude. Thank you so much. Please tell the children thank you too. I now have a lot of golf balls, so please do not buy anymore for a while. The neckties come in handy too. Did you get the tea I sent you? Today I sent you a pen point and candy and toys for Hiromu. As I was making the cows and horses, a man who has a child about the same age told me that a three year old would not be satisfied with such a toy, I guess before I know it, he has grown up and learned things and is no longer the baby I think he is.

Lately it snows a lot. Some of the icicles are more than two inches wide. The scenery is very beautiful on a clear day, so although it is winter, my heart does not get gloomy. We are probably living a more carefree life than you are imagining, so please do not be concerned. This will probably be my last letter to you for this year. Please take care and have a happy New Year.
Affectionately, Katsuchika

January 6, 1944 *(original in Japanese)*
My dearest Umeno,

I received the two letters you wrote at the end of the year and I am sure you were able to greet the New Year in good health. I feel very lonesome having spent my second New Year away from you, but I am very well, so please do not be concerned, I received the mochi, peanuts and almonds yesterday. It was very good. We received shoyu from the repatriation ship (from Japan) so our nimono (cooked food) tastes very good. I am doing my best to be reunited with you. I have no desires beyond that and I understand your feelings very well, so I will never do anything to betray you.

There is no hurry but please send me about $30. Please give my regards to all the people that I have not written. Will close for today. Take care.
Affectionately, Katsuchika

January 11, 1944 *(original in Japanese)*
My dearest wife,

Today it is overcast, but quite warm. Please rest assured that I am well as usual. I am sure that school has started for the children. Are they both happily going to school? I am sure Hiromu is learning both good words and bad words. All children go through this phase so it can't be helped. The family reunification plan is gradually taking place but it is not proceeding very fast. I sometimes become envious of the men being reunited with their families, but I tell myself that it is useless to get irritated and I try to patiently persevere and wait for the day to come, 1'm sure you encounter many hardships and problems, but please take care of your health and devote yourself to the children's education. Will close for today so take care. Until I write again.
Affectionately, Katsuchika

January 17, 1944 *(original in Japanese)*
My dearest Umeno,

It's an unusual nice day for January and the sun feels so good. The golf course is covered with snow and probably won't be able to play until March. I received the package from you on Saturday. Thank you very much. The knitted socks are very nice and the size is just right for me. This stationary comes in handy too. A few people got notices to go to Crystal City but I have not received anything. Good to know that Hiromu is well now and that Yot-chan and Mut-chan are well and attending school. Well, until I write again··· Sayonara.
Affecionately, Katsuchika

January 19, 1944 *(original in Japanese)*
My dearest wife,

We are having our usual good weather. The winters here are not so bad. Please do not be concerned as I am quite well. The other day we ordered buri (yellowtail) from San Diego and had it as sashimi and cooked fish.

There are quite a few men leaving here, so I am restless and troubled, but I try to calm my mind and wait for the day. The other day, I was asked some questions, so I told them honestly that living together with my family is my first choice. At any rate, it is the biggest relief to me that you and the children are healthy and safe. Please give my regards to everybody. Until I write again.
Affectionately, Katsuchika

January 26, 1944 *(original in Japanese)*
My dearest wife,

The snow has been falling steadily since last night. But it is not too cold, so besides not being able to exercise outside, it does not bother me. Are you all well? I am very well so please do not be concerned.

The Stockton men have left one after another, so there are not many left here. My case seems like it would be decided soon, but it seems to be dragging on and on and no decision has yet been rendered. I am so irritated and cannot help but feel uneasy and wretched.

I am not in a hurry, but did you get my letter asking you to send me money? Sometimes, they (?) forget about it so I am inquiring, I hope everything is well with your Nii-san's family.
Affectionately, Katsuchika

January 30, 1944 *(original in Japanese)*
My dearest Umeno,

Today is Sunday and after a big snowfall, it is a clear day and the sun is shining through the windows. From your letter, I am grateful to know that you are all safe and well. I understand there are already some families that have been relocated to Crystal City from there and so you must feel quite uneasy, but I am sure that decisions will be made soon, so please be strong and wait patiently a little while longer. Every time I say goodbye to a departing internee, I always think how happy I would be if I was one of the departing men. The men from Stockton have left one after another and now I am the only one left. But under the present circumstances, I think it is best not to make any noises about it, but wait patiently for their decision. The one thing we are blessed with is that we are all quite healthy and we must be very grateful for this.

Well, I will close for this morning. Please do take care.
Affectionately, Katsuchika

February 5, 1944 *(original in Japanese)*
My dearest Umeno,

Thank you for sending me the money. That will be plenty for quite a while, so until I ask you again, please do not send me any more. Your question regarding Tule Lake and Crystal City··· as far as the weather is concerned, I hear that Tule Lake might be better, but I am concerned about your long travel with the children. If we cancel the repatriation to Japan, it would be most convenient if we can all return to Gila and that is my desire, but I have no way of knowing whether it will be decided in our favor. No matter what the decision is, we must abide by it and do the best we can. Either way, it shouldn't be too long now, so I plead with you to please be cheerful and persevere a little while longer.

I am quite healthy and am happy and relieved to hear that you are all well too. Will close for this morning.
Affectionately, Katsuchika

February 9, 1944 *(original in Japanese)*
My dearest wife,

How have you been since? I am very well, so please do not be concerned. We had continuous good weather for about ten days. It was spring-like warm weather, but now it is cloudy and looks like it might snow. The days go by without any notification, so I feel terribly anxious but there is nothing I can do about it. Of course when I look at the big picture, I shouldn't be despairing about my personal hardship, but being human, I can't help but be concerned. I am sure you are very worried about many things, especially since you have small children with you and my heart goes out to you.

Next time you write to Okazaki-san, please give my regards to him. Are the Takemoris, Teshimas and Nii- san all well? Will close for today. Please do take care.
Affectionately, Katsuchika

February 11, 1944 *(original in Japanese)*
My dearest Umeno,

I read your long awaited for letter of February 4th and was glad to know that you are fine. I am fortunately very well, I have not heard anything more since. I am sure that it is to one of the three places, but since they make the choice, there is nothing I can do. From a letter we received from a man who went to Crystal Spring. Crystal Spring sounds like a very nice place. Of course, he hasn't experi-

enced the summer there yet and I am told that it gets quite hot there too. We are having many warm days now and it's nice since we can exercise outdoors. I understand it has warmed up there too, but you must take extra care during the changeable climate. Until I write again, take care.
Affectionately, Katsuchika

February 16, 1944 *(original in Japanese)*
My dearest wife,

Is everything all right with you since? I am very well as usual so please do not be concerned. Today, I signed the papers for Tule Lake. I don't know the definite date yet, but I am sure we will eventually all relocate there. I believe you and the children will be going there first. I am sure you will be hearing something there, but please keep in mind that that is the intention. I am concerned most about your traveling with small children, but under the circumstances, please endure everything and do your best, I know it will be hard for you to part with Nii-san and Takemori-san and the children will lose their friends so it will be sad, but please understand that it cannot be helped. Will close for today.
Affectionately, Katsuchika

February 23, 1944 *(original in Japanese)*
My dearest wife,

Are you all well? For me, the most happiest thing is that you are all well. It is needless to say that health is the most important thing for our happiness. I am quite well.

What I wrote you the other day is not definite yet, but I'm sure it will materialize, I think the families will move first and then we will be going there. From what I've heard, I think the weather is better at Tule Lake than at Crystal City so I think it will be better for the children. I can't help but worry about your long trip with the children, but please try not to worry too much and do your best. Have you heard anything there yet? From the Stockton rural area, there are two men going there. Both men have families there (Gila) so I believe we will be moving together. If the move happens quickly and you don't have time to let me know, it's all right to write me after you get there. Will close for today. Sayonara.
Affectionately, Katsuchika

February 25, 1944 *(original in Japanese)*
My dearest Umeno,

I read your letter of February 21st with sadness. That day was certainly a most grievous day. Two years has passed without not being able to do anything about it. I immediately wrote a petition asking to go to Gila and then proceed with you to Tule Lake, I will do my best from here, but if it does not happen, please try not to worry and do your best. Mrs. Mikami and Mrs. Mizuno should be going together with you so I asked them for their help. Especially since Mrs. Mikami does not have children, I'm sure that she will help look after yours. And Yot-chan and Mut-chan are now old enough to listen to reason. I will repeat petitioning.

I'm in a hurry today so will close for now.
Affectionately, Katsuchika

March 1, 1944 *(original in Japanese)*
My dearest Umeno,

I have not received any further notification. If families are moving out from there, I think it would be best to try to go with them. I am trying all I can on this end, but everything seems to take time, so if you can leave, I think that would be best so things won't be delayed any further. I fully realize the move is not going to be an easy task for you, so if my petition that I submitted the other day goes through, it would be so wonderful.

I take it you are all well, I am quite fine as usual. The weather here for the past several days has been like spring and so I can't complain.

Things that seem at first insurmountable, many times turn out not as bad as anticipated, so I beg you to not worry yourself too much in anticipation of things to come.

Affectionately, Katsuchika

March 3, 1944 *(original in Japanese)*
My dearest wife,

Before dawn, it began to snow and it is still falling. The cold is not so severe and I am well as usual. The one thing that bothers me is that I have not yet received a response to the petition I submitted. I pray day and night for a quick decision so that I will have a chance to see you again, but I don't know what's going to happen and I feel like I am engulfed in thick clouds or fog. I am sure that you must feel the same way.

Are all the children well? Even though I am not allowed a temporary visit with you, if other families are leaving, I think it would be best for you to be with them. As long as you can get a man to help you with packing your belongings, I think you will be able to somehow handle the travel. I am trying my best to come there and then go to Tule Lake with you but that might delay things··· rather than delay things, I think it would be better for you to go there first if possible and settle in.

Affectionately, Katsuchika

March 5, 1944 *(original in Japanese)*
My dearest wife, .

Yesterday was an unforgettable day for me. When I came back into the barracks from the outdoors, there was a note on my bed stating that a certified package had arrived for me. I wasn't expecting anything, so I was curious and wanted to see what it was so I hurried to the office which was just about closing Saturday afternoon. I watched the clerk as he went through the pile and picked up this package that was rather small, so I couldn't imagine what could be inside. It first had to be inspected, so I watched intently as he opened the package··· all the while my heart was filled with delight from expectation. When the case appeared, I thought it might be a watch, and when he opened the case and I saw this splendid Bulova wrist watch, I was so stunned that I couldn't talk, I have no words to express my happiness at receiving such a magnificent watch which seems to have fallen from the blue sky··· I just had not expected this at all. What I can't express to you in words, I hope you can guess my feelings.

I did receive your much awaited letter dated February 26. Am so glad that you are all well and safe, I am fine too, I haven't heard any more (regarding the family reunification).

Affectionately, Katsuchika

March 11, 1944 *(original in Japanese)*
My dearest wife ,

Nice spring-like weather is continuing. We've started work in the gardens. The flower gardens have been maintained nicely, but since there still might be frost, we haven't started planting any seedlings yet. Received your letter of March 6th. I am very grateful and relieved that you are all well, I fortunately too am quite well. I have not heard anything more since. I just pray that we will be able to see each other again soon. When the men that I've lived with since Bismarck leave here, I am filled with this indescribable loneliness. Please give my regards to Takemori-san, Teshima-san and Nii-san. And when you write to the Yamasakis, please give them my regards too. Well, will close for today. Until I write again.

Affectionately, Katsuchika

March 16, 1944 *(original in Japanese)*
My dearest Umeno,

Hope all is well with you. I am quite well so please do not be concerned. Three days ago, there was a strong wind with a sandstorm, so yesterday we spent the entire morning doing a big clean up. There are all kinds of rumors, but no official notice yet. Have you heard of any definite schedule of the move to Tule Lake there? I still haven't received any response to my petition, which I submitted the other day. How wonderful it would be if I could suddenly go there. Men that are being reunited with their families are leaving here one after another, so I am getting very nervous about being left here. I am sure that you are feeling the same. But there is nothing we can do. Please be brave and wait a little while longer. Say "hello" to the children.

Affectionately, Katsuchika

March 21, 1944 *(original in Japanese)*
My dearest Umeno,

I said that spring was here, and actually we were having nice spring-like weather, but yesterday it snowed and today it seems like we're back to winter. Of course, I don't think this will last very long, and as soon as it clears up, I'm sure it will warm up again.

On Saturday, March 4th, I was surprised with receiving that unexpected wristwatch, and last Saturday, the I 8th, I received a picture of Mut-chan in a kimono··· I am so happy. Mut-chan looks so nice and she has grown so much that my heart is filled with deep emotions. Although you are living in an inconvenient environment, it is important that the children not neglect the cultural arts and studies.

I take it you are all safe and well. I am also quite fine and waiting for the order to leave here. Until I write again.

Affectionately, Katsuchika

March 28, 1944 *(original in Japanese)*
My dearest wife,

I don't know why, but I'm sorry that the letter was delayed··· I immediately sent a condolence telegram to Mrs. Masuda. Mr. Masuda was a very nice person and I am much indebted to his kindnesses and assistance. I am so sorry about his passing. Please convey my condolences to his bereaved family.

I have not heard any further, I nervously await for the day, resigning myself to the fact that there is nothing I can do about it. My only consolation is that you are all safe and well. Am in a hurry, so will close for now.
Affectionately, Katsuchika

April 2, 1944 *(original in Japanese)*
My dearest Umeno,

The stars were twinkling last night as I walked back to my barracks after the twice weekly movies, but early this morning when I woke up, it was snowing. Though as I am writing this letter, it is again very clear and I expect a nice day. It had been warm for several days so although the snow on the ground is melting, the bare trees are still covered with snow and it is a very beautiful sight. I suppose, since we are at a high elevation, what would be a spring rain turns to snow.

I received and read your much-awaited letter of March 29th. I am of the same thoughts as you, and if I had known it would take this long, I would've requested to go to Crystal City. I feel very irritated, but when I look around and see these older men or some with sad family situations still here, I feel unlucky of course compared to those who left here earlier, but I have my health and you are all safe and well, so I shouldn't really complain and try to bear it. I realize your anxiety, but please do not become irritated from worries, and try to be cheerful waiting just a little while longer.

I've heard that manners are getting very bad and how is that affecting our children?
Affectionately, Katsuchika

April 19, 1944 *(original in Japanese)*
My dearest wife,

A second April 8th has arrived since we parted and I'm surprisingly reminded that Hiromu is now three years old, I never even dreamed that we would be in this situation when Hiromu was born three years ago. It is so memorable. The other day, I received notice that I can go there so I think I can leave soon. This is such a wonderfully happy thing. Some people have had to wait a month, but I'm praying that it will happen soon. Lately, the weather is very nice and I am getting along very well so please do not be concerned. According to the letters from the children, they seem to be very healthy and I am relieved. I take it that Nii-san, Takemori-san and Teshima-san are all well. Please give them my regards. Will close for now. Sayonara.
Affectionately, Katsuchika

April 14, 1944 *(original in Japanese)*
My dearest wife,

Read your much-awaited letter of April 8th and thanks for being concerned, but I am quite healthy, not even catching a cold, so please do not worry. I am very happy to hear that you are all well too. As I told you in my last letter, I have been notified that I can go there, so finally after more than two years, my wish will be realized soon. It is only a matter of time. For me, there is no better news than this and makes me very happy. Have you received notification yet? It (the move) has taken some people one month after notification. If possible, please ask the officials there to hasten things.
Please take care of yourselves and wait for the day we can happily meet again.
Affectionately, Katsuchika

April 19, 1944 *(original in Japanese)*
My dearest Umeno,

How are you? I am as usual quite well, so please do not be concerned, I guess you can call it hazy springtime skies, but lately we have these cloudy days that look like it might turn into rain, but it starts snowing. Of course, it's usually just short snow flurries that melt away quickly and the cold is not that bad. This past Sunday, we had our first baseball game of the year. Right now, all I am doing is praying that the departure day will come soon. We've been separated for over two years, so I'm sure you can imagine my feelings of wanting to fly over to see you. I have turned over my responsibilities here to others and waiting only for the day I'm ordered to leave. I'm sure it will be very soon, so please take extra care of yourselves and be strong and wait. Will close for now. Sayonara.

Affectionately, Katsuchika

April 27, 1944 *(original in Japanese)*
My dearest wife,

I am quite well so please do not be concerned. I am eagerly looking forward to the day, but have not heard anything definite yet. I know I am not the only one, but they sure are trying our patience. I wonder why they are not letting us leave soon.

Are the children all well? I even dream about our home, and can't settle down and put my heart into doing anything anymore. Lately it's windy, so can't play golf too well and all I do is pray that they will let me leave here soon. Will close for today.

Affectionately, Katsuchika

May 1,1944 *(original in Japanese)*
My dearest Umeno,

I am as usual fine and eagerly waiting for the notice to depart. It is already May now and I have been here almost a year. How quickly the days go by!

Are you all well? The weather has turned quite warm here··· it must be almost hot there, I don't know if I can get it or not but I will do my best so let me know if there is something you want. Since you are sending me the Gila News constantly, I am aware of all that's going on there.

Will close for today. Please give my regards to Nii-san and others.

Affectionately, Katsuchika

May 5, 1944 *(original in Japanese)*
My dearest wife,

This morning, it is a rare, lovely day and from a high place, the surrounding scenery is especially beautiful and I cannot help but feel gratitude for my health and my life. I am sure that you are all doing fine. The departure date has not been announced, but I am sure it is very soon. Please wait patiently. This is a very short letter, but I wanted to let you know that I am fine.

Affectionately, Katsuchika

NOTE: The family was reunited at the Gila River camp in May 1944 and the letters temporarily stopped. Katsu and the family left for Tule Lake, California shortly thereafter. When the war ended in the summer of 1945, Umeno and the children were released and left for Lodi. However, Katsu was detained until March 1946 and his letters to Umeno follow.

TULE LAKE, CALIFORNIA

October 1945–February 1946

The following letters are from Katsuchika Tamura at Tule Lake, California, to Umeno.

October 7, 1945
Dearest Umeno,

Today is already the 7th. Since then, the weather has been fine and there have not been any cold days. I have completely recovered from my cold.

How was your train trip? I worried about many things, but hopefully you reached your destination safely the next day. How are things? You must be awfully busy. How are the children? How are Hiromu and Osamu? With those two your daily life must not be easy. Anyway, please relax and do the best you can under the circumstances. I wrote a letter to Matsuo-san and his wife, but please tell them yoroshiku from me.

Mr. and Mrs. Yamamoto, the block managers, left here yesterday morning. Besides them, no one else has left. Our neighbor Fujii-san married last night and will live in Yamamoto-san's barracks. A young neighbor named Honda-san says he is leaving soon, so I will be surrounded by empty barracks. Suddenly, people are leaving and especially at night, the loneliness is very depressing. I read or listen to the radio until ten o'clock or so and try to fall asleep.

The following day, I went to get a SMA (probably powdered infant formula for Osamu), but was told , "Instead of today, I gave you two yesterday," and wasn't given one. I will send you what I have here in a few days. Did you get all of your shipped goods all right?

I have not received any word yet concerning our situation. The departure of the people who have been leaving here morning and nights had been postponed for a few days due to a bus strike or something. Doesn't look like the Yamazakis have gone yet.

I'm sure there are many changes, but please pay attention to Hiromu's naughtiness. Well, I'll close for today. Please let me know how things are going there.
Katsuchika

October 10, 1945
Dearest Umeno,

It is now after 9 p.m., and some people have moved in after the young people left next door. They are making knocking noises and I can hear people talking. Perhaps it is better than silence, but loud noises can be bothersome too. I went golfing yesterday, and my ball fell into a concrete ditch. When I tried to retrieve the ball, my foot slipped into the water, and I came home drenched from the waist down. Perhaps because I got chilled, I didn't feel too good, but I am okay today. I came home carrying my golf bag, dripping wet like a sewer rat··· was certainly not a very pleasant sight.

The soldiers have left here and agents from the Immigration office have taken over. For three days now, every evening, we have lightning and thunder and it rains, but during the day, it is clear and warm. Since you left, we haven't had one day of morning frost, so the stocks have started blooming.

Mrs. Mitsuyoshi says she will be going there in a few days. Mutsuko and Hiromu's coat came back from the cleaner but my hat has not··· it has been 40 days. I go to the mess hall for my meals, but I can't always hear the bell ring so it is a problem .
Katsuchika

October 12, 1945
Dearest Umeno,

How have you been since? I'm sure you are quite busy. How is your sister's family?
For three days now, we have had evening showers and it had been overcast, but this morning it has cleared, but the fog is thick and reminds me of the San Francisco mornings.
There has been little change in my life here. Yesterday morning, Sasaki-san stopped by and told me he is leaving here on the afternoon of the 15th for Lodi.

I talked about many things with Sato-san from Sacramento the other day and he said our case was a matter of time and we shouldn't be too concerned. Not only from my conversation with Sato-san, but from all the rumors I have gathered here, I think his thinking is correct, so if you have not already talked to people from around Stockton about us, I think you should wait a little while more. People that don't know our situation might think it rather strange if we ask favors now, so I think it is best to wait. As you know, Mizuno-san and Sumida-san who have applied earlier have not heard anything yet.

Since you are out there, I'd like to get out of here as soon as possible, but there is nothing we can do but "gaman" and wait. Matsuo-san must be very busy too, so while everything is still up in the air, I'm sure it is difficult to discuss. This is the situation so if you agree with me, please put it off for a while.
Katsuchika

October 15, 1945
Dearest Umeno,

Yamazaki-san came to visit me Saturday afternoon and told me he went to Lodi and French Camp and met with you and brought me the omiyage you entrusted him. I was so happy to receive such unexpected "mezurashii" (unusual) hard to come by goodies.

According to Mune-san, during the grape harvest season, it is awfully busy there. With Hiromu and Osamu with you, I can imagine just how terribly busy you must be.

This morning, Mrs. Mitsuyoshi left. I believe she is going there. I gave her a senbetsu (farewell money). No other families have left since. Today, I received the underwear. For this fall, I think that is adequate. If it gets colder, I will wear my thicker underwear that I have. The climate has been warm since. Tonight, after sunset, it began to rain. The stock in the yard is green and a few of them have purple flowers.

When it is a nice day, I go golfing for half a day so it isn't so bad during the day, but the nights are terribly lonesome. What are Yot-chan and Mut-chan doing these days? Are they happy? Hiromu is at an age where he learns both good and bad things, so please keep an eye on him. How is the ear? Is it getting better? Please don't "muri" and take care.

I am doing everything possible to get out of here. According to Mune-san, Matsuo-san is going to Stockton in a few days. It may have happened before you get this letter. I wonder what the outcome was?
Goodnight, Katsuchika

Sunday, October 21, 1945
Dearest Umeno,

It was clear this morning, but it started to cloud up and finally it started to rain this afternoon. It is a dreary day. Is everyone well and happy? That is my fervent wish.

I am sure you have already read it in the papers, but this camp, like the others, is going to be closed by next February 1st. Every day, there are people leaving here, and I'm sure that number is going to increase.

On the 19th, I met Mrs. Matsumoto on my way to the shower, and she looked surprised to see me and said, "Tamura-san, an internment order was issued to people on parole again. Tsuji-san, Katayama-san, Tanikawa-san all received a letter. Did you get a letter?" Hearing this, I anticipated more troublesome problems, and went to see the block manager. Indeed there was a letter for me. It was written by the immigration agent stationed here, and it said simply that our parole was canceled and we were now interned. Upon further inquiry, we learned that it was only a name change, and we would not be transferred soon out of here. We were parolees of WRA, but since WRA was dissolved, they had to change our status. Anyway, this makes me want to aggressively work towards my release. I must get ?? from Yoshimi-san or Shin-san? so I can submit a petition. I did get the statement from the mess operations, but all it said was that I worked hard··· I don't think it is going to do me much good. This is very troublesome and I don't know what to do. This is the situation that I am in now, and it isn't as easy as I had imagined. It will probably take time, but if I try my very best, I believe things will somehow work out.

Kusumi-san who was the warden in Block 8 (the man who lived with Tanaka-no-ojisan) is leaving here soon, so he persuaded me to be the warden, so I will be taking over as warden tomorrow. There was talk about my taking over Hori-san's job, but since Hori-san's release date is not definite yet, and if I'm not doing anything, I'll be put backpacking in the mess hall, so I decided that it would be best to take the warden's job.

The first three weeks since you all left, the weather was rather nice so I was able to play a lot of golf. But it will start raining more and snowfalls and the cold will probably prevent outdoor activities. I thought there would be more people who would like to play "Go," but it seems like everyone has their own work or hobby and no one is coming to play "Go". Poor Yamasaki-san seems quite restless··· it's understandable.

Goodbye for now, Katsuchika

October 24, 1945
Dearest Umeno,

I received the almonds yesterday. It's the first time I had almonds roasted in the shell··· it is very oishii, and it is tanoshimi.

There has been no change··· everyone is saying that it is just a matter of time before we can leave here. I'm working as a warden since Monday. It's from 4 pm to midnight, but there is not much to do. I work five days and get two days off. Luckily, I have Saturday and Sunday off. Of the five working days, there is usually one day of extra work. The daytime warden has to stand in front of the grammar school and watch for the cars so the children going home are safe. The nighttime warden has to go monitor the evening activities at the high school. Last night was my turn, and so I wore that black cap (warden's) and stood watch. It was a Japanese movie called "Botchan." I very seldom go to see movies on my own, but since it was part of my duty, I watched it. But I had to wear that black warden's cap inside the gym and felt a bit self-conscious and embarrassed when seen by someone I knew. The Hawaii group teased me saying they were wondering who it was in that warden's cap and told me I looked good in it.

Recently, the canteens are stocked well with cigarettes, and we can buy almost anything. I can buy cigarettes by the carton now, so I don't think I'll have a hard time obtaining cigarettes from now on. But it will be very inconvenient when the canteen closes down. My hat has not been back yet. They tell me that I'll get it before the place closes down. Right now, there is nothing that I need.

Today, I received a letter from Takemori-san. They said they are still doing the same work. Since things are expensive there; they say they are barely making it on $250. Their son, Hitoshi-san, will be graduating from high school next spring, so they won't know until after that whether they will be coming back here or not. Anyway, until next July or August, they have decided to stay in Chicago. The Kamimotos and Teshimas are still working in Seabrook and Roy-san is now an optometrist. Heard Hikita-san is working for the WRA in Chicago.

Are the children all genki and happy? Hope Hiromu is not fighting. Please yoroshiku to Matsuo-san and your sister.
Katsuchika

October 29, 1945
Dearest Umeno,

It seems like the weather cycle here is three weeks of nice weather and then it turns bad. Since you all left, until several days ago, we had morning frost but the daytimes were nice, but now the clouds are hanging low, the wind is blowing and it rains off and on these days.

Are there a lot of people working? Taking care of the little children, helping with the kitchen, etc., you must be terribly busy. Please don't "muri" and take care of yourself. How is your ear? Matsumoto-san got out early so it was good, but Sasaki-san was late so that was too bad. I imagine Sasaki-san will eventually be leaving here.

Mune Yamasaki-san left this morning by himself. The house built after the fire is small, so he is going to add on to it and then call his family. He left here at 4:30 a.m. so I did not get to see him off.

Our neighbor, Tanabe-san, left to go to the hospital for surgery. Heard Dr. Terakawa also had surgery the other day. Nobody from this block has left since. When you were here, you used to return with rumors and gossips you heard at the laundry and shower rooms, but I don't know what is happening any more.

Today, Nakano-san in #54 came by. He said he is letting his wife leave here first. These days, I feel I did the right thing to have you all leave here first.
Will close for now, Katsuchika

October 31, 1945
Dearest Umeno,

I received the letter you sent with Naniwa-san. As far as my case is concerned, I don't know exactly when, but they will probably have a "hearing" for me. As I have told you, I'm pretty sure everything will be okay, but I think you should do everything you can on your side.

The people listed in the enclosed paper are people I've met not personally, but in public. So I don't know if they will write me a "character witness" statement, but I certainly would like a letter from them if at all possible. If that is not possible, a letter stating how much I personally or publicly cooperated in community activities such as Community Chest, Red Cross, USO, etc. in Stockton area would be very helpful.

It would be very good to have people like Ayao-san who have U.S. citizenship and ?? write a statement. It would also be good to submit a petition to Mr. Ennis from you too.
Katsuchika

November 3, 1945
Dearest Umeno,

Yesterday, about 320 people bound for Hawaii left here. Next will be the second ship to Japan, which was scheduled to depart on Nov. 7th but was postponed until the 16th. Heard that 5,000 can board this ship, so I'm sure many people will be going from here. Nakatsui-san, Shokuro Yoshida-san are getting ready to leave. Tsuji-san wants to leave too, but it looks like his wife is pregnant, so they won't let them board unless the ship has a hospital bed, so he says he is going on the next ship. Camp close down is nearing, so many people are busy getting their things together to leave or go to Japan. We have not heard anything official yet. We keep hearing "soon" but no definite date has been given us. At this rate, it is doubtful whether we can get out of here before Christmas and New Year.

Since many people left, the mess hall is run by volunteers. I will probably have to start going to help too. Anyway, it is very troublesome for those of us left behind. The canteen is going to close at the end of November, but it will be run privately to sell every day goods so there is nothing to worry about.

Have the people living there decreased some? But if you are still feeding a lot of people, it must be quite a task feeding them. Are you finding things being very inconvenient? Is Osamu growing up okay? You must have depleted your SMA by now. Hope the children are all okay. Please take good care of yourself.

Katsuchika

November 5, 1945
Dearest Umeno,

How are you all since? Are the Okazaki's all well too? Please give them my best regards. Have things settled down a little so that you are less busy now? They say the world is so large, but really is so small. I was so surprised to learn that people far away, that I had no idea they knew about you, already knew you had all left here. Arima-san and Fujita-san had heard that I had left here too. Mrs. Nakatsui stopped by to see me yesterday afternoon. Because of her relations with young people, she applied to return to Japan, but talked to me about paying her own way to go back. She is worried because people that have family are restricted to the amount of money and goods they can take back. They have not announced how much they can take with them, but it is a big concern for them. Because of these circumstances, Fukaniki-san says he is going back to Stockton first.

The Hatanakas left here for Los Angeles on the afternoon of Nov. 2nd on the same train that you took out of here. Mrs. Fukunaga will be leaving here this afternoon. Her children will probably be going to Japan. Only Mrs. F. will remain here. It is very sad, but shikataganai (cannot be helped).

Saturday and Sunday was very nice, but today, it has been raining since morning. I had been thinking about paying a visit to Murano-san and Yoshida-san, so I am going to do it today.

So long for today. Please take extra care of yourself.

Katsuchika

November 10, 1945
Dearest Umeno,

I received the certificate that Mr. Speckens wrote. He wrote about me very nicely, so I'm sure it will be a big help. I deeply appreciate his kindness. Please tell Matsuo-san how much I appreciate his efforts in obtaining this statement. I immediately went to the WRA lawyer yesterday morning and asked him to write the petition he had promised me. But he said that since I petitioned for a hearing already, it would be better to submit the certificate at the time of the hearing, so I agreed to the lawyer's advice. And I don't want to rely on just that one statement··· I would like to be able to submit others too. So please write a letter to Mr. Ennis from your side explaining my situation.

The snowy weather has continued for a week now. It doesn't continue snowing, but it snows before the snow on the ground melts away, so today we have three inches of snow on the ground. The surrounding mountains are white.

This morning at 9 a.m., Hori-san left for Utah. The Itamuras are still here. I forgot to mention to you, but according to the letter from Takemori-san, Jimmy Teshima is with the army in the Pacific. I'm sure Mr. and Mrs. Teshima are praying for the early discharge of Jimmy. Yesterday, Sato-san of Stockton came by, so today we are going to visit Arima-san (SF).

How are the children? Hope Hiromu hasn't become mischievous. Hope the baby is genki too. Please take good care of yourself.

Katsuchika

November 18, 1945

Dearest Umeno,

Hope you are all well. Hope all is well with the Okazaki family too. The weather here is the same. The snow falls off and on, but does not stack too thick on the ground, and the wind is always blowing. As for us, no word yet. The Hawaiian families and single people are departing from here soon. The Hawaiians for Hawaii and the single ones to Japan. From this block, the Iharas and Shirais are leaving and Yasui-san, Tanaka-no-ojiisan (the man who sells kamaboko) and the three Fukunaga brothers are departing for Japan. I haven't seen Hisatsune-san yet, but he is probably going too. Haven't heard from Sumida-san and Mizuno-san, but they are probably leaving together.

Yesterday, Hirokane-san stopped by to thank me for the candy that Mut-chan sent Kimiye-san. It's very cold outside so I have been reading books and playing go. There aren't really good go players, so I just play sometimes with Harauchi-san.

I hope you received the SMA and other things that I sent you the other day. Yesterday I sent you some candy. I'm sure you can buy all you want there, but to kids, things being sent are something special.

This year, I don't want to catch a cold so I am being very careful so please don't worry about me. Hope you all will take care of yourselves too.

Katsuchik

November 20, 1945

Dearest Umeno,

I received your letter dated the 16th. I am so glad to hear that things are going well for you. Please convey my gratitude to Matsuo-san.

There is no official announcement yet, but it looks like we will definitely be able to be free by Christmas. Perhaps we won't have to go through a hearing. I am so happy.

On top of taking care of the children and busy working, you have had to do a lot of running around for me··· but we were able to do a lot so I am relieved.

The Nakano family has already returned to Los Angeles. According to Nakano-san, the $2 I loaned him towards school material, he donated it.

The canteen will close down in ten days··· they are selling everything for one third of the wholesale price, but there is nothing I really need, so I have not bought anything. They have given us a certificate for the reimbursement, but have told us they can't pay us so probably the membership fee is the only thing coming.

Well, I will notify you as soon as I get official notice. Will close for now.
Katsuchika

November 25, 1945
Dearest Umeno,

Hope you are well. Yot-chan and Mut-chan seem to be happy with school and friends, but how are Hiromu and Osamu doing? Osamu must have grown quite a bit. Is Osamu still a good baby?

I get so tired of this nasty wind blowing. I'd rather that it quietly snowed instead.

Last year, we didn't have turkey at Thanksgiving, but this year we got turkeys. We got 15 or 16 turkeys just for this mess hall, so we all got plenty to eat.

On the morning of the 23rd, we sent off the first group of people leaving for Japan. There were about 400 some people from here and according to the radio, the ship has already left Seattle. Mr. and Mrs. Matsuno have since left for Suisun··· only their son is left by himself. Mrs. Fukunaga left this camp for Oakland, but her three sons are going to Japan so she came to visit them. She wants to take her daughter to Oakland, but she can't do it right now. Matsumoto-san came back and left with his family. Yesterday, I went to see Murano-san. He says he is quite a bit better, but perhaps because of his illness, I was surprised at how he has aged. I also stopped by to see Yamasaki-san but Mrs. Y. was not there since she went to see some people off. I guess Murano-san is not ready to pick her up yet.

Well, we haven't received any official word yet. I guess they are very busy with the Hawaii returnees and the people going to Japan. Please take good care of yourself.
Katsuchika

December 6, 1945
Dearest Umeno,

Since this morning, sometimes the sun peeks through the clouds, but the wind is still blowing hard, so I seldom go outside unless I have to. The luggage for the people leaving for Japan on the 16th is being taken to the high school gym for inspection. It's not a very difficult inspection, but they have to take out the packed belongings and, after inspection, have to pack it back which is hard work. Wooden boxes are too heavy so many are packing it in big bags. I'm sure people like Seino-san and Ogawa-san are going to have a difficult time.

Fujimura Sensei sent us a newly published newspaper from Chicago called "Hohrin". He is now a minister attached to the Midwest Buddhist Churches. You probably read the Japanese papers and know more about what is going on than I do. Anyway, I was happy to hear that Sensei was actively ministering over there.

The bottom of my black shoes needed repairs, so I took them to the shoe repair man that took over the canteen, and was told it would cost $3.50.That was not a very good pair of shoes, and if I had known it would cost so much, I would've gotten a new pair. He's probably making a lot of money, since he owns the shop.

Received a letter from Gosuke Sasaki-san. Looks like he is in Florin. He needed a guarantor at the Immigration Office so he had to hustle a lot. That procedure is gone now so we don't have to go through all that anymore.

Looks like Fukanogi-san finished his packing so he's probably leaving in a few days. Doi-san is leaving this afternoon for the Sacramento area.
Katsuchika

December 10, 1945
Dearest Umeno,

Are you genki? How are the children? I am well. Last week, I was sent to the hospital one night. There was a young woman who lost her mind and killed her child. Another cute 11 month old daughter only had minor injuries and survived. My heart went out to the family and I could only feel compassion. The situation is so unsettled here, that this is the result of the anxiety and stress.

Originally, 5,000 people were scheduled to leave for Japan, but that has been cut to 1,500, so many are going to have to wait for the next ship. People like Seino-san and Ogawa-san, whose husbands are over there already, are going to have to wait for the next ship. They have already put out their luggage and it is in the high school gym, so they will have to go and sort it out. What a job.

Yesterday was my day off, so I went and volunteered at the mess hall. I had to wash the pots and pans but I got to rest between 1 p.m. and 4 p.m. so I wasn't too tired.

This morning, last night's snowfall packed 5 inches, but fortunately there was no wind and it was relatively warm. One of these days, I'd like to write a letter to Katsu-san, so if you know his address, let me know. Will close for now.

Katsuchika

December 13, 1945
Dearest Umeno,

It is very cold, but other than that, there is no change. The Fukanogi couple left here yesterday for the Stockton area. They said they would temporarily settle into the church on Manro? Street. Nakao-san (Alice's mother) had a baby. I thought for sure that I could leave here by Christmas, but we have not had any official word yet, so I don't know what to think any more.

As you know, there is no way I can get Christmas presents here so I am sending you $20. Please buy something for yourself, Yot-chan, Mut-chan, Hiromu, Osamu and the three Okazaki children from me. As for me, there is nothing I need right now.

For breakfast only, I bring the food back to my room and make my own coffee. A jar is almost full with sugar. Lately, they give us grapefruit often. Lunch and supper, I eat at the mess hall. The number of people working in the mess hall have decreased, but with volunteers, things are running as usual. The canteen sells newspapers, magazines, bread, fruits, peanuts butter, etc., so I don't feel any inconvenience.

Are you feeding Osamu vegetables and egg? Will close for now, but let me know when you receive the money.

Katsuchika

December 15, 1945
Dearest Umeno,

I was very surprised since I had no idea that Matsuo-san would come to visit me here. It was Saturday morning and since it was my day off, I had gone to the mess hall to help, so I wasn't home when he dropped by. When I returned home briefly around 10 a.m., my next door neighbor, Tanabe-san, handed me a package saying that it was left by a man from Lodi. He did not get the name of the person, but that person was going to be at Block 29 until evening. It was snowing pretty hard, but I hurried to #29. Unfortunately, no one was home, but there was a Nash parked outside, so I figured it was probably Matsuo-san who came to see me. I looked around but it didn't look like he was in the neighborhood, so I came back disappointed. Right after lunch, Matsuo-san came by to see me and we chatted for about an hour. Chatting with him, I learned many things (about you all), and I felt much relieved.

As for the Christmas presents, if I am still around here at Christmas, I'm not going to open it till then so I lined them up on the counter. The 2 pounds of butter probably came from Matsuo-san··· I had it for breakfast this morning. Real butter tasted so good! He gave me a big striped bass also, so I saved half for myself and gave the other half to Arima- san. He was so appreciative that it was worth sharing it with him. Arima-san won't be able to eat sea bass when he returns to Japan. And there is no way we can obtain sea bass here so I can understand his joy. He said the rice served in the mess hall was not good enough to eat with the delicious fish, so he cooked some rice in his room. In the evening, I went and got some rice from Arima-san and had sashimi with it. I still have some left to eat tonight. The snow has not melted the last ten days, and it keeps on falling on top of it, so I used the snow to pack the fish so it will last for many days.

As I've told Matsuo-san regarding my situation, there has been no official word yet. Hopefully, I'll hear something this week. People who renounced their citizenship are having a hearing and will be able to get out. Naniwa-san says he is going to Lodi, so I asked him to take this letter to you.
Katsuchika

December 20, 1945
Dearest Umeno,

I received your package yesterday. When I opened it, I was surprised that it was full of presents. I wasn't expecting to receive so many gifts. I am so happy and feel very fortunate. With the ones that Matsuo-san brought me, there are now altogether 11. I have lined them up on the counter and am anxiously waiting for Christmas morning. I gently shook each package, so I can imagine what's in there, but if I open it now, I feel like I will be doing something illegal, so will not open it until Christmas.

It snowed a lot the morning that Matsuo-san came, and it has been very cold and snowing since, so the roads look like it has been applied with white cement. Yesterday morning was the coldest, and the iron fence looked like a solid white screen, and the telephone wires looked like white thread. If it was like this last year, I'm sure the children would have really enjoyed it.

I have not heard anything more. Same with Mizuno-san and Sumida-san. At this rate, it will probably be next spring. I realize you are as busy as I had imagined. Please try not to worry too much, and be patient a little while longer. More than anything else, I'm glad to know that the children are happy there.

5,000 people will be leaving on the ship sailing on the 28th, so until then there will be a lot of confusion around here.
Katsuchika

December 20, 1945 (in its original English)
Dear Milton,

Thank you very much for the Christmas presents. I have not opened them yet. I think we should not open our packages until the Christmas morning, don't you think so? Well, I'll write again and tell you what I got after Christmas.
Goodbye, Father

December 26, 1945

Dearest Umeno,

I imagine you had a joyous Christmas. I opened all the presents that you all sent me, and appreciated your thoughtfulness as I opened each one. There were so many delicious goodies, that I am looking forward to enjoying them.

Yesterday, I sent you money by registered mail. I also enclosed a picture of Hiromu. I'm sure you have received it by now. Your letter dated the 17th mentioned receiving the photo, but nothing about the money so I am concerned.

Some of the people going to Japan left here yesterday, and the others are leaving tomorrow. Sometime tomorrow, Nakatsui-san and Yoshida-san will be leaving. From this block, it's Tanaka-san, Ogawa-san and Seino-san. It's really going to be lonely around here.

I will write a thank-you letter to Takemori-san. According to a letter from Yamagishi-san in Crystal, his hearing is completed, but he does not yet know the outcome of it. The hearing will probably start here next spring, but we have not been given any dates.

My health is good and I really don't have any complaints, but the weather is so terrible that I am confined indoors, so am very bored. When you get this letter, please ask Yot-chan to buy the January 1946 Readers Digest and send it. Will close for now,

Katsuchika

December 31 , 1945

Dearest Umeno,

Today is the last day of the year. I feel very happy that you will all be greeting the New Year in good health. I am as always, well too. I feel relieved that you received the money that I sent you. Regarding the Readers Digest that I asked you to send me, please disregard it if you have not bought it yet, since I bought it at the canteen. I knew I was asking you a troublesome favor, but the canteen here is not very reliable, so that is why I asked you.

Since all those people left for Japan, it has become very lonesome around here. They've closed half of the mess halls. Since Christmas, the weather is quite warm, and so I can go golfing sometimes. I believe we had several sunny days around this time last year too.

I received a New Year's card from Kaya-san. It was from Glendale, Arizona. I sent him a card too. Happy New Year to all!

Katsuchika

Morning of January 2, 1946
Dearest Umeno,

I feel grateful to have welcomed the new year in good health. The weather was also fine and I played golf all day. This year, we had cooked and were given all the food on the 31st, so it was very convenient. We bought turkey with the block money; Sugimura-san made the saba-zushi and there was anpan and lots of other gochiso.

Our mess hall will close on the 4th, and block 8 will go to 11, and 7 to 12.So I must go from one end to the other end for my meals.

Day before yesterday, about 4:30 p.m. on the 31st, a fire broke out in the high school auditorium, and that large auditorium totally burnt down in two hours. Fortunately, there was no wind, so it did not spread to the adjacent buildings. There are many rumors as to the origin of the fire, but we won't know the official word until the newspaper comes out. Up until now, we never had a fire here··· to have a fire near the closing of the place··· it was sad to lose such a nice building like that.

Many people have left now, but there are still about 7,000 left. The free people must leave by the end of the month, so there will be a lot of people leaving. It will be a busy place. Heard that some people will be getting "free to leave" papers soon. If everything is not settled by the time WRA leaves at the end of the month, perhaps the Justice Dept. is taking over. I feel very anxious, but there is nothing I can do but to wait. Please take care of yourself,
Katsuchika

January 7, 1946
Dearest Umeno,

Are you all genki? How about the baby? I hear it's been raining a lot there. I am well as usual. Since yesterday, a terrible wind is blowing and it's very cold so I am confined to my room.

I was terminated from my job as warden at the end of last year, since not many people are left here, and a warden is not needed. I'd rather be working instead of doing nothing, but the job openings are all for very hard work. And of course I may be released soon, so I don't know what to do. About ten people have received their notices. Sumida-san received word that he can leave on the 5th. I submitted my application quite a bit later than them, so that is probably the reason for the delay.

It is not easy doing nothing when the weather is bad. Dr. Terakawa passed away at the hospital last Saturday evening. I feel very sad. I am enclosing a New Year's letter from Fujimura Sensei. Do take care of yourself.
Katsuchika

January 12, 1946
Dearest Umeno,

I am still waiting. They have not sent me anything yet. Sumida-san left yesterday for Sacramento. Hearings have begun for those that renounced. Harauchi-san next door has finished his hearing, but he doesn't know the results. Yesterday, Sato-san came from Sacramento and said that the hearings for the Isseis will be after the 20th. I have not applied for the hearing so I think I can be released without going through it, but it is sure long in coming. People that are in the same situation as me have not received any notice yet so I am relieved.

Thank you so much for my birthday present. I am so grateful that you all remembered my birthday. Last year, because of the circumstances, we couldn't celebrate your birthday, but I hope we can celebrate your birthday together this year. There are not many people in the block so I had to help with Terakawa Sensei's funeral. Because of the circumstances, there weren't very many at the funeral, but it was a very solemn Christian service. I was the MC. His family will be leaving for Los Angeles tomorrow. The widow's parents are there.

Are there still people going to work packing celery? If there are people working during winter, cooking the meals for them must be quite a task, keeping you very busy. According to Yot-chan and Mut-chan's letters, the children seem to be quite content and happy. That is wonderful. Well, I will close for today.
Katsuchika

February 1, 1946
Dearest Umeno,

I read your letter dated January 28th, and realized how deep your anxiety is. I imagined day and night how you must be worried for a long time, but the situation is such that there is nothing we can do. Until towards the end of December, no one was freed, so there was a feeling of resignation among us, but like I mentioned in my previous letter, some people received notices on Saturday, December 29th. About a week later, on January 5th, Sumida-san and Tojima-san received notices, so I looked forward to one, too··· but it has been three weeks since and no word yet. Katayama-san made an inquiry to Washington, and was told his case was under consideration, and so just wait for the notice to arrive. At first, I found myself patiently waiting, but recently it has surpassed the feeling of sorrow, and the whole thing seems so absurd.

I know you're leaving here early, without me, which put you through a lot of hardships, but when I look at the whole picture, I think it was better. By mid-January, all the free people, whether their husbands were internees or renouncers, were all released. Hamada-san and Sato-san's wives were all released. In this block, Mrs. Takiguchi is a renouncee, but Mr. is free, so he took one son and left here early. Since you left here, this has been a place of confusion, what with people returning to Japan, etc., so this would not have been a pleasant place for you and the children. I have repeatedly been relieved by the thought that you and the children are settled out there and not here (in this confusing environment).

Since you left here early, you were able to run around Stockton to get "character reference" statements, etc., for me and I'm sure your efforts has helped my case. As I mentioned the other day, the hearing board for the Isseis began on January 21st and they were gone by the 26th. There were no hearings for me and several other people. I think it was because of the letters you got from Mrs. Ford and Mrs. Brown. Otherwise I would've had to go before the hearing board too. The letters that Nakano-san and Mizuno-san's wives and the letter you received were different, so your efforts made a difference. I'm sure if you had not gotten out early, and did not run around getting those statements, I would be having a difficult time. Those ladies were not someone I was really close to, so if it was not for your seeing them and asking them personally, getting a statement from them would have been very difficult.

We both are experiencing difficult times now, but as long as the children are happy, that has to be a consolation. Your feeling of impatience and longing, I feel too. But right now, there is nothing I can do to alter the situation. Please be calm and wait patiently. That is my sincere wish. I will close for now.
Sayonara., Katsuchika

February 11, 1946
Dearest Umeno,

I hope you are well and in good spirits. I know you are busy raising the children and worrying about me, so it's hard to be very cheerful. But there is nothing we can do, so please try to live cheerfully each day. I am quite genki as usual, so please don't worry about my health.

We were told to ship out our luggage while WRA is still here, so I spent all of yesterday packing my belongings. It came to three boxes. I packed one box with chinaware, blankets and books. The second box, I put my trunk and will ship by freight. In the third box, I put my golf clubs and carpenter tools. They haven't come to pick them up yet, but I'm sure they will in a few days. If it should take a month to get there, and if it gets there before me, please accept the boxes.

I must move to Block 11 this week. Because of the decrease in population, we have to move to the middle block. It's so troublesome to have to move now, but nothing we can do about it. Fortunately, the packing is all done so I just have to move the bed and my personal things.

Another ship is leaving for Japan on the 20th. Tsuji-san was looking forward to getting on this boat, but their baby was born a few days ago so they can't board this ship. I feel so sorry for them. There are some warm days, but it seems colder than last year. It has snowed for several days now and feels like winter. Will close for now… until I write again.
Katsuchika

February 21, 1946
Dearest Umeno,

Hope you are all well. No official word yet, but have heard that our cases will all be settled by the first part Of March, so I should be free by then. For untold reasons, it has taken so long and I know you have experienced indescribable hardships. As you know, there was nothing we could do and have waited anxiously for almost six months. According to rumors, WRA was busy processing the people returning to Japan and the renouncees, that they were unable to get to our cases until the January 21st hearings. The WRA has decided to put out all the residents here by March 15th, so I should be free before then.

Of the renouncees, the men who have received notices will go to Santa Fe, and families and women will go to Crystal City soon.

On Sunday the 17th, I moved from block 8 to block 11. The stoves were removed when the barracks became vacant, so we had to carry in the stoves and install them again so it was a big job. Even if it's only for a week or two, we couldn't live in a rat-infested like place, so we spent two days cleaning the place. We had to do the moving ourselves so we had to help everybody clean their place and install the stoves so that alone took a whole day.

The tooth that I had been having worked on since last year, kept giving me trouble, although it wasn't hurting… I finally had it pulled. By the way, how is your ear?

Yesterday, I received a letter from Dr. Akimoto in New York. He says he left Rowher around last year mid-November. It sounds like he heard from Takemori-san that I was still here. They seem to all be well. According to Akimoto-san, Tadao Miyata-san suddenly passed away in Oregon. I had heard that he wasn't in very good health, and that he was receiving all kinds of treatment, but I had no idea he would die at such a young age. I feel so bad.

On Tuesday, probably the last of the people leaving from here for Japan has left. From my neighborhood, Dr. and Mrs. Fujii left. Altogether, there were less than four hundred people.
Will close for today··· at any rate, it shouldn't be much longer so please take care of yourself and try not to worry and keep a cheerful mind. Please "shimbo" a little while more.

Since you have been receiving help from Matsuo-san and his wife for such a long time, shall I write a letter to them?

Katsuchika

February 25, 1946

Dearest Umeno,

Received your letter dated February 19th. I was so happy to hear that you are all well. I received a letter from Hori- san in Utah. Hori-san tells me he stopped by to see you when he was in California the other day. The Sugimura's older son and daughter are still here, so was concerned about them.

Glad to know you received the boxes. For the Sacramento and Lodi area, we were able to contract ourselves with the shippers, so that is probably why it was quick. Heard one of the trucks overturned and some people lost their shipment.

The young Yokoi couple became free recently, but we have not heard anything yet. It is so disappointing. Please give my regards to Tokuo-san and his wife. If it weren't for the strong winds, we are having some spring like days here once in a while. The Tsujis had a baby boy. That's why they couldn't get on the ship that left the other day, and they will temporarily be going to Crystal City. I am going to work as usual every day. Mizuno-san was working as a boiler man until the other day, but now all the boiler men are Caucasians. I suppose because processing is taking longer than WRA expected, and getting food supply orders aren't as easy, the meals are not as good. But we do get a lot of turkey these days. Well, take care of yourself.

Katsuchika

HANDWRITTEN LETTERS

JULY 2, 1942 – DECEMBER 20, 1945

Original letters in English from Katsuchika to Umeno and children

July 2, 1942

Dear Milton & Nancy

How are you? Hope you are well. What kind game do you have there? At our place we have soft ball, table tennis and horse shoe pitching. I can't play golf any more so I play table tennis very often, but I am not very good at it yet. Nancy do you eat plenty of vegetables and drink lot of milk. They are most important food for you. Too much sweet things are no good.

Say "hellow" for me to Henry, Fred, George, Masako, Sadiko, Tayeko, Barbara, Marion, Takeo, Johny, his brother, Jimmy, Yukiko and Misako.

Be nice boy and girl. Good-bye.

Affectionately yours

Father

W. D., P. M. G. Form No. 4

July 3, 1942

My dearest wife,

How is everything with you? Have you already moved out? If you have, how hot is it down there? Are children all right? We were transfered to a new place again. This place is away down in the south. It is pretty CENSORED than the place we have been. Trees around here are mostly pines. Their needles are much longer than those in California. I am doing fine and you have nothing to worry about me. From now on until I let you know, I wish you write letter to me in English. Japanese letters are permissible, but it takes too much time to reach me. Don't forget to let me know where you are, how you are getting along right away. You know how anxious I am to know what kind place you had to move and how you all are.

Affecionately Yours
Katsuhiko Tamura

W. D., P. M. G. Form No. 4
February 17, 1942

August 3, 1942

Darling,

How is everything? Are children all right? How was train travel? Did you have very hard time? I wish I were with you. What kind place is it down there? Guess It is very hot, is it not? Did Takemori and your brother take their dwellings near you? I feel very helpless. When you needed me most I was away from you and you had to carry all burden alone. Why? why? why? Forever I ask and get no satisfactory answer. Only thing I can do is to keep my chin up and take our fate with fortitude. I miss you though.

CENSORED

We get shower often in summer season and sure it helps to keep CENSORED. Pine trees around barracks are lovely to look at but they make poor shade. I met only one friend from CENSORED Well, I must bid you good-bye now, dear. Take good care of your health. Yours ever

Katsuichi

August 6, 1942

Dear Umeno,

I just received your letter dated Aug 1. Am very glad to hear you all are in good health and spirits. It was indeed fortunate you ~~were~~ were still there to receive my letter otherwise it would have taken a long time before I hear from you. I am becoming more accustomed to new surroundings and getting along very fine. Last week we had an exhibition of internees handworks. There were curious stones, tree roots carved as flower vases, water color painting, wooden sculptures and many other things. Two letters you mailed on July 24 and 30 respectively I have not received yet. No doubt they will foreward them to me from McCoy but if they are in Japanese it will take a little time before they reach ~~them~~ me. Well I must say good-bye now until next time meanwhile take good care of your self.

Yours ever
Kakuichi Tanaka

Mrs Umeno Tamura
21-3-D
Rivers, P.O.
Pinal County, Arizona

Katsuchika Tamura
ISN-23-4-J-1012-CI
3RD Internee Co
Internment Camp
Camp Livingston
La.
Aug 18, 1942

Dear Umeno,

I have just received your first letter since you arrived at Gila River Relocation Center. It makes me very happy to hear that everything went well on the train and the trip was a very pleasant one. Children must have had a wonderful time. The heat in Arizona must be very hot. Take good care of yourself and children. Until you get used to the new climate and adjust yourself to the new surroundings, go easy and don't be over ambitious to do two much work. I think it is fortunate to share the room with your brother. It is nicer this way than you take one alone. I have received all you letters

except two which were written in Japanese and reached at McCoy right after I left. I am sure they will come by and by. I feel I can't express my thanks enough to the Kamimotos, Takemoris, and Teshimas who so kindly looked after you. Give my best regards and extend my sincere gratitude to them.
Until next time

Always yours,
Kitaoka

Mrs. Umeno Tamura
21-3-D
Rivers P.O.
Pinal County
Arizona

Katsuchika Tamura
ISN-23-4-J-1012-CI
3rd Internee Company
Internment Camp
Camp Livingston
Louisiana
Aug. 21, 1942

My dearest Umeno,

How is everything down there? Hope you and children are in good health. Have you become used to the new place? Is the heat very hot yet? I hear you get sand storms too. Is it pretty bad? Can the children take the heat? Write me soon. I am waiting to hear from you.

I am doing fine as usual. The weather is changeable but it is cool in the morning and evening.

It may sound awfully selfish, but sometime ask Mr Takemori if he can spare a few golf balls and one or two iron clubs for me. It is not regular course, but a sort of miniature course we made. I think it would be nice if

I can have them here. You did not take along mine with you, did you? Oh well, it is ridiculous question to make. However, I am sure, Mr Takemori has a few extra ones besides his regular sets. If I am asking too much at this time, don't bother it now. Take good care of yourself. So long.

Yours ever,

Katsuhika

Mrs. Umeno Tamura
21 - 3 - D
Rivers, P.O.
Pinal County
Arizona

Kakuchuka Tamura
ISN-23-4-J-1012-CI
3rd Internee Co.
Internment Camp
Camp Livingston
La.
Aug. 24, 1942

Dear Umeno,

Hellow. How are you? This is eight o'clock in the morning. It must be seven in Arizona. Is the heat very hot yet? It is much cooler here and I wish your place too. The day before yesterday I received your letter written July 27 in Japanese. I wonder what has happened to the other you said you mailed a few days before this one. It seems you wanted something to tell me in that letter. As I haven't received it I wish you would write me again telling what you wanted. In this letter which is lying before me you seem worrying about our children who are picking up bad manners and becoming unmanageable. It is pretty bad. Though we can't do much to correct them under the present conditions do your best. It's one good thing that they are in good health. Tomorrow I will write to them telling to mind you. Well, let me hear from you soon. Until then, I am

Yours ever
Katsuchika

Mrs Umeno Tamura
21-3-D
P.O. Rivers
Pinal County
Arizona

Katsuchika Tamura
ISN-23-4-J-1012-CI
3rd Internee Company
Internment Camps
Camp Livingston
Louisiana

My dear Umeno,

Your letter and Masaru-san's, written July 26 and 25 respectively, have finally reached me yesterday, and I came to understand what you wanted to tell me. Well, about repatriation I'm doing my best, but it is unlikely we get our turn this time, for there are too many applicants ahead of us. However, don't be discouraged by this disappointment. In the present conditions we must forbear many trials and afflictions. In a few days I will write you in Japanese. Though it may not reach you as quick as English one I can express myself better in it. Wish you do the same besides English ones, as to hear from you

is my happiest expectation
here. Will you extend my
cordial thanks to your brother
for his kind letter.

Always yours
Kakuchika

August 30, 1942

My dearest Umeno,

A few day ago I received your letter of Aug 23, telling me that you were going to move to Camp # 2 from Camp # 1. It made me very happy as always to hear from you. I wanted to reply immediately, but as I had used up my two letter a week allowance in writing you in the

CENSORED

surroundings. I don't

CENSORED

? Give [illegible] rt-felt thanks for her kindest, excellent manner in which she does it for you.

W. D., P. M. G. Form No. 4
February 17, 1942

16—27540-1 U. S. GOVERNMENT PRINTING OFFICE

Always Katsuchika

September 9, 1942

My dearest Umeno,

This is Sunday morning and we had our breakfast at 7:45, an hour later than week days. It consisted of fresh peaches, dry cereals, fresh milk, bacon and an egg, bread and butter, and coffee. We get prenty of sugar, too. Our barrack being next to the messhall, we always know what we are going to have for the next meal in advance. Roast chicken and apple pie a la mode for this noon. Doesn't it sound it good? Your letter of Sept 2 was handed to me yesterday and it made me very happy as always, to hear from you and to know everything is fine and well with you all. I have nothing to complain about, but miss you terribly. How are our children behaving these days? Is Hiromu getting bad and mischevious as you said he is? Don't be too ambitious about obtaining a job. Your health is the most important thing for all of us and you should take good care of. As for golf clubs, if you haven't written for them yet do not bother any more. I might be able to obtain them here.

Yours ever
Katsuchika

September 16, 1942

Dear Umeno,

Glad to hear all of you are fine. So am I. So they had cut off so much from my letter of Aug. 30 that you could not make out head or tail of it. Well as long as you learned what I wanted to say from my Japanese letter, it didn't matter much. You surely did right thing by taking out the application there. Though I neglected until now I wanted to suggest you to do it. At present you have nothing else to do. Just sit tight and wait till the time comes. You could send me any amount of money, but do not do it until I ask you to. I have still ~~still~~ fifty dollars deposited in the hand of military authorities. When I was at Bismarck I bought a small trunk and a pair of own shoes. Then I ordered a cloth cover and a few small items at McCoy. Well, dear Umeno, this is all for today. Goodbye and good luck.

Always yours

Katsuchika

Dear Umeno, September 21, 1942

Hellow! How is everything with you? The weather here has changed since yesterday. It became so cool that many of us started wearing a sweater. I rather like this kind of the weather as it is invigorating. A few day ago I received a very kind letter from Matsuo San and Satsuma San, urging us to go back to Japan. I wrote them a letter immediately thanking for their sympathetic considerations for our situation. I think you know, dear Umeno, that they are soon going to move out to Arkansas, an adjacent state to Louisiana; a quite long way from California, isn't it? Thank you for the first edition of the Gila News Courier. I enjoyed it every bit; it is so interesting and informing about the camp life and its activities that I feel I know pretty well the relative aspects of your new home. Remember me to the Kawamotos, Takemoris and Teshima and tell the children that I am always thinking of them. Wishing you all the luck.

Yours ever
Katsuchika

W. D., P. M. G. Form No. 4

September 28, 1942

Dear Umeno,

How is everything with you? Received your letter of Sept. 22, but not yet Japanese one. Heard that they send them to an Eastern Office for censoring. This is likely reason for their delay. After I mailed my last letter to you I've got two more camp newspapers. I enjoy them very much. Now I think I know much about your camp. By the way did you hear that they caught a rattlesnake at the Canal Camp other night. Well, you have to look out, as there is no assurance that there is none at the Butte Camp. Last night it rained cats and dogs out here, and this morning the air is so fresh and clean; but before the sun was up it dropped to 43°F and ~~was~~ we felt cold. Hurriedly we set up the stove in our barrack and started fire. Otherwise everything is all right with me. This is all for today. Meanwhile let us all take good care of ourselves. As usual please remember me to all our dear friends.

Yours ever

[illegible]

W. D., P. M. G. Form No. 4 16—27540-1 U. S. GOVERNMENT PRINTING OFFICE

October 7, 1942

Dear U,

This is a rare fine morning. Yesterday I worked in the kitchen and stayed in bed later than usual this morning. This job comes every fortnightly and everyone has to work. I hope you are feeling fine. How are children? Has school started already? You know you must let them do what they can do themselves. I received the camp papers no. 4 and 5. Some people seems worrying about the table manners in the mess hall. The youngsters are apt to acquire bad habits very easily; so you must see to it that they would not run away from your reins. The outlook of our situation is just about the same as before. I am in the best of health. Remember me to the Kamimotos, Takemoris, and Teshimas. I am waiting your Japanese letter but up to date I've not received it yet. Well, I must say good bye now. Take care of yourself. Always yours

[illegible]

October 12, 1942

Dear Umeno,

This is Monday morning. I have just finished listening in radio news after our breakfast. The weather has been fine for a week. As the temperture is mild now, I gave up most of my reading and do more outside exercises. Yesterday we had two representatives from the International Youngmens Christian Association. They promise more athletic equipments. Well, how is everything with you? I suppose Yokichi and Mutsuko are going school now. How is Hiromu? Does he talk much now? Well, take very good of yourself and children and keep your chin up. I am always thinking of you and waiting patiently for a day when we shall be reunited again. My kindest regards to Kimimotos, Mrs Takemori and Mrs Teshimas. So long until the next time. With love

Kakuichika

October 22, 1942

Dear Milton and Nancy,

Thank you, I am fine. I am glad that your school has started. You should study hard and be good pupils. I see Miss Sato teaches Nancy's class. Who is Milton's teacher? I am proud of you both for writing such nice letters. They surely make my heart warm. Will you, Milton, thank Ukiko for me for his giving Hiromi a tractor. You are lucky to have Akira and Hitoshi to play with you all the time. Nancy dear, you have quite many subjects to carry this year. I bet you like music best. I long to hear ~~to~~ you sing. Please give my love to Mom and tell her to take good care of herself. I did not forget her birthday, but I could not send her a birthday cake this year. So long, both of you, and be good children. With love

Postcard front and back,
October 24,
1942

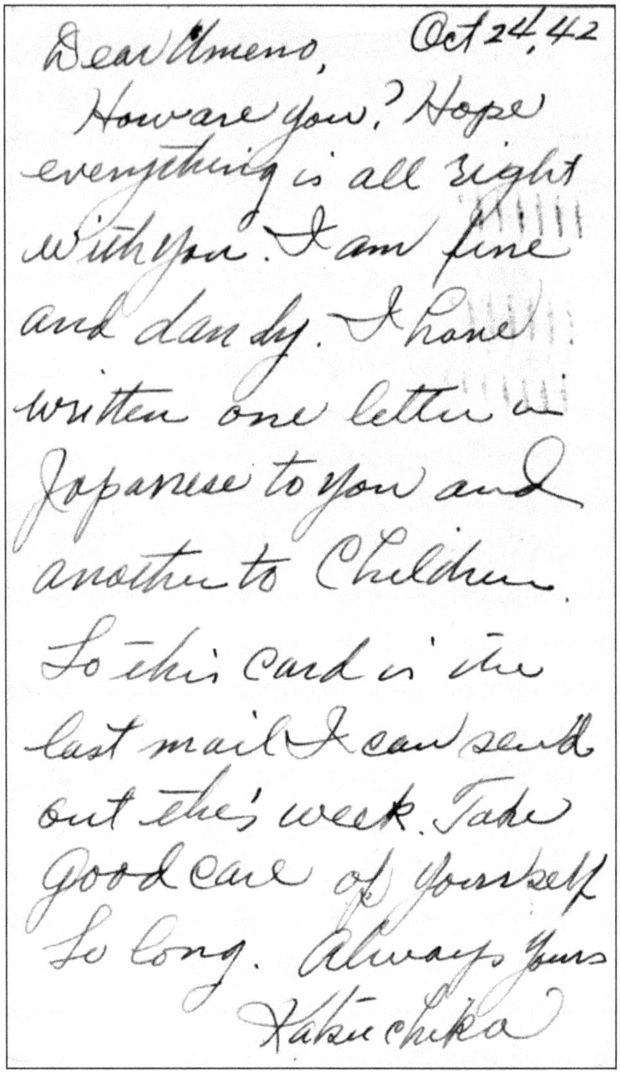
Dear Umeno, Oct 24, 42
How are you? Hope everything is all right with you. I am fine and dandy. I have written one letter in Japanese to you and another to Children. So this card is the last mail I can send out this week. Take good care of yourself. So long. Always yours
Katsuchika

KATSUCHIKA TAMURA
(husband)
ISN-23-4-J-1012-CI
3RD INTERNMENT CO.
CAMP LIVINGSTON
LA

THIS SIDE OF CARD IS FOR ADDRESS

CENSORED
WAR DEPARTMENT
Camp Livingston
Internment Camp

MRS. UMENO TAMURA
~~63~~ 65-3-D
RIVERS, ARIZONA

October 29, 1942

Dear Umeno,

How are you and Children? I am doing fine. The weather here is very unsteady these days. One day its' cold and the next day warm. An autumn weather I guess. Oak trees are mostly bare now, but pine trees are as pretty as ever. Zinias which we sowed after we arrived here are now profusely blooming. I hope you are contented as I am here. I wonder if you could get two pairs of every day pants for me — I mean work pants of denim or jean. Didn't I have one at home. My waist size is 30. Could you cut it to my length. Khaki color is prohibited for us to wear. When you send them I wish you would send me a small scissors too. Today I received letters from Milton and Nancy, written last Sunday. Take good care of yourself and don't catch cold. Then until next time, Goodbye.

Yours ever.

November 11, 1942

Dear Umeno,

Thank you for your letter of Nov. 4 and two pairs of pants. They fit me just fine. They are of nice material and ones I just desired for coming winter. Though I speak of winter the weather here has been warm and we haven't been using stoves for a month. I am sorry they haven't installed stoves in your barrack rooms. Poor Hideo and Hiromu! I can see their chubby icy fingers and pale lips in chilly mornings. How are other children getting along in their school? By the way, did you ask the people now live at our house to send my golf clubs? I remember I wrote you not bother once, but as it is kind of hard to get them here I might as well get my old ones, if it is not too much trouble for you. Forgive me for asking one thing or another when your hands are full with the cares of children.

With love

[illegible]

Postcard front and back,
November 14
1942

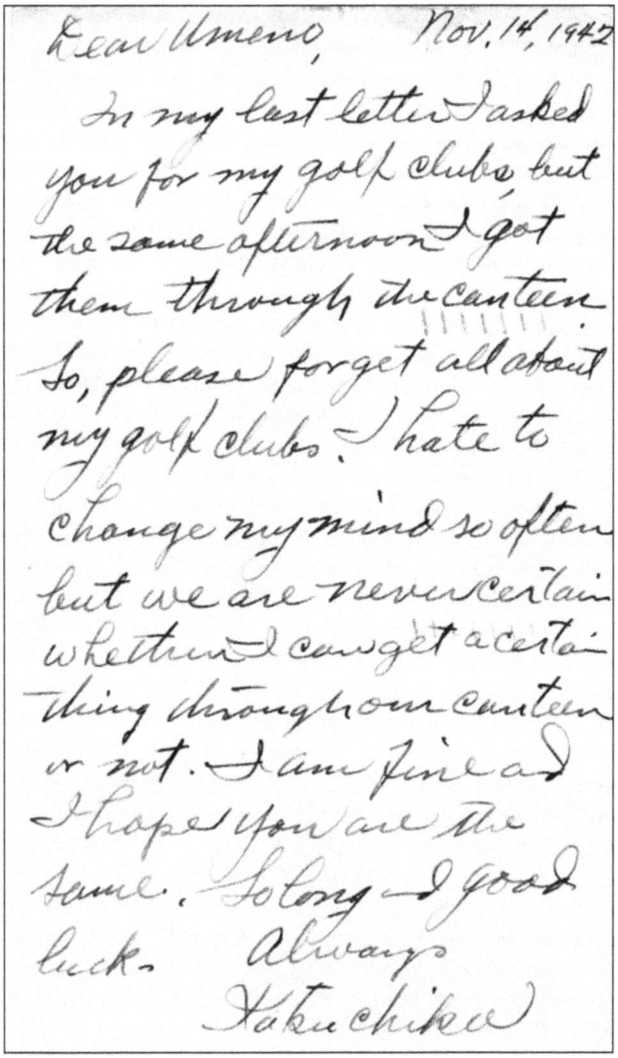
Dear Umeno, Nov. 14, 1942

In my last letter I asked you for my golf clubs, but the same afternoon I got them through the canteen. So, please forget all about my golf clubs. I hate to change my mind so often but we are never certain whether I can get a certain thing through our canteen or not. I am fine and I hope you are the same. So long and good luck.

Always
Katuchika

KATSUCHIKA TAMURA
ISN-23-4-J-1012-CI
3RD INTERNMENT CO.
CAMP LIVINGSTON
LA.

MRS. UMENO TAMURA
65-3-D
RIVERS, ARIZONA

November 23, 1942

Dear Umeno,

How is everything? Maybe you have been wondering why you haven't received any letter from me for sometime. Well, the fact is I haven't received any letter from you for a week. The reason is that they have changed the manner of handling our letters and they send all our letters, either English or Japanese, to an Eastern Office for censoring. So, do not worry though you haven't heard me for a while, as I am in good health and spirits. How are the children? Are they behaving all right? I hope by this time they installed the stoves in your barrack. What become the water situation? Do you get enough water all the day? This is all for today. Take good care of yourself and watch out that the children don't catch cold this time of the year. So long and good luck. Always.

Kotaro Sileo.

November 30, 1942

Dear Umma,

Hellow! How are you? I am getting along fine. The weather here is still nice and we can exercise a lot the out-doors yet. Did you have a nice dinner on the Thanksgiving day? We are fortunate in having an excellent cook in our kitchen. He used to work in Chicago and has had a long experience in gastronomical art and cooked us everything in perfection, from mock turtle soup to mince pie.

Yesterday I received your two Japanese letters, one of Oct. 12 and another of Oct. 16. They made me very, very happy as I did not hear from you in Japanese for long while. I suppose you haven't received my letter lately. Well, I haven't from you either except these Japanese letters which took more than forty days to reach me. Anyway don't worry. You will get my letter pretty soon. You see they don't censor our letters here any more. With love

December 11, 1942

Dear Umeno,

This is raining morning and still dark at 8 O'clock. How is everything with you? Yesterday I received your Japanese letter dated Oct. 22. By that letter you seemed enjoying a nice mild weather, but it's is pretty cold in mornings now, is it not? Do you get post there these days? No, we don't get much post here yet. I think you are wondering why you haven't heard from me lately. As a matter of fact I am writing you every week but our letters take much more time than before to reach either way. The letter, I mentioned, took almost fifty days to reach me. However, do not worry because I am treated well and in the best of health and spirits, and keep on writing whether you get mine or not. Otherwise, you know, I shall be very lonely without hearing from you at all. How are the Takemori's, the Kanemats and Teshima's? Will you give them my best regards.

Yours always.

[illegible]

May 1,
1943

Dear Milton,

Thanks for your letter of April 19. I am very glad to hear you are well a f going School everyday. It is very warm here these days but I am just fine as ever. Other day I had a long hiking too and cought a big eel. It has four little feet and looks terrible. We made a sort of aquarium and keep it in it. There are many turtles too. I wish I could sent you one of them. Don't you think it would make a good play thing for Hiromu. As hot days are coming again you have to be careful not to have your nose bleed. Do you remember you suffered from slight sun stroke a few years back. Be good boy and nice to your mother.

Your loving father
Kakuchiro Tamura

W. D., P. M. G. Form No. 4 ... U. S. GOVERNMENT PRINTING OFFICE

Tule Lake
Nov. 8, '45

Dear Muchan,

How are you getting along now? Is everything all right? You happy? How far is your school? I suppose you made a lots of new friends.

Everything is O.K. with me except I miss everyone of you. I am wishing that I can join you before very long.

The most of families in this block are still here. Only the Hatanaka left for Los Angeles. Your friends, Kimiye Tanbara, Ogata, have not moved yet.

Now we have a real wintery weather here. Last Monday we had the first snow this year - I mean this winter. The wind is very cold and everything is freezing. Naturally I can not play golf for a while.

Be a good girl. Wish you lots of lucks. Dont forget to write me a letter.

With love

Father

Tule Lake
Nov. 8, '45

Dear Milton,

How are you? Are you getting along all right with your school? I want you study hard for you will be in senior high in a couple of years.

I am doing fine except I miss everyone of you. I am working as a block warden. Since last Monday this has been a nasty weather. Snow, Cold, north wind — everything.

The most of your friends ~~&~~ in this block have not move away yet. Terakawa, Sugimura, Nanba, Ueda, Miyakawa and Arima are playing around as usual.

Your birthday is coming pretty soon, and I am sending you one dollar with which you buy anything you wish. I can not get any present here. The Coop will close at the end of this month and their stores are almost empty already.

With Love
Father

Nov. 18, '45

Dear Nancy,

How are you? Is everything all right with you?

I am getting along fine. Golf? No I can not play much these days. The weather is too nasty for that.

Other day I met Reiko Ogata. She said she and her family were going to Denver pretty soon. She wanted me to write "Hellow" to you for her.

Kimiye Hirokane certainly delighted with candies you sent to her. It was very nice of you to remember your dear friend!

Good bye & good luck

Your Father

12/20/45

Dear Milton,

Thank you very much for the Christmas presents. I have not opened them yet. I think we should not open our packages until the Christmas morning, don't you think so? Well, I'll write again and tell you what I got after Christmas.

Good bye

Father

BISMARCK, NORTH DAKOTA

February–June 1942

Original letters in Japanese from Katsuchika to Umeno

The first Japanese internees at Ft. Lincoln were aliens mainly from the Terminal Island area in Los Angeles. Arrested December 7th and 8th, 1941, they were sent across country in prison trains, and unloaded under armed guard at Ft. Lincoln, December 18, 1941. Courtesy of John Christgau.

Unloading Japanese inside enclosure, main gate. Kimmins, with his back to the camera, Jim Maloney, helping a man step down. Courtesy of John Christgau.

英文ですでに申上ましたっ通り私共の日々の生活も思っ
たより楽で少しも心配することはありません。汽車の上での
食事は大層上等でしたからそれに比較したらこゝのは何共か
落ちますがそれでも空腹を感じる様なことはありません。
七時半 十二時 六時が食事時間です。家室も私共のは
レンガ造りですし室も廣く窓も二重ですから寒いことは
ありません。只今の處何の不足もありませんから御安心下さい。
斯く私の方は御心配に及びませんが留守中の家のことが苦
労になります。他の方々は心配はあるにしても生活上の
保証のある方がよいのですが私達の様に充分の用
意無く弘も居るのでどうしてお暮しかと案じて居り
ます。成る可く気を楽に必要以上骨を折らぬ
方がよいと存じます。出来得れば誰れか一共に住ん
でもらったら温り淋しい目に逢はぬと思ひます 何れにし
ても気苦労するのが一番よくありませんから充分気を
附けて下さい。子供達の生活は出来れば今迄位にしてやっ
らどうかと思ひます。極端につめて暮さすのは将来の
為めにもどうかと案じます。私の方からの手紙は一週二
回で英文一通邦文一通許されます。紙数は一度で
す。邦文だと検閲官が一人ださうで幾分後れると思
ひます。では今日はこれで只々も心配してはいけません
吉見 田中 竹本 竹森 元さん 岡崎さん 達へよろしく

一九四二、三月一日　勝用

梅乃どの

如何が御暮しですか 萬事うまく行って居りますか
立のきの善の不楽もありましたが私共がこゝで知る事の
出来る範囲ではつねは立のく様になると思ひません。
典ちゃん睦ちゃん弘ちゃんは元気ですか、もう今月で弘の
誕生日ですね。今誰れか来て共々起居して居りますか
成る可く淋しい思ひをせぬ様にした方がよいと存じます。
そちらからの手紙には別に制限は無いと思ひます。日本語で
よいのですから時々様子を知らして下さい。飛行郵便で出す人
もありますが速さは左程かわらぬと思ひますから三仙の
普通郵便でよいと思ひます。先日は御送り下さった品
々を確と受取りました。下着は早速着ました。他の品々も
暖かさうで大層有難く感じて居ります。
其後スタイン地方の様子はどうですか 上田さん其他の様子は
一寸新聞で知りましたが現在何處にどうして居るのか知りま
せん。此處での生活もまだ仕事はさせません。尤も食事料
理とか理髪とか無報酬で奉仕せねばならぬ仕事は有
ります。昨日は日曜だったので朝食には アップル一個 ボイルド
エッグス二個 コーンフレクス、ミルク、ブレッド、バター、じゃみ、コーヒー
昼食はローストポーク、マッシュポテト。レタス、ブレッド、バター
茶、夕食は ハンバーガーステーキ、サラダ、ライス スープ等
でした。朝のコーヒーにはすでに砂糖とミルクが入れてあるので困ります。
自動車を売った方がよいと思ひましたら其の様取運ん
で下さい。長い間ほって置くよりは其方がよいと思ひます。 勝田
梅乃 より

御変りありませんか、子供達は健康で暮して居りますか。
今日は日曜日ですが昨夜降り通した雪が何もかも白くおふて居ます。
室内は七十度からで丁度よくってあります。またこれと云ってきまった
仕事はありませんので室内の掃除を皆でする位のことです。先週
おたよりをしてから手紙二通とラルナフトを受取りました。御心使の程を
深く感銘致して居ります。鐘枝さん始め皆さんへは貴女から宜し
く御禮を申上て置いて下さい。私から直接禮状を出すことは此際さし
控へねばならぬと思ひます。本の事もありますが多数の同居なの
で御手数を掛けて送って載いても心をこめて讀むことが出来るかどうかと
案じて居りますから何れ御願ひする迄待って下さい。
過日の御手紙にもありました通り貴女なり子供達が健康な事は
何よりと存じます。どうぞ過り将来に就いて取越苦労せず心晴かに
日々を送って下さい。子供によい習慣はしよう勵し悪い習慣は
早くなほしてやるようにせねばならぬと思ひます。誰れか一共に
住んで呉れて居ますか、淋しいでせう。過日申上た自動車は誰
かに相談して賣れれば賣った方がよいと思ひます。日會からのは
宮田さんに願って居きましたから呉れたらもらって居ればよいと
思ひます。手紙も一週一度でしたら日本語でよいと存じます。忙しい
時間をさいて解らぬ事を書いて載く必要はありませんが簡單に變りない
事を知らして下さい。貴女からの手紙が一通私の手に着かなかったかと
思ひます。弘はもうじき歩むと思ひますか。共ちゃん睦ちゃんに手紙の
禮を述べて言ふて下さい。

三月十五日

勝用

梅乃殿

最初に英語の手紙を受取り其後日本文のを三通 子供からのを一通受取りました。最近のは十二日の消印で私の手には十六日月曜日に到着致しました。おたづね下さった氣候の事は当地方三十年来の暖かさださうで今日など窓から雪が見あたらぬ位とけてしまいました。殊に室内は七十度位の温度がたもってあるので誠にしのぎよいのです。スタクトンの人々に送ってくる品物も通りあたたかいものでどうする事も出来ず送り返すひとさへあります。私のも御心ずくして充分ですから御願する迄決して御送り下さいますな。日用品は売店があるのと シヤーローバグが一週一度出張して店を開きますし注文も取って呉れますので何の不自由もありません。煙草も止めようと思って居ますが巻く煙草を一袋宛呉れますのでつい止められません。皆さんが御親切にして下さるさうでまことによろこばしく存じます どうぞ呉々も宜しく御禮を申上げておいて下さい。度々申上る様ですが将来の事は過り苦労する事無く其日々を心ほがらかに暮して下さい。苺も今年は充分肥料を入れぬと出来ないでせうね。典ちゃん睦ちゃんにもおとなしくよく勉強する様に申して下さい。家から遠くはなれて居ることは一番つらいのですが周囲の人々を見るにつけても過り勝手は云いません貴女からのおたよりを何より樂しく待って居ります。

ではこの次まで 御身体も御大切に さようなら

勝男

三月十七日

梅乃殿

三月十七日附の御手書を三月二十三日月曜日に受取りました。
此処に居ります吾々の将来もはつきりして居りませんのでこれと申す仕事もなく
単調な生活を繰返へしてかれこれ一ケ月になります。快晴の日には室外で運動を
しますが其他の時間は取留もない話に聞き入らねばなりません。私の様にさうした
話題に興味を持たぬ者は過ぎさつた事に想が走ります。モントレー、ギルロイ
サンタクルーズ等も浮んで来ます。予期して居つた事とは云へ二月二十三日の
夕も忘れる事の出来事の一節です。
弘の熱もじき去る事と信じて居ります。先日こゝでも予防注射を致し
ましたが弘も出来る丈早く衛生局で注射をしてもらうとよいと存じます
竹林さんでも兄さんでも頼む事が出来ませんか。日会よりの金の事
は今の所望が無い様になつたと思はれます。あの方面の不親切からで
どうする事も出来ません。生活費に就いて一番心配して居ります。過り
無理せず止まる様でしたら私に知らして下さい。御親切に種々心配して
下さる方には呉々もよろしく禮を申上げて居いて下さい。受信には別に
制限は無いようですが發信は一週二通にきまつて居りますので一々私から
御禮を出すことは出来ません。コーヒー其他お送り下さる物を御た
づね下さいましたが先便にも申上ましたる通り此処での待遇は非常
によくこれ一つとして不足を感じるものはありませんから決して御案じ下さる
事なく私から御願ひするものだけを御送り下さい。スタクトンの人々
漸へも御宅から必要のないものを澤山送つて来るので困つて居ります。
こうした所に就いて近所の人々がかれこれ云ふのは全然風聞である
で跡形も無い事です。私は一番苦痛なことは貴女方からはなれ
て居ることです。典ちやん睦ちやんに出来る丈自分の事は自分
でする様申傳へて下さい。

三月二十四日

勝用

梅乃殿

三月廿一日、二十三日附の御手紙をそれぞれ落手致しました。萬事都合
よく行って居ります由で何よりと喜んで居ります。当地も四日程はげ
しい雪風吹で本当のノース、ダコタ天候を味ひました。御送り下さった
厚い下着が感謝されました。御手紙の度毎に皆さんから御世話になる
事を承知致しますが私から一々御禮を差出すことが出来ませんから
どうぞよろしく御禮を申上げて置いて下さい。又新しい規則で日系市民
でも行動不自由になったと存じます。時が時ですからお互に
最善を盡すより方法ありません。自動車のことは一寸御参考
迄に申上げた丈で貴女がよいと思ふ手段を執って下さい。お金のことは
まだ必要ありませんが来月に入りましたら御願ひせねばならぬと
思ひますが何れにしても私から御願ひしてからにして下さい。子供達
が健康であることは何よりだと存じます。弘もじき歩みさうださう
ですね。御誕生にはどうでせう。受取る手紙に制限はありませんが
差出す分は一週間に英文で一通日本文で一通となって居り
ます。それでこれからは日本語の一通と英文で子供宛一通を
出すことに致します。何れ立のきが実現するかも知れませんが
それまでは心晴れやかに楽しくお暮し下さる事を心から祈って
居ります。では今日はこれで

勝用

梅乃殿

今日は四月四日です。もう四日で弘の誕生日ですね。自由でしたら飛んで
行き度い様に思ひます。貴女はじめ子供達も丈夫でほがらかに暮して
居りますか。種々なうわさがあるので御心配なことだと推察致します。
立退問題も大分近よった様ですね。あゝこう申上げても私が
居りませんではどうする事も出来ません。重荷ではありますが貴女
が最善だと思ふ方法を執って下さるより仕方ありません。土地の
事はWCCAとナショナルファームローンのスタクトン事務所に
相談してごらんなさい。立退其ものには御心配無用だと思ひます。
総て其筋の行為を信頼して~~鎮~~沈着に行動して下さい。各商店で
捨売等ありますが必要以外のものは求めぬ方がよいと思ひます。もとく無い
金ですが出来る丈現金でもって居った方がよいと存じます。私は相変ず
元氣で暮して居りますから安心して下さい。渥美さんが私の下にねて居り
ます。何一つ不自由なものはありませんから御懸念下さいますな。
且し御金を二十弗程銀行のチェックで送って載けますか。
近所の皆さんはどうですか。吉見さんへもよろしく申上げて下さい。
兄さんはの、島へ行って居るのですか。竹森さんはの、店を閉め
ましたか。日米新聞を讀みますか。此の週間はこれでもう日本語
の手紙は書けません。長っく様な氣がします
ではこの次まで御健康を祈って

勝用

四月四日

梅乃殿

御変りありませんか私は相変らず丈夫で暮して居ります。博さんから手紙と二十円受取りました、私からも禮状を出して置きましたが貴女からもよろしく申上げて置いて下さい。島の方が都合よく借人があるさうでよろこばしく存じます。私のもので大事な物はありませんから箱にでも入れておけばよいと思ひます。トランクやスーツケースは皆お使ひなさい私のブラウン色のも使へると思ひます。先日手紙で申上げて置きましたお金の事はどうなりましたか立退き前に出来る丈も出る様に宮田忠雄さんか藤森賢三弐は岡本勉さんに頼んで下さい銀行からは出してよいと云って来て居るのですからこの人達にまかしきりでほって置いてはいけません。私の方は日用品は共いられますがそれでも幾莫かかゝります。立退き後はむづかしいと存じますからこの金か手に入るか自動車か責れましたら五十円程送って置いて下さったら非常に心強いと思ひます。お互の事情を知って居る私からこうしたお願をするのは大変心苦しい事ですが先がわかりませんので御願して置く次第です。

弘も随分手が掛るでせうね。フロワーの上を匐ひ廻って遊ぶと云ふのが目に見える様です。典ちゃんや睦ちゃんはよいこですか、

今日はこーも雨が降って居ります。寒さは大分ゆるやかになってローンも追々青くなって行きます。

心晴れやかに何事も御心配なさらぬ様に

では次の通信まで皆の健康を祈りながら

勝用

四月十八日

梅乃殿

四月十五日附の御手紙を受取りました。
リースペーパーの下書が出来ましたら送って下さい。
差支へありません。但しタイムが無くてそれの出来ない
時は博さん博行さんを信頼してサインされてよいだ
らうと思ひます
先は右要々まで
四月二十三日
勝用
梅乃殿

April 26, 1942

四月二十日附の御手紙を拝見致し元氣で御蕃の由で安心
致しました、子供達も丈夫ださうで何よりです。二十二日の
日米を当地で受取りいよ〳〵立退の日が決定した様承知
致しました、案外早く来たので種々混雑する事と思ひます
何事も子供達を中心として沈着に行動して下さい、私の事については
過り心配なさらぬ様にすでにしておいて下さった丈で充分です。百弗
受取ったさうで安心しました立退く前にあの方々に願って五月の月に百
弗立退いた處へ送って呉れる様たのんで置きなさい。この手紙が立退
前に到着しタイムがありまだ私の夏物が送ってなかったら紙の箱に
ざっとした品物を送って下さい。夏のスーツも入れて置いて下さい。スーツケース
は当地で買ひます。私の所へのお金の事は其後の手紙で御承知
の事と存じます　あれ程は必要ないかも知れませんが適当に送って
載いておけば充分です。
この次は立退かれた所へ通信する様になると思ひますでは
それまで心朗かにすべてにあたって下さい。

勝周

四月二十六日朝

梅乃殿

追信　先日の手紙に子供の写真を送ったとありましたが手紙の中に
ありませんでした。途中で紛失したのでせうか

May 5, 1942

五月四日月曜日すでに十時四十五分の消燈時間もすぎて床に入って居ります
と隣の室の八木さんが田村さん手紙ですよと持って来て呉れました。多分夕
刻配布すべき分から落ちて居たのでせう。起きて廊下の燈のついて居る
所へ讀みに行きました。

土地のリース、立退の登録や準備、銀行等とさぞ忙しいであったらう
とほんとうにおさっしします。前々からこうした時の事を案じて居りました
何と云っても本人でなければ用の足りぬ事が澤山起って来るのに小さい
小供があり便が思ふ様でなかったらさぞ難儀であったらうと同情致して居ります。
この手紙も都合よく行けば立退所に達すると存じますが兎に角差上げて居
きます。先日は寫真を受取りました。大層よく寫って居ると存じます。幸福
さうに寫って居るので安心しました。弘も相変らずふとって居ますね。五月二日
金田のりつちゃんから手紙と五十弗の小切手を受取りました。随分世話になって
居りますねよろしく御禮申上げて居いて下さい。私からも返書は出して置きました。
夏物の小包も確と受取りました、あれで充分です、もう何もいりません。
種々御心盡しで感謝に堪へません。

今度はおまへは立退所で生活して居られるかと御案じ致します。何かと不便で
苦労の多いことと推察致しますが追々なれて来るでせうから忍耐して心強く
晴々して氣分で御暮しの程を祈って居ります　では又の日まで

勝周

五月五日

梅乃殿

DETAINED ALIEN
ENEMY MAIL
EXAMINED
U.S.I.&N.S.

本月五日の消印の附いた書信を九日に落手致しました。案じて
居りましたが無事落付かれた由で安心致しました。種々
不なれの事多く御心痛の事と存じますが子供達の為めまた
より以上不幸の人々のある事を心にとめて最善を盡して下さる
事をお願いして置きます。先は解らず私共も何時迄こうして
居るのかと思ふと氣もめいりますが此際お互に心強く諸事
事態に打勝たねばならぬと思ひます。私達男子でも食事
時はうるさいのですから貴女方特に子供があれば随分つらい事
が多いと御察しします。

昨日吉見の節代さんから手紙をもらひました。過日家へ歸ったさう
ですね。私達の家へも来たさうで弘や共ちゃん睦ちゃんの事など書いてあり
ました。

金曲のりつちゃんには先日禮状を出して置きました。
貴女たち子供達が丈夫だと云ふ事が何よりのよいたよりです
どうぞ今後も總てに元氣を附けて病氣をせぬ様注意して下さい。
紙本さん親子さん竹森さん竹森の典さん方へ呉々もよろしく
申上げて下さい。隣近所はどなた方か其内に知らして下さい。
では今日はこれで

勝用

五月十日

梅乃殿

ながらへば またこのごろや しのばれん
うしと見し世ぞ 今は戀しき

DETAINED ALIEN ENEMY MAIL EXAMINED
23-2

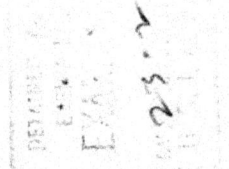

五月十二日附の消印のある手紙を今日受取りました。昨夜は雨だと予想して居った空もようが今朝起きて見ると大雪に変って居ます。尤もこれと申して屋外の仕事は無し家屋は永久的に建てた煉瓦造りの立ぱな建物なので寒いと思ふ程ではありません。集合所の生活がさぞ不自由であらうと心掛りになって居りましたし食堂通ひの経験は私自身味はったので心から御同情致します
お互にこうした時代にめぐり合せたのですから忍耐して何事も解決して行かねばなりません。弘も今が一番手が掛ると思ひます。ねては居ずそれかと申して一人置いてはあぶないし そのかはり今が一番かはゆい時代でもあると思ひます、典ちゃんや睦ちゃんも丈夫だそうで此上もありません。エルクは三男さんもらってのましたらよいと思ひます。さうした所の生活は今迄の様に近所の人々に気兼ねない生活とちがって種々心使ひをせねばならぬので御心配の多い事とお推察し致します 食事、洗濯入浴等が中々めんどうな問題ですね。
先日私共のルームから一人帰りましたが今の所はっきりした事は解りません 楽かん的に申す人もあり悲かん説の人もあります。私自身では帰れる様に信じて居ります。何をぎせいにしても帰りたいと思ひます。集合所たり収容所の生活は仁たりよったりの生活と思ひますがそれでも早く帰って一共に暮したいと思ひます。竹森御夫婦吉見さん紙本御夫婦方、呉々もよろしく申上げて下さい。

勝甫

五月十六日

梅乃殿

ワーダイからスーツを受取りました禮と受取を出して置いて下さい

May 26, 1942

今朝は昨日一昨日と續いた不愉快な風が止んで静かな好天氣になりました。朝食をすまして窓に立って外を眺めますと三ヶ月前此處に到着した当時同じ窓から眺めた時とは雲泥の差があります。見渡す限り荒涼を感じさした眺望も今は萬々とした芝生と青々とした木々に依って美しく晴々した公園になりました。黄色いたんぽぽが加州のポピー様に至る所に咲いて居ます。建物の前にある大きなカットンツリーの上にろびんが巣をつくって居ます。

私は幸で健康で順調ですが別段不平の無い生活を送って居ります。唯一の慾望は一日も早く歸り度いと云ふ事です。皆んな恙無くお暮しの由でこれよりよろこばしいたよりはありません。氣兼ねの無かった生活から急にさうした所に入って種々氣苦勞なることと察し心から同情致します。忍耐して最善を盡して下さい。

では又次のたよりまで近所の皆さんによろしく

勝周

五月二十六日

梅乃殿

五月二十五日附の御手紙を子供等のと一共に受取りました。恙無く
御暮しの由で安心致しました。ほんとうに早いものでお別れしてから
早三ヶ月になります。だれも一日も早く平和の日が来る事を祈って
居りますがどうする事も出来ません。キャンプも追々整って来まし
たが、食事はどうですか。スタクトンの人々からのたよりでは野菜が
充分で無いと不平を云って来る様です。弘のたべ物はどうして居
ます。ベビーのキャンものは自分で買ふのですか。売店の様
子は如何です。竹森さんや紙本さんは何かに働いて居りますか。
私は幸と丈夫です。気候がよく変ります。一日春の様なうら
やかな日があるかと思ふと翌日は冬の様です。今朝も空は暗
く雨も降り温度も低いのでヒーターを再び入れて居ります。
相変らず読書したり遊んだりして同じ事を繰返して居ります
近頃石をひろってあるくのが流行り出して誰れかれも
めづらしい石、きれいな石をひろったりまたそれらをみがい
たりして居ります。私にはする気がしません。一昨々日は午後
三時間ばかり庭のスペードイングに行き昨日はケツナン
へ働きに行きました、交たいで誰れでも行かねば成りません。
誕美さんはサツクに行き常穂さん「大阪屋の主人」はベーカリー
へ行きます。吉見の節代さんから手紙を受取りました。立退前
に五日ばかり家へ帰ったさうですね。衛生に気を附けて
丈夫で暮して下さい。ではこの次まで

五月三十日

梅乃殿

勝田

CAMP MCCOY, WISCONSIN

June–July 1942

Original letters in Japanese from Katsuchika to Umeno

CENSORED

五月五日附のお手紙を受取りました。なつかしいおたよりは何時も嬉しく存じます。結局戦時中は帰れぬ様に決定して別のキャンプに移されました。帰る人もありますので種々御心配下さるでせうがこうした時代でやむを得ぬ事ですからどうぞ心強く力を落さぬ様して下さい。此度の私共の仲間にも私達以上氣の毒な方もありますがみなあきらめねばなりません。
私も貴女方の事を非常に心痛して日夜祈りましたが今は総てがすむ迄はどうする事も出来ません。私としては貴女が確として決心し子供の養育に専念して下されば、これ以上のことはありません。写真を見る度に心にもあるした晴れやかな母、ゑみのある事を願って居ます。時に今でも日本へ帰れる機會があるかも知れぬと云ふ人があります。家族も一共です。其かゆく俗に云ふ「裸一貫で帰らねばなりません。貴女の考を次便で知らして下さい。此度場所は変りましても生活は別に変らず以前と同じくよいたいぐうをされて居ます。十一月午後ビスマークを出て東へ東へ走りミネソタのセントポールから南へきれて當所に着きました。ウイスコンシン州のキャンプマッコイと申します。山の中で景色のよい所です元氣で暮して居りますから其点は案ぜずに下さい思ひは色々にはせて僅かに氣持が取止めなく浮んできますが書き表はせません。よろしくさっして下さい。

母へ　文　十二月十三日　勝用

御変りありませんか。私は元氣で暮して居ります。近い内に貴女方も他に移る様聞及んで居りますがどうですか、どうぞ氣候のよい場所ならばよいと祈って居ります。子供達があるので移るにも一方ならぬ困難のあると心痛致して居りますが兄さんや竹森さん方によって最善を盡して下さい。限りの無いと思ふ悪い天候もいつか晴れる様に樂しく逢へる日がきっと来ます。私の事に就きましては決して心配して下さいますな。新しいキャンプ生活も悪くありません。シカゴに近い山間にあって現在は氣候もよく食事取扱等少しも不平はありません。唯一つ貴女からはなれて居る事丈けが心を暗くします。家族と一共に住める様になると云ふうわさもありましたが一寸あてになりません。兄さんや竹森さんは如何ですかよろしく申上げて居いて下さい。私共は今所　　程です。スタクトンからは私一人です　何れまた来るかも知れませんがどうか解りません。御身体をたいせつに子供達にもよろしく

八月十六日

勝用

梅乃殿

其後お変りありませんか。御手紙を十日程いただかないのでどう御暮しかと案じて居ります。只今奥地へ移らねばならぬので御多忙のことと推察しております。子供も皆丈夫ですか。今頃は帰ってお手助が出来るかとはかない望を持って居りましたがこうした事情で誠に残念に思いますがまた浦野安井両兄のことなどおもってやむを得ぬことあきらめて居ます。度々申上げる様ですが心晴れやかに最善を尽して下さい。吾々の一生にはつらいと思ふことも後には精神的に貴い経験になることがあります。私は幸と元気で暮して居ります。係の方々も大層よい人達で私達も幸福です。柏の木と松の木の繁った小山にかこまれた山間で今朝の様に晴々した朝は誠に気持がよいのです。当方へ移る頃こちらへ移った当時は貴女のことや子供のことをおもって実にくるしい思をしましたが。今日此頃はむしろ健康で暮して晴れやかにまた逢ふ日を待たうと出来る丈衛生に注意して日々をすごして居ります。では呉々も御身体御大切に。御手紙を待って居ります

六月二十四日
勝用
梅乃殿

W. D., P. M. G. Form No. 4
February 17, 1942
16—27540-1 U. S. GOVERNMENT PRINTING OFFICE

先週手紙を差上げた後二十日附御手紙
二通二十三日附一通合はせて三通のおたより
で御無事で御消光の由を存じこの上も無い
ると存じます。私も幸ひ元氣暮して居ります
一昨日はひどい雷と降雨でした。此附近では
夏には度々あるさうです。今日はうららかな
日で嵐の後の静さです。秋本ドクター
も此處に来る事になったさうですか
ビスコークで仕事がある故かまだ来ません。
御手紙にあった様にツレラレーキの方へ
行ける様でしたら幸だと思ひます。皆さん
の話ではレーキがドライアップしたあとで
砂地で暑いかも知れませんが加州の冬です
から氣持だけでも他州に行くよりよ、
かも知れません。竹森さんにも何かと世話
になると思ひますがどうぞ呉々も御礼
を申上げて置いて下さい。岡崎さん一家
はスタクトンへ行って居るのですか。どうぞ
よろしく申上げて下さい。平野さんは
ほんとうに御氣の毒でした。私からも謹しん
でおくやみ申上ますと御傳へ置き下さい。
御近所の方フレンチキャンプの方々へよろ
しく申上げて下さい。

六月三十日
勝用
一田ら 父

其後は皆々健かに御暮しですか。弘も大分歩ん
様になりましたか。口もきける様になりましたか。
典ちゃんも睦ちゃんもよい子ですか。学校へ行っ
て居りますか。貴女もキャンプ生活になれました
か。私達の家にはどんな人が入って居るのです
アンオンも案外安かったさうですね。吉見さん
田中さん、竹本さん方でも変りありませんか。よろ
しく申上げて下さい。兄さんは何かの仕事をして
居られますか。英夫さんも大きくなったで
せうね。静子さんは。竹森さんは一足先に
何をして居るのでせう。ツールレーキへ行く事
はどうなりました。アリゾナ方面へ行った人
は随分暑いさうです。貴女の目方は近頃ふえ
ましたか。弘は何斤ありますか。当地は近来
になく涼しださうで楽です。食物もよく
司令官は親切で貴女方に別れて居る事
以外に不足はありません。日本行もまだ手
続して居りません。竹森さんや兄さんはどう
考へるでせう。初めに来たので皆さんの
事を種々世話して居ります。元の仕事
の様に一面うるさい仕事ですが皆さんの
為めに奉仕する事は決して望ましくない
事ではありません。では次のたよりまで　勝男
七月九日
丹ろ　父

W. D., P. M. G. Form No. 4　　16—27540-1　U. S. GOVERNMENT PRINTING OFFICE

御手紙を受取りました。典ちゃん睦ちゃんの手紙
も一昨日受取りました。弘も一番可愛い時と存じ
誠に残念と思います。此處も二三日来暑くなり
ましたがそれでも其處の百度以上の暑さから
比らぶれば楽だと存じます。別段予想して
居った様なえらい事はありません 司令官は
じめ皆よい人達で私達も身心共に健全で
暮して居ります。[illegible]さんはまだ来て居りません
十日程前に来た手紙ではまだビスマークに居
る様でしたがあすこも大分人が移動して居る
ので近頃の様子は知れません。朝は六時に起き
て冷水浴を取り七時に朝食です。十二時が昼
食で夕食は五時です。人数が少ないので食堂も
混雑しませんし食るも兵士と同様ですから中々
上等です。アイスクリームも時々あります。朝も
果子フルーツ、シリアル(コーンフレーキス其他)ミルク、コーヒー
トーストバター等家で喰べて居ったようにビックブレー[illegible]
ハストを執ります。立木も柏と松が沢山あっ
て涼しい木影が沢山あります。冬は寒いそう
ですが設備がよいからすごしよいと思います。ハット
オーターも充分ありますから入浴や洗濯は何
時でも出来ます。皆さんによろしく。御身体を
御注意なさい。

七月十七日 勝用

梅乃殿

16—27540-1 U. S. GOVERNMENT PRINTING OFFICE

一寸二日程暑くって又この二三日涼しくなり
今朝は寒い位に感じます。貴女の手紙
でも承知し且つ吉晃の節代さんが送って呉
れた新聞の切ぬきに依ればアリゾナの
ギラリジャーと云う所へ移る様に存
じます。暑い所でせうが健康に悪い所
とは思はれません。萬事に注意して身体を
大切にして下さい。多分ターラフクで受取る
手紙は之がしまいと存じますから、あちらへ
到着したら新らしい所書を早速知らし
て下さい。それから節代さんが巻煙草を
一箱送って呉れました。山の方へ見舞
旁御禮を云って下さいませんか。子供が
少さいので移動するに非常な御苦労
だと御察し致して居ります。兄さん
竹森さん、呉々よろしく御たのみして
居って下さい。まだスタクトンの人が一人
も来て居らぬので淋しく思います
それでは皆無事で新らしい所へ移る
様祈り居ら　　　　勝田
一九四三年七月二十日
梅乃殿

CAMP LIVINGSTON, LOUISIANA

July 1942–MAY 1943

Original letters in Japanese from Katsuchika to Umeno

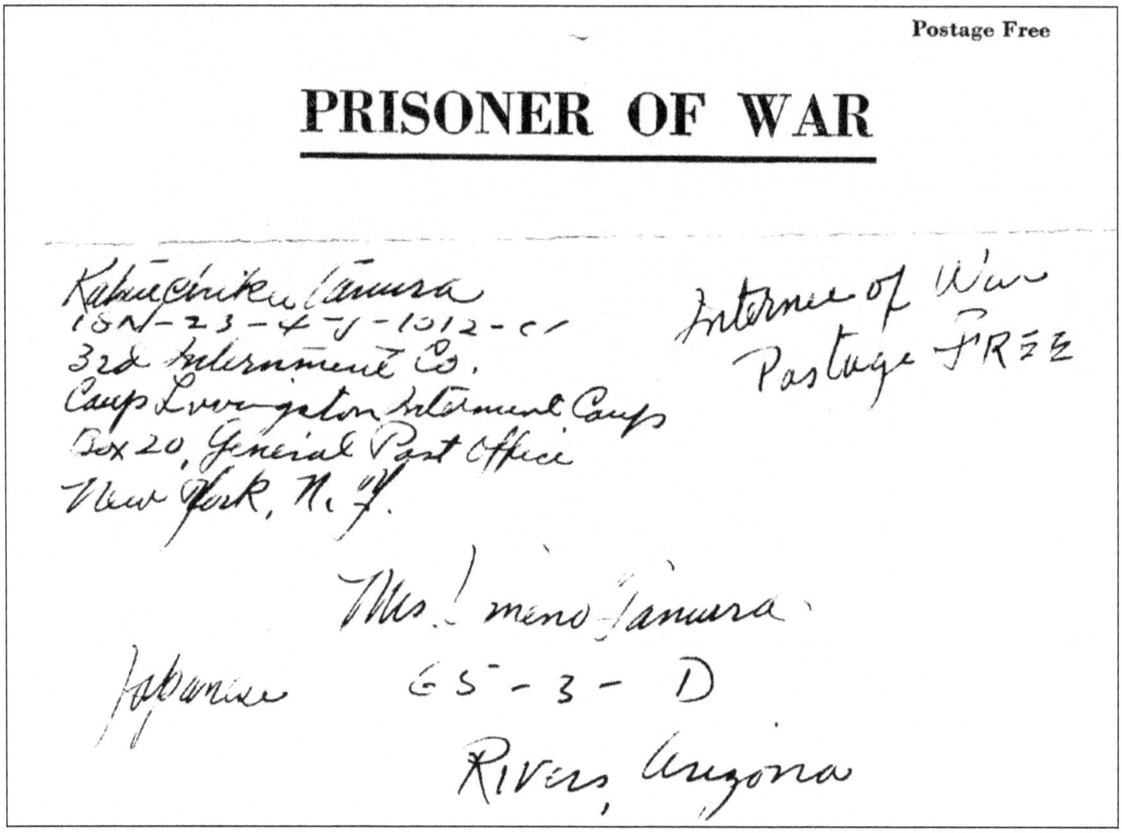

Postage Free

PRISONER OF WAR

Katsuchika Tamura
ISN-23-4-J-1012-CI
3rd Internment Co.
Camp Livingston Internment Camp
Box 20, General Post Office
New York, N.Y.

Internee of War
Postage FREE

Mrs. Umeno Tamura
Japanese
65-3-D
Rivers, Arizona

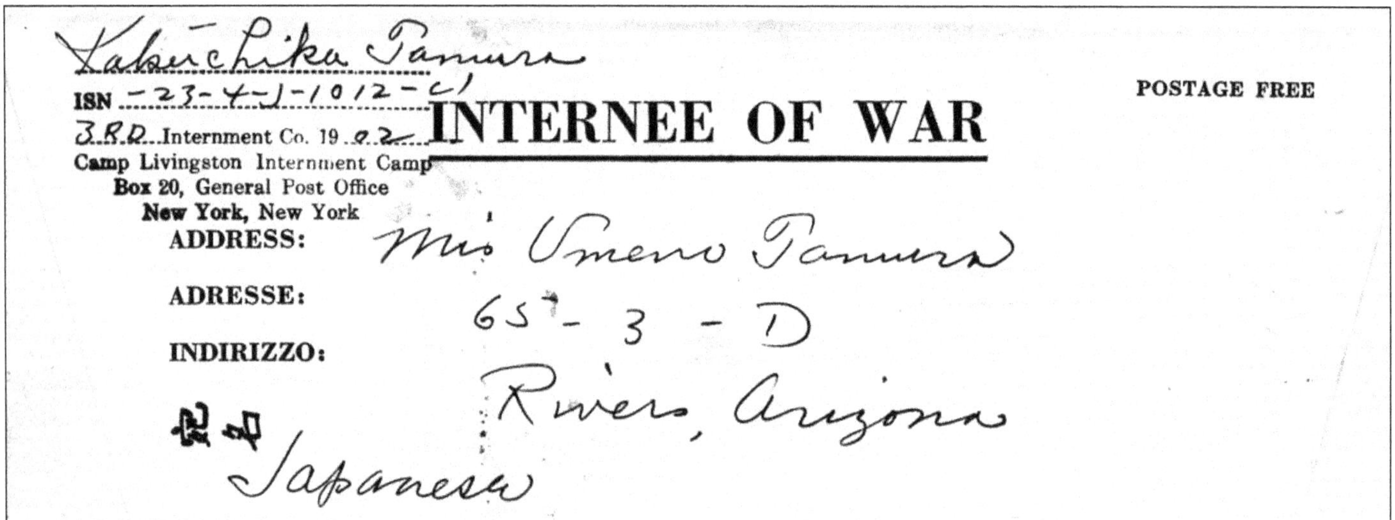

Katsuchika Tamura
ISN -23-4-J-1012-CI
3RD Internment Co. 19 02
Camp Livingston Internment Camp
Box 20, General Post Office
New York, New York

INTERNEE OF WAR

POSTAGE FREE

ADDRESS: Mrs Umeno Tamura
ADRESSE: 65-3-D
INDIRIZZO: Rivers, Arizona

Japanese

JAPANESE

Mrs. Umeno Tamura
65-3-D
Rivers, Arizona

Katsuchika Tamura
ISN-23-4-J-1012-CI
3rd Internment Co
Camp Livingston Int. Camp
Box 20, General Post Office
New York, N.Y.
April 12, 1943

手紙が後れはせぬかと案じて居ります。先日出た手紙が途中から返って来ました。元氣で暮して居りますから安心して下さい。昨日の弘の誕生日には些少でも降誕花祭が行はれ私も私等の隊を代表して参列致しました。心から皆の無事息災を心から念じました。土曜日には活動がありましたがあまり面白い写真は近頃ありません。先日手紙にあった子供のチキンポックスはどうです子供達からうつらずにすみましたか。聞く所によれば其他の病氣もはやるさうですが本当ですか。暑くなると水が多くいるでせうが今年も制限がありますか。子供達の学校は何時休みになります。私はこの次から皆の世話をして居るので忙がしいのですが日曜にはゴルフも遊びます。一日も早く一緒になれば安心します。それまでは暑さ寒さにかゝわらず案ぜられます。

ヒラの新聞も順次来て居りますから大体の
様子は知れますが時々は皆さんの様子を
知らして下さい。子供達の其日々にも御心配なさ
るでせうが最善を盡し過りに氣を短かく
せぬ様にして下さい。では今日これで さよなら

Katsuchika Kimura

いろかしこ

妻へ

W. D., P. M. G. Form No. 4
February 17, 1942

16—27540-1 U. S. GOVERNMENT PRINTING OFFICE

皆元氣のことと存じます。私も恙ありません。ビスマークで
インターンと決定した時直ちに歸國手續をする様すゝめ
た方もありましたが私一人の考ばかりでは行かぬのと急にマッコイ
へ移されたので其儘にしてあったのです。其後貴女の氣持も
よく解りましたが歸ってからのこともあり同時に吾々と家族
を一共にすると云ふ案もあるのでもう少し様子を見てと思
って居りました。尤も早く申込をして居たにしてもよほど早くした
のでないと申込者が二倍もあるさうで第二回船と云ふ譯には
行かなかったと思ひます。近頃特に七月二十六日附の子供の手
紙、兄さんからの手紙等によって子供の教育等もあり
ますから歸國する様手續しました。尤もこれも變更は
何時でも出来ますから貴女の考が變りましたら知して
下さい。わづか十五ヶ月程でお別れし早や半ヶ年にもなり
私も一日も早く逢ひたいと希って居ります。政府は家族と
一共にする計画があるにしても何時するか其結果もどんな
ものか解りません。アリゾナが随分暑く砂嵐があるさう
ですし随分困難なることと心からおさっします。子
供のしつけも困ったものですね。弘までがどうしたのでせう。
若し萬る都合よく行けばこの次には乘れると思ひますから
何事もこらへて心倖して下さい。今回は兄さんへ手紙を
差上ませんから宜しく申上げて下さい。竹森、手嶋さん
へも呉々も。身体を大切に　　勝用
九月一日
梅乃殿

九月廿日附の手紙を受取りました、英語の手紙は切りぬかれてよく
解かなかったさうですね。別段差支へあるのは書かなかったつもり
でしたが。貴女もそこで申込んださうで さうして置けば何より
と思ひます。お金の方は送ればどれ程でも送れますか
今の所全然必要ありません　軍部に預けてあるのですが
まだ五十弗程あります。小さいトランクと着物を
掛けて置く大きな袋とラバーシューズを買った丈で後は
残って居ます。帰る時でも貴女がもって居ればよいので私に送る
必要はないと思ひます。荷物は三十二立方尺で小型の手さげ
は持込む事が出来ると思ひます。何れにしてもまだ／＼先の
解らぬ事ですから余り心配しないでよいと思ひます。氣が
付いた事があったら通知します。私としては一日も早く貴女方
と一緒になりたいと思ひます さうで無いと汽車での途中も
心配になりますから。重ねて云ふ様ですが子供の事に付いて
余り取越苦労してはいけません。健康に出来る丈け
注意して時期の来るまで待って下さい。これからは急な用
の無い時は日本文の手紙を次から次と書いて下されば順に
受取る様になると思ひます。英語で書いて戴くるも
忙がしい時は御氣の毒だと思ひます。ゴルフのクラブは
こちらで買へぬ事になりました。若しすでに来て居まし
たらNo.7、8 とPUTTER（パッター）の三本とボールを
送って下さい。今日はこれ丈け　さよなら

九月廿四日
梅乃殿
勝用

W. D., P. M. G. Form No. 4
February 17, 1942

16—27540-1 U. S. GOVERNMENT PRINTING OFFICE

其後変りありませんか　子供達も元気ですか　大きくなった
でせうね。色々心配はするもの、どうする事も出来ぬ状態
です。船もまだ出ませんので私達の番に何時来るか解りま
せん。こうした事情の下にあっては気を落なけて時期の来る
のを待つより仕方ないと思ひます。大分土地にもなれましたか
先日送って下さったキャンプの新聞に依ると一年の八ケ月
はよい気候だと云ふではありませんか。何かといろいろする
事でせうが健康に注意して日を送って下さい。働
きの[illegible]も子供があるので無理をしてはいけません。今日
此頃は気候もよし何一つ不足は無いもの、皆んなと別
れて居るのが悲しまれます。運動や催しもあり
成可く気をまぎらす様つとめて居りますが私す
性格からこうした生活は非常に苦しく感じます。
松雄さんから深切な手紙をもらいました。アーカンサス
の住所が解ったら知らして下さい。兄さん、も手紙を出
さねばならぬと思ひ乍ら後れて居ります　呉々も
よろしく申上て置いて下さい。英語の手紙は静子
さんに書いてもらふのですか、どうぞ御禮を申述べ
て置いて下さい。竹森さん手嶋さんへもよろしく
ではこの次まで
勝用
十月八日

今日は十月十九日です。月日の立つのは早いものです。明暮御身の上を案じて居ります。現在では大きな流れにながされて居る様なもので流れに従って時の来るのを待つより仕方ありません。お互に心を晴やかに持って逢ふ日を一日も早かれと念じませう。僅の間とは云へフレンチキャンプでの生活は忘れる事の出来ぬ楽しい思出です。又我等もあなたや子供達があるので大きな希望があります。帰国が可能になれば一人三百弗とありますが私の知って居る範囲では、これは大人（三十才以上）に對する高だと思ひますが過り先の事は心配せずに落ちついて待って居て下さい。私の今案じて居るのは貴女方の旅行です。其前に何とかして一緒になれたら非常に都合がよいと思ひます。荷物は大人一人に對して三十三立方尺だと申して居ります。勿論大人子供共に一つ位づつのスーツケースは常に身のまはりにけいたいする事が出来ると思ひます。今週は日本文の手紙を先に書きました。到着は後れると存じますが後にするとついおこたり勝になります。少しはその生活になれましたか。あなたの気分には向かないでせうねでは今日これで皆々も壮健で愉快に日を送る様つとめて下さい。

勝田

梅乃 殿

W. D., P. M. G. Form No. 4
February 17, 1942

16—27540-1 U. S. GOVERNMENT PRINTING OFFICE

今日は十一月二十七日です。一ヶ月程雨がありませんでしたが数日前一日降って翌日は再び晴れて寒さが増し今朝は丁度加州の土用はじめ頃の氣候です。すごしがたいと云ふ程では無く大氣は心地よいほどすんで居ます。知って居られるでせうかまだ二回船も出て居りませんから近い将来に私達の家財が来るとは思はれません。あなた達が健康で不足勝とは云へ無事で暮して居られると信じて心安く暮して居ります。過日ゴルフの競ぎがあったので出ましたら運よく一等賞をもらひました。勿論上手と云ふのではなく運がよかったのです。学校が始まったので二人は一日の大部分を学校で暮すると思ひ今迄の様に一日遊んで居るよりよいと思ひます。弘はどうですか大きくなったでせうね。夜中によく起きますか。私の方は一般によい健康状態で大して病氣する人もありません。私も其後風一つひきません。こう云ふ際で誰れもかれも苦悩させねばならぬのですから皆す健康を第一として心晴れやかに暮して下さい。私は夜も昼もあなた達に差なかれと祈って居ります。夢から醒めて近かった様に思ったのに事変は以前として遠くはなれて居るのでがっかりして淋しくなります。では又

勝用

梅乃殿

今朝は曇って居りますが暖くスエター無しで丁度よい位です。日本文の手紙は近頃大分後れますが何時かは到着すると思って書きます。生活は別にこれと申して変ったこともなく今迄に申上げた様なことを繰返へして居ります。貴女も子供達も元氣で暮して居られると承知して居りますが何よりと存じます。種々不便もあり貴女の氣分にはあわぬ生活でせうがこうした時代に逢って誰れも忍ばねばならぬ運命ですから忍耐して處して下さい。時に岡崎一家はアルカンサス、行ったのですか。送って下さるそこの新聞にスタクトンからの人々が来たとあったので或は其處、行く様願ったのではないかと思ひました。明暮貴女方のことのみ心に浮びます。写真を見て二人は左程変らぬにしても私はあの時から見た丈随分大きくなったでせうね。共ちゃんも睦ちゃんも学校が始まったので大分よくなったでせう。近頃の氣候はどうですか朝は寒いでせうですね。早く平和の日の来るのを祈りながら今日はこれで

勝田

皆さんへよろしく

十月六日

梅乃殿

昨日英文の手紙でパンツを受取った通知をして置きました。大層よい品物でよく合ひますのでよろこんで居ります。天候もよく身心共にすこやかに暮して居りますから御安心下さい。今の所別れて居る悲みの外には何も不足はありません。胸の内であれこれ繰って見ても不平よりも感謝すべき
多い様思はれます。第一身体は健康ですし心もこうした状態にたへ得る丈の心組は持って居ります。此處での吾々の生活も決して苦痛などはありません。食料もよく湯水も充分ですし家屋便所なども清潔で今日の安らかならぬ世界の状態の下に住む人の内では幸運中の幸運者だと思って居ります。お互の案じは子供の教育だと存じますがこれも最善をつくすより仕方ないと思ひます。貴女も子供等も健康でせうね。弘も随分大きくなったでせう。いたずらですか。交換船も今の所何時出るやらわかりません。何れにしてもお互に身体を注意して一日も早く逢へる様念じませう。兄さん静子さん竹森夫婦手嶋一家によろしく申して下さい。フレンチキャンプの方々も皆一共ですかでは次便までさようなら

十一月十二日　勝田

懐しき妻へ

明暮あなたの事のみ想って居ります。すべての事を共に處し行き度いと云ふ事が私の唯一の願ひであったに不思議な運命でこうした長い間別れ々れに暮さねばならぬ様になって残念です。時の立つのは早いものでもうじき一ヶ年になります。あの頃を想ひ出すと胸に痛を感じます。心に一つのやましい事は無いとは云へこうした不安の世にあって罪あると無いとにかゝわらず運命にもてあそばれいくらあがいてもどうする事も出来ません。時々は希望のある様なうわさも出ますがそれもいつかは水面に落ちた白雪の様にきえてなくなってしまいます。従って私の今の唯一の願はこの世界的風雲が晴れ渡る迄貴女も子供達も心晴れやかに健全で忍耐して待って居て呉れる事です。そこの生活には少しはなれましたか子供達の近頃はどうですか 学校が始まって少しはよくなりましたか。さうした所に生活する人の常としてよく不平をならべますがものは心の持ちやう事ですからその氣持で暮して下さい。では御身大切に

勝四

十一月二十日

梅乃殿

W. D., P. M. G. Form No. 4
February 17, 1942

16—27540-1　U. S. GOVERNMENT PRINTING OFFICE

先日申し述べた通り英文の手紙も来ます、検閲の
為め行くので私もこの二週間程おたよりを
受取って居りませんがそちらでも同様だと
存じます。然し皆も御健全と推察し私
も常の如く丈夫で暮して居るからお互に安
心して日を送りませう。近頃朝は一寸寒
くなりますが日中は暖く心地よい気候です。
近頃家族と一共にする様な話があります
が実行されゝば此上もなうると日夜心に
念じて居ります。其地へ帰るのか別に
キャンプを建てゝ一共に集めるのかよく
わかりません。これも今迄の様に早く呼
だけかも知れませんので過し期待は出来
ません。岡崎さんはアーカンサスへ行ったの
ですか。たよりがありますか。兄さんは何を
して居られるのですか。ブラフクの副支配
人をまだして居るのですか。竹森さんは、其
處にはゴルフコースは無いのでせう。
子供達は学校へ行く様になってから
少しはよくなりましたか。種々の人の見
まねしてなかなかむづかしいでせう。では
身体を呉々も大切にして暮して下さい。

十二月廿七日　勝田

梅乃殿

W. D., P. M. G. Form No. 4　16—27540-1　U. S. GOVERNMENT PRINTING OFFICE

近頃手紙が来ないので淋しく感じて居りましたが昨日は十月二十二日附今日は二十六日附の手紙を受取りました。両方とも長文で誠に嬉しく拝見致しました。弘も今が一番可愛い頃でせうか早く見たいと思ひます。あなたも友達も無く心淋しいでせうがこうした時代の常として誰れもかれも種々なるに耐へねばならぬのですからどうぞ忍耐して心晴やかに暮す様つとめて下さい。こうした事にならうとは夢にも想はず楽しく共に暮せると信じて居りましたのに人間の一生には種々予期せぬ事が起るものです。私の此処での生活も何一つ不足は無いとは云へ、あなた方の事のみ明暮心に掛ります。

クリスマスも近くなり子供も贈物を予期して居るでせうが今年はどうする事も出来ません。よろしくそちらで買求めてやって下さい。當方も一週間程前まで割合に暖かかったのですが二三日朝夕一寸寒く感じます。とは云へ何と云っても南方の州なので春居ったノース、ダコタ等とはくらべ物になりません。只、建物が余り上等でないので外界の暑気寒気をよけい感じる様です。

今日はこれで皆さんへよろしく

どうぞ丈夫で幸福に暮して下さい。

十二月九日　　勝周

なつかしき梅乃殿

W.D., P.M.G. Form No. 4
February 17, 1942
16—27540-1　U. S. GOVERNMENT PRINTING OFFICE

近頃和英書信共に後れるのでこまったものです
私からの手紙も僅かなるで歸って来ましたらさ
ぞ案じて居られると存じます。この手紙もこう
して書きますが何時着くかたよりも無いのです
何れにしても健全で暮して居りますから安心して下さい
日本手紙も三通受取りました最近の分
は十月十日附です 気候もよく皆丈夫で暮
して居るさうで此上も無いよろこんで居ります
日々はいって居ます 受取の手紙は其際書い
鉄もパンフも確に受取りました。よく合ふの
たのですが過日もどって来たので再び書添へ
て置く次第です。申上げた様に常識で
解するる出来ぬ様な審査の仕方
なので何を書くるも出来ません。何故
必要の無い せさせるのか意か
知れません・昨日下駄を四足 タブレット
ペンシル キャンデイを送って置きました
到着すればこの上もありません。
今日はこれ迄に
寒さに気を附けて幸福に暮して
下さい。
十二月十六日 勝男
梅乃殿

16—27540—1 U. S. GOVERNMENT PRINTING OFFICE

和英両文共に同じ時を要するので日本文で
したためます。何時この手紙がとどくかそれも
ばく然として居るのでたよりないのですが大丈夫で
平和な日々を送って居られる事と推察して
案じない様つとめて居ります。そちらでも
同様私からのたよりがつかぬので心配して
居られると存じますが相変らず壮健で
暮して居りますからどうぞ案じない様にし
下さい。一共になれると云ふ話もあるので其
日の一日も早く実現するのを日夜祈って
居ります。　当方はまだ氣候もよく
天氣も續きますので日中はゴルフを遊
んでやるせない思ひも出来るだけまぎら
す様つとめて居りますが一日も早く逢ふ事
が出来たらと願ふ思ひは一時も心をはな
れません。讀書もしたらよいのですがこうした所
の生活には落付いて目的ある讀書も出来ぬの
で輕い時間つぶしの讀物にふける位です。
一般的には何一つ不足云ふ事はありません。
幾度繰返しても同じ事ですがわかれ別れ
暮して居るのみ云ひ知れぬ悲しみ
です。では此次まで。

勝周

四二・十二月十八日
梅乃殿

W. D., P. M. G. Form No. 4
February 17, 1942

16—27540-1　U. S. GOVERNMENT PRINTING OFFICE

昨夜はベエドに入ってから雨の屋根にあたる音を
きいてねましたが今朝はまれに見るよい天氣で
空氣は清く空はあをくとし松林も生き生き
して居ます。一共でしたらどんなに樂しい事で
せう。昨日十一月十六日附のお手紙を受取り
ました。近頃は通信に時日を要するので
近信は中々ゆかず何となく案ぜられますが
皆んな元氣だそうで安心しました。ゴルフ
クラブも心配掛けてすみませんでしたね。何か
の手紙に書いた様今二本此處で手に入
りましたが出來れば [redacted] がもう
一本あればよいと思ひます。ボールが容
易に手にはいらないのでお願ひ出來たら
六個程送って下さればと希って居ます。
上手には一向なりません。保険の事は
よいようにしたと存じます。現在の状態
ではそうして置くのが何よりです。通信
は英文和文変りませんから其つもり
で。總ての事は一番よいと思ふ方法を執
って置いて下さったら満足です。では
身体を注意し幸福で暮して下さる
様に。

十二月二十三日　勝周

梅め殿

明日はクリスマスです。此処でもそれぞれお
祝の仕度をして居ります。子供達の学校
も休みになったすでせう。お正月も数日に
せまりました。去年（本当は今年でしたね）の
こゝをおもって何となく淋しく感じます。
今朝は曇って九時とは云へ何となく暗らいで
心がよけいめいって来ます。もう一年近くも
お別れして居りますから無理もありません。
おもひめぐらせば想出深い一年でした。戦争の
もたらす悲しみの一つとは云へ心に一つ暗いとこ
ろ無く家族と別れてこうして暮さね
ばならぬと云ふ事はあきらめやうと務め
てもあきらめきれぬものです。近い内に
は家族と共にすると云ふ話しもあります
が実現するまでは何とも云へません。さうし
たらになれば此上もないです。早くさう
なる様ひたすら念じて居ります。
この手紙が年内に着くとは思は
れませんが書いてる私は此日が晴々しい
楽しいお正月を迎へる様心から祈って
居ります。

十二月二十四日

勝田

[illegible]

梅乃殿

今年も今日か終りです。何と想出多い年で
したらう。健康でどうやう年を越せる
るを感謝して居ます。あなた方もどう
ぞ幸福でよい年を迎へて下さい。先日
はクリスマスプレゼントを有難う
御座いました。何もかも直ぐ役に立つ
もので大層よろこばしく存じました
子供達にもよく云っておいて下さい。
小包類は割合早く着きます
保険の書留類は一時止まりましたので
サーンして早速送って置きました。種
々早く送って来れる様たのみました
が駄目なので例の様に一ヶ月位
掛ると思ひます。いたし方無いと
思ひます。
今日は取急ぎますのでこれまで
どうぞ身体を注意して下さい。
近頃英語学校を教へ始め
ました。

一九四三、十二、三十一　勝田
Kakuchuka Tamura
梅乃 殿

お互に健康で新年を迎へたるを慶びます。昨年は私共にとって忘れ難い悲しみに満ちた年でした。今年は苦労しても共々に暮せればよいと日夜念じて居ります。三日はよい天氣で一世に祝賀し二日の夜には芝居がありました。こうした所では予期しなかったよい芝居でした。大丈夫で暮して居ますから安心して下さい。

クリスマスのプレゼントを有難う御座いました。靴下は早速役に立ちました。睦ちゃんはみがきも使って居ります。煙草も私のすきな物でもうありません。大曽立はな暦が出来ましたね。新聞も次から次に着くのでそちらの事情がよく解ります。十二月二十六日附の和文と二十八日附の英文の手紙を受取りました。しばらくぶりで大曽日懐かしく拝見しました。通信に時間が掛るので困りますね。後れる理由はすでに御承知の事と存じます。私は毎週二通は必ず書いて居りますから追々受取られると思ひます。ハサミは確かに受取りました。保険の書類も送って置きましたが早い方法が無かったのが残念に思ひます。では寒さに氣を附けて幸福な日を送って下さい。

一月七日

Kakuchika Kimura

梅乃殿

如何ですか。子供達は丈夫で學校へ行きはじめ
ましたか。先日家族の中で病氣の人があると言つて
見舞に行つた人があるので心配になります。皆さん
身体に注意して下さい。當地は三日間雨が降り
續いて寒くなりました。やがてはじき寒くなると
思はれます。周圍の山はたしかに雪が降りました。
通信に時間をとるので誰にも無沙汰して居
ります。近頃だよりがありましたが、あちらでも
皆丈夫だそうです。近頃散歩も始めて居ります
今日も午後一時からあるので其の準備をせね
ばなりません。以前から手紙が無いので困つた様
行きません。過日は野外であつた活動も近
頃は室内であります。しかし寒くなるので
二、三週に分けてやります。私共は昨夜行き
ました。何を見ても一人では面白くありません。早
く一緒にして見られればよいと言ふ事を祈つて
居ります。先日ある人にはよい通知が來
ましたが私には來ませんでした。どうしてかと
いろいろと心配して居ります。長い間共に樂
しさをともにしてきたのに苦しく感じます。
相變らず元氣でおられることだけは安心
して下さい。ではこの次まで

Katuchika Tamura

一九四二年十一月八日

柏田乃殿

W. D., P. M. G. Form No. 4
February 17, 1942

16—27540-1 U. S. GOVERNMENT PRINTING OFFICE

御機嫌よく御消光のこと存じます。近頃、
御地の気候は如何ですか。ストーブは入りまし
たか。此頃時報で見ると朝は大分寒いさうで
すね。霜が降りますか。当地も寒さが一
週間程續いた後昨日から暖くなりま
した。御別してから一ヶ年近くになりますがな
んと長い一ヶ年でしたらう いろいろのこともあり
悲しい經験も致しましたがあなたも同様と
思ひます。住みなれたフレンチキャンプをはな
れ、君らはターラック、行き再びアリゾナ
へ転さし子供をつれてさぞ困難であったらう
と御察し、ます。先日此處を訪問した人の
話ではインターニーの家族随分私共の
身の上を心配して居る様云って居りました
が。さうした心配は絶對無用です。家族
と別れ別れに居る淋しさ以外生活上の
苦痛は全然ありません。これは今迄度
々申上げて置きましたが近頃外部から来
た人の話で思ひ出して重ねて申上げて置き
ます。どうぞ私の此處の日常生活には決して
心配せずに心やすらかにして下さる様に
ではけふはこれで
一九四三年十一月十日
梅乃 殿

Kakuechika Tamura

一月もすぐに中ばになりました　今朝は曇って
うっとしい空あいです。昨年お別れして以来、
の私の胸の内の様、近頃は兎角曇り勝ち
です。でも待てば何時か晴ると思って忍耐して
其の日を待って居ります。大丈夫でせうね、子供
達はまめで学校へ行って居りますか。皆驚
く程大きくなったでせうね。皆の目方と身長
を知らして下さい。弘は毎週クリニックへ行くの
ですか。睦ちゃんはものぎらいせず何んでもたべま
すか。青物は充分でせうね。歯はどうです。歯
科医に行きますか。典ちゃんは時間を忘れず
歸って来ますか。近頃は風をひくのはあ
りませんか。体を大切にして下さい。私は相変らず
です。時がたてばたつ程別れの生活の淋しさにた
られぬ気がします。一週に四日英語を教へ
ます。運動にはゴルフを遊びますが近頃ボール
が無くなって困って居ります。この手紙を受取る
頃私がまだこゝに居る様でしたらボールを二三
送って下さいまし。皆さんへよろしく
では呉々も健康に暮す様に祈りながら

一九四三年一月十四日　Katsuchika Tamura

梅乃殿

両三日前から北風で寒かつた気候も今朝は風もやみ日中は暖くなりさうです。すでに洗濯をはじめた人もあります。通信の往復が不規則で何か物たらぬ感じがしますが皆が健康で幸福に暮して居ると信じ又祈つて居ります。前週には貴方と睦ちゃんに手紙を出して置きました。弘も大きくなつたでしやうね丈夫ですか。あなたをパパと呼ぶのはなほりましたか。家族と一共のキャンプへ入れると申して居りますが一日も早ければよいとそれのみ念じて居ります。総ての運命はいさぎよく受けやうと観念はして居るもの、日毎夜毎心に掛るのはあなた方のことで一日も早く共に暮せればとそれ以外の慾望はありません。そちらの近頃の気候はどうですか。子供があるのですから働かうなどと無理をしてはいけません。キャンプの新聞はひらき封の方が早くつきます。不幸にも書きかけに今の検査に来ましたから今日はこれで

では御機嫌よう

Katsuchika Tamura

一九四三、一、二八

梅乃殿

皆元気ですか　私も幸ひ恙なく暮して居り
ます。昨夜ねてから雨の音を聞きましたが
今朝は晴れて寒さもゆるみ日中は暖い
だらうと思ひます。朝は六時半に起き食
るのは六時四十五分です。今の所朝食の時は
まだ暗いのですが日は一日一日長くなって行き
ますからじきに遊ぶ時間が長くなる譯です
そこではそんな人はないでせうがある轉住
地ではインターニーの家族をだまして金にする
人がある様聞きました。あなたも知っての通
り私は暗い所は少しもないこうした所
に居る理由もありませんが現在の所誰れに
どうする事も出来ないのですから一共の
キャンプにでも入るのを唯一の希望として
いたづらに人の口に乗らぬ様にして下さい。
保険のペーパーを送って置きましたがもう
すでに受取りましたか。受取ったら出来
るだけ早く始末して置いたがよいと思
ひます。今日午後は英語の組があり
ます。個人的に習ってあげる人もあり
ます。運動には相変らず下手な
ボールを遊びます。では　Katsuchika Tamura
[illegible]年十一月十九
梅乃殿

W. D., P. M. G. Form No. 4

昨日二通の手紙を一共に受取りました。一通は昨年
の暮他の一通は今年のはじめしたためられた
ものでした。待って居ったので大層よろこば
しく讀みました。あなたも子供等も元氣で
暮して居られるさうで此上もありません。子供、
共の成積もよでしたら満足だと存じます。
別れて居り此處に居る人の家族に病人など
ある話を聞きますとあなた方が健康のみ
が氣になります。子供が三人もあると何
から支障が起り易いものです。もう三週
間程でお別れしてから一ケ年になります。永い
く間別れて居った様な氣がし住みなれ
た家を後にターラック アリブナへと
子供を連れて不自由なキャンプ生活に
さぞ心労されたるとお察しします。
パンフとはさみは早く受取りましたから
御安心下さい。私も相変らず善
ありません。氣候も大層よく近頃
では夜野外で活動があります。
皆さんへよろしく 身体を御大
切に

Kakuchika Tamura

妻へ

私共にとって手紙は楽しみの楽しみですが昨日は三通共
に来たので私には嬉しい日でした。知っての通り検閲の
為め別々に出した通信がこうして一共になったのです。何れも
懐かしく其時々の心持がよく現はれて居て日常の態
も目に浮び皆が無事で暮して居ると感謝せず
にはおられません。家族キャンプの話も子供の其学校
や友達を失ふ事を思ふと何となく不安にも思
ひます。私からの小包はクリスマス前に着くやう
出したのですが忙しいので後れたと思ひます。何
れにしても到着して何よりでした。比良時報も皆受
取って居ます。過日は比良から造花をもらって
皆嬉んで居ます。餅はどうしたのかつきません。
此處もこの三四日非常によい天氣です。この手
紙も春の様なうらゝかな日のもとでしたゝめて
居ます。窓硝子を通じて青々とそびへた
松木を通じて雲一片無い空を眺めると
氣も晴々します。早く平和になって一共にこう
した自然を楽しめる日が来ればよいと思ひ
ます。其ちゃん睦ちゃんにも手紙を受取た
からと申し傳へてもっと書く様云って下さい。
兄さんはじめ皆さんへよろしく

Katsuhiko Tamura

なつかしき
妻へ

手紙を二通一共に受取りました。書信も追々早く到着する様になりましたが最近のものはつい先日したゝめられたもので殊になつかしく繰返へして読みました。子供達が無邪気に育って行くのはまことに嬉ばしいことですがあなたが晴れ晴れ無い心で悩んで居られる様で案じられます。無理もないですが私共の様なる情の下にあるものは種々現在なし得事に就いて考へさせられ悩まずには居られません。何と今日吾々が遭遇して居る様な動乱時にあっては誰一人として其餘波をかうむらぬ者はありません。そして過去の同じ様な過度期に身体精神共に強健であった者が生き残ってあらゆる困難に打勝って来た様に私共も子供達の為めに忍耐してこの試練に打勝たねばなりません。或程自由を拘束されて居るは云ひ知れぬ苦痛ですがそれも心の持様では軽くする事が出来ます。此頃時報の記事に依れば近所で望ましからぬ出来事が起った様ですね。私も驚きました。あなたの心が暗くなるのも無理ないです。ある詩人が云った様に人間と云ふ者は弱いものですね。時に昨日煙草を一箱受取りました。有難うございました。私がまだ煙草を止められぬのもよく知って居ますね。近頃は遍りすいません一箱あれば一ヶ月はあると思ひます。では御機嫌よう

一九四三年、十二、十八 Kakuchika Tamura

愛する

妻へ

今月の月はじめの手紙を受取りあつこばしく拝見しました。皆恙無く暮して居られて何より此上もないです。弘は元気になりましたか。典ちゃん睦ちゃんの手紙も受取りました。手紙は私達の楽しみにして居るものゝ一つです どうぞまた書くやう申して下さい。週二回の新聞は順次受取つて居りますおかげでそちらの様子がよく解ります。先日は美しい造花を譚山受取り各食堂を飾りました。

餅も来ましたが遅れたので青かびが生へてとしてたべられるのはありませんでした。いろいろ心配掛けましたがクラブはもう思切った方がよいと思ひます。只今年許にある糸のボールを送つて見て下さい。何故フレンチキャンプの人は私のクラブを送つて呉れないのでせう。時に支給された以外には靴が家を出る時はいて来た一足だけです。はやく買つて居けばよかったのですが。もし機会があったら一足買つて居いて下されば嬉しいのだと思ひます。無理をしないでようございます 又どうにかなるでせう。なつなつで幅の廣い方がよいのです。どう想像して居られても別れ別れ居るのかなしみ以外には割合に平和で安気な暮しをして居りますから必ず案じて下さいますな。

なつかしき 妻へ

Kakuchika Tamura

十日程前の手紙を受取りました。通信が早くなって
何よりの事です。今日は日曜ですが三日大層暖かか
ったのと昨夕雲り出し今朝は雨になりました。天氣な
れば午後ベースボールがあるのですがそれも無いので終日
屋内で暮さねばならぬと思ひます。幸いラジオが
ありますし讀む本もあるのでたいくつはしません。手
紙にある様今頃フレンチキャンプに居れば色々の
花が咲きそろふのですが誠におしい事です。今も
寫眞を出して見いってたゝぬ想出にふけって居
ます。一生忘れる事の出来ぬ樂しい生活でした。
二三夜續けて夢を見ます。別段悪い夢ではありま
せん。過り氣にするので皆の夢を見るのでせう。弘
がねんねこで背はれて居る様でした。
共ちゃんと睦ちゃんは大きくなったのに驚きました。
多分大きくなったのでせうね。今日は二十一日です
今もあの夜の事があり〳〵浮びます。あの夜
は一睡もしませんでした。数人はすでに家族と一共に
なったのですが少数だけが今でもこうした生活を續
けねばならぬわけです。お氣の毒に思ひますが
どうぞ忍耐して今しばらく待って下さい。近い内に
家族と一共になる運びになると申して居ります。
今日はこれで　Katsuchika Tamura
妻へ

二月十日附の手紙を戴きました皆恙が無く暮
して居られるとの事何よりと存じます。典ちゃんも
睦ちゃんも元気で学校へ通って居るさまが
想はれます。野菜も色々出来る由でよい
ですね。私達にも少々と云ふ程ではありませ
んが自由に多くあるのを取って食卓にのせる
様な譯には行きません。野菜園の計画
もありますがはたしてよいものが出来るか
どうかうたがわれます。家族と一共に住む
様には間も無く實行される事と思って居り
ますが今迄度々失望させられたので過
り期待は出来ぬと思ひますが本当に一日も
早くさうなればよいと日夜祈って居ります。
お互に生活に不安は無くともこうした生活を
して居りますと心のなやみが種々起り
勝ちです お互に心けんごにいたづらに
なやませられぬ様つとめて子供達の将来
をみてやりませう。皆さんへよろしく
典ちゃんと睦ちゃんの手紙は受取りました。
健康に務めてよく勉強する様申して
下さい。ではこの次まで

梅乃殿 Katsuchiku Tamura

近頃は通信が早くなってつい先日の手紙を受取り誠になつ
かしく皆も元氣の由で安心致しました。私も相變らずで
大丈夫です。二三日の雨が昨夜から北風に變って今朝は
一寸寒う御座いましたが空ははれて午後は暖くなると
予期して居ります。いろいろ案ぜられると存じますが
繰返へし申上げた通り私達の生活には申分無く
幸にしてインターニー ハミリー キャンプへ行っても別に變
つたるは無いと思いますから人々が心配する様な
案じは決してありません。ゴルフボールの煙草の丈
った小包を確と受取りました。感謝しよろこんでは
居りますが御めんどうでせうから煙草は送って下さら
ないでもよう御座います。それから小包は當キャン
プ直接に送って下されば受取れますから其のつもり
で。キャンプ新聞も順次受取って居ります。アルカン
サスに來て居る家族の人がだいぶ逢に來ます。
而しこれもよしあしで少さい小供等を連れて來
ると何も知らぬ小供はお父さん一共に歸ろうなど
申して父としては随分つらいさうです。ぼつぼつ
ハミリイキャンプへ行く通知を受けた人もあるので私も
氣が落付きませんがいよいよ一共になるまでは過
りぬかるこでも出來ません。念ずるのは日夜
そうなるのみ祈って居りますでは又身体に注
意して下さい

三月三日

梅乃殿

Katsuchika Tamura

手紙を有難う何時もなつかしく拝見して居ります。興ちゃんも睦ちゃんも元気に通学の由弘も喜ぶ会って行くので誠によろこばしいのです。さぞ可愛いことでせう他人には解りませんがどうして一共に居らぬ子を残念に思ふかお解りのことと思ひます。手紙にあった通り去年の二月二十日はお互に忘れ得る事の出来ぬ日ですあれこれおもひ乍ら夜るお別れした時は「こともおもって居たる事を云はづにお別れしてしまひました。心に一つも暗いところ無く其点に旅で胸は軽かったとは云へ、あなたと二人の子供を残して運命に従はねばならなかった私はあの夜一睡も出来ませんでした。其次に一番つらかったのはビスマークでインターンの命令を受けた日です。其筋の人々の公平を信じて居った私も一度に不平は胸に充ちて誰れに語ることも出来ずひとりなやみになやみました。過去の悲しみのみ申上げて申訳ありません新しい野菜が澤山だそうで何よりです。私達も食するに就いては申分ありません。今日も午後農学校があります。では次の手紙まで

三月八日　さようなら

なつかしき
貴女へ

Kakuchuka Tamura

手紙を有難う十月程で着きました。皆元気だそうで何より嬉しかったのです。私も丈夫で暮して居ります。まだ家族と一共になるため移動した人はありませんが通知を受けた人はあります。私には何の通知もありません。もう少しは運がめぐって来さうなものとじれったくなります。随分しんぼうして待ったのですから今頃は一共にして呉れてもよい頃と思ひます。日本行を申込んで置いたのが又別扱ひを受ける理由かも知れませんがそれにしても早く一共にして呉れたら誠に都合よいと思ひます。おそくも今頃迄には一共に暮せると思って居ったのに一向當てがつかぬので少々気が短くなって来ました。ゴルフクラブやボールのことは心配して下さいますな。今あるので充分です。靴のことも遠り案じなくともよいのです。日常は支給されたものをはいて居ますし家を出る時はいて居ったのが(もう一足)ありますから若し出来たら買って居いて下さればよいと思ったのです。買っても私の頃へ送らずにそちらへ置いて下さい。キャンプニュースはもっと短い帯封で此處へ直接送って見て下さい。ニューヨークへ廻すのは書信だけです。表書の印紙の所はこの上書き様書いてもらって下さい。

梅乃殿　三廿七日

二月附の手紙が昨日つきました。元氣でお暮しの由で何より
です。典ちやん睦ちやんの手紙も讀みました。二人もあ
つてたよりして呉れるそうでまことによろこばしく存じます。
すでにファミリーキャンプへ先發したものもあるそうで氣
が落付きません。氣ばかりいらくしてもどうする事
も出來ませんからなり行を待つよりほかありません
が一日も早く逢ひたいものとそれのみ念じて居ります。
弘も困らすそうでこまったものです。ベビーの時は
さう湯あみをきらうやうでもありませんでしたがどう
して顔や手を洗ふのをきらふのでせう。でも小
供はみなこうして育つのでせう。手紙を讀んで弘の
いろくだだこねるさまが心の目に浮んで思は
ず頬を笑ますにはいられません。別段必用の
ものはありませんから典へは心使ないやう。
重ねて云ふやうですがどうぞ心だけを晴や
かに持つてたとへ萬事が思ふやうにならずとも
平靜に押し通して下さい。典ちや睦ちやんにも
一度に返事が書けませんから一つ一つ出すやうにします
からさう申して下さい。睦ちやんの作ったカレンダーは
大變きれいによく出來て居りほんとうによろ
こばしく存じます。では今日これで皆さんによろし
く。

Katsusuke Tamura

梅乃殿

御手紙拝見御壮健の由誠に嬉ばしく存じます。私も
相変らず元気で暮して居りますから御安心下さい。
今朝は空暗く雨が降ってうつとうしい日です
私の今の心にふさはしいかも知れません。晴れた日
はよく庭でゴルフ等をして忘れて居りますが こうして
家の中に とじこめられて居ると やるせない想ひに
なやみます。家族と同居するも追々実現せら
れて来ますので 私等も近い内と希望して居り
ますが子供達が生れた坊やの友達に別れねばなら
ぬ事等想ひ及び可愛さうに感じます。陸ちゃん
はダンシングのレッスンを執って居るさうですね。
新聞に出て居った温習會に出たのですか。典ちゃんも
大きくなったでしやう。皆が元気なのがなによりです。
弘の二たんじようにはとても御目に掛れないで
せう。日々いたづらになって行く様ですね。可愛
い頃、相見ることが出来ず今度逢ふ時はさぞいぶ
かることでせう。オレンジやグレープフルーツが
沢山食卓にあがるさうでよいですね。私達に
これらの果物や菓子が充分與へられる様なり
ました。種々不平のあるのが吾々の位置に置かれ
た者の常とは云へ、色々の点へ感謝せねばならぬ
事もあります。お互に心強く暮しませう。では

三月廿五日

妻へ

Katsuchiku Tamura

昨日事務所から小包を取りに来て下さいとの事
で何かと思って行きましたら思ひがけなく
澤山な美しいゴルフボールを受取って
ほんとうによろこばしく存じました。二打（ダーズン）
ありました。よく買いましたね。長い間
新しいボールを見なかったので其の時の驚き
とよろこびはこゝに言ひ表はせぬ程でした。
ゴルフボールだけは百萬長者になった様な
氣がします。心盡しをまことに感謝致し
ます。私は相変らず元氣です。急に
暖くなって午後は暑い位です。野外に出る
と種々な花が咲いて居ります。夏になると
悪い蠅がふえますがそれが無いので今が一番
心地のよい時です。子供達は丈夫ですか
身体を大切にしてもうしばらくしんぼう
して下さい。もうすでに出発した人もあります
から私達も遠からず知らせがあると
信じて居ります。過ぎた一ヶ年何日は
十年も長かかった様感じました。では
今月はこれでゴルフボールを呉々も有難う
皆さんによろしく

三月廿一日

Katsuchika Tamura

妻へ

三月二十六日附お手紙なつかしく拝見し皆々御変なく御消光
の由何よりと嬉しく存じます。私も元氣にて出来る丈愉快に
日を送る様つとめて居ります故御安心下さい。すでに一部
の者はハミリーキャンプに移動しましたから、この次は私の番で
はないかと予期して居りますがさして待遠しいです。
明日は私のたんじょう日です。二年前のあの頃を想ひだし次
から次となつかしい想出にふけります。氣候は大分暖く
なりました。この週間にストーブも取のけるようになって居
ります。昨年居った処とは雲泥の差です。チキンポックス
が流行って居るさうで困ったるですね。出来る丈注意して
それでかかれば仕方ありません。子供は種々な病氣を一度
せねばすまぬ様です。子供の学校の成績は遠り御配
ならぬ様、男の子は皆そうしたけいこうがあります。従つ
てとくによくない時はほかは遠り叱ってはいけません。ごん
つボールを受取ったるは御知せして置きました。すでに前の
日曜に一つおろしましたよいボールです。安心して使ってますか
又と云って待手にはいるかどうか解りませんから大切に
して居ります。何もこれ以上必要な物はありませんか
ら其の実は安心して下さい。写真のお話がありました
がこのキャンプではさうした便宜がありませんので一寸だめ
と思ひます。私も残念です。では今日はこれ
で呉々も氣を附けて晴やかに暮して下さる様

四月七日

妻女へ

Yasuchika Tamura

四月一日附手紙拝見皆々元氣にて御暮しの由
まことに嬉ばしく存じます 弘も何か悪いことを
おぼへさぞかしお困りの事でせう。御手紙で様子
を知りおかしくもあり思はず笑はされます。
吉見の節ちゃんからも先日手紙をもらひました
相変らず加州に居る様ですがあの方がかへ
って幸福なのでせう。私も大丈夫で暮して居り
ます。三月程むし暑く心地悪い天氣でし
たが今は良く晴れことにそよ風が吹いて近頃
になりました。今日思ひ掛けなく加州ランド
リーをして居った徳永さんから菓子一箱
面會の人にことづけて送って呉れました。こう
して忘れずに居て呉れる人があるかと思ふ
と誠に感謝にたへません。ゴルフクラブが
来ましたら御めんどうでせうが七番の
鉄の人分を一本だけ送って下さい。ファミリー
センターへ行くのは一日も早くと念じて居
りますが仕度に手間が掛る由で数日の
内とは予期出来ません。子供達にも
よろしく申して下さい。では身体を大切に
次の時まで

四月十五、

Katsuchika Tamura

梅乃殿

皆んな変りありませんか。大分暑くなったろうと推察致します。私は相変らず元気ですから安心して下さい。数日来暖かったのでストーブを片付けてしまった所急にまた涼しくなって寒がりの私にはへいこうです。晴れたら又暖くなるでせう。あの後まだ家族と一共になれる通知が来ません。追々来ることは思ひますが準備に手間取ると思ひます。過ぎた日曜にはゴルフの會がある筈でしたが雨でだめでした。本を讀んだりラジオを聞いて暮しました。屋根にあたる雨の音を聞くと淋しくなりあふたや子供のことを想って心も暗くなります。共ちゃんも陸ちゃんも丁度大切な時で種々心配のこともあるでせうがこうした時代に相遇した私達ののがれぬ運命とあきらめ過りやかましく云はぬ方がよいと思ひます。私もどんなきゅうくつにあっても心晴れやかにひがまず暮したいとそれのみ念じて居ります。世間では食料品なども随分節約せねばならぬ様なことを聞きますがこゝはおかげですべて充分で其の点は一つも不足云ふことはありません。では今日はこれで呉々も身体を大切にして下さい。

四月二十一日

Katsuchika Tamura

御手紙をなつかしく拝見しました。皆日健康に御暮
の由何よりと存じます。子供達もイースターで学
校が休みでよろこんで居るでせう。色附の玉子さ
がしもあつたのでせうか。今朝はまれなよい天氣
で實によい氣持の日です。現在の状態の常とし
て種々な出来事が起り不安に思ふ時もあり
ますが幸ひすべてが思つたより平静で過ぎて
行きます。私も何か實質的なる事を習得
したいと望んで居りますがこれと申して得る所
も無く讀書やゴルフで日がすぎて行きます。
せねばならぬ仕事もありますがそれはさほど
苦にする程するではなく萬事都合よく行
つて居ります。ゴルフのクラブを一本御願ひ
しましたがとどきましたか。手に入つたと云ふ
クラブはフレンチキャンプから来たのですかそれと
も此度買つたのですか。送つて下さる新聞は
次から次へ着きますから様子は知れますが
長くなると其處もあきるでせうね。ファミリ
ーキャンプも仕度がはかどらぬので後れて居
るのだと思ひます。弘は相変らず
困らせますか。では今日はこれで御氣嫌よ
う。皆さんへよろしく

Kazuchika Tamura

四月二四日
なつかしき
妻へ

朝夕は丁度よい氣候ですが日中は暑い位になり
ました。相変らず元氣で暮して居りますから
御安心下さい。ゴルフのクラブを昨日受取り
ました。有難う。これですべてそろひボールも澤
山あるので安心です。今日此頃には逢
へることそれのみ楽しみにして居りましたのに
未だ其實現を見ず誠に待遠しく思ひ
ますがこれも今日の事情下にあってはやむを
得ぬると存じます。お互に心強く来る
日を待ちませう。子供達は丈夫ですが
段々暑くなりますから充分注意してや
らぬといけません。殊に典ちゃんは以前
暑さにあたった事があるのですから出来る
だけ氣を附けてくせをつけぬ様せぬと
いけません。學校は何時から休みになり
ますか。餘り日かげ等も無いのでせう
か。泳ぐ所がありますか。弘も随分
大きくなったでせうね。相変らず困らせ
ますか。こまったものです。
では今日はこれで。呉々も暑さに氣
をつけてき嫌よく暮して下さい。

五月四日

Kazuchika Tamura

甚る牛の場、雨が降ると元気になる先生の話を聞いて感心しましたが、曇天でもそういうこともありうるはありません。今朝の様に雨の後、晴々とした日は何と無しに元気が溢れてきます。四月の三十二十九日付のお手紙を正に受取り、うれしく拝見しました。此回文子ご苦していたら、私にはこれ以上(まっ)だらはありません。予期も一日一日と、どう元気がつらくなる時もありますが、一々陰自分の気持ばかりも出来ませんので時期の来るまではけんどご待っている他ありません。兄さん竹林さん手紙をまたも御無理無い様に静かにしていらっしゃい。ゴルフボールもあかくわたくが高価ですせう大切にしていますからなるべく節約するます。この一二十日にはたつかった位う。あるので思う様に出来ず、運動の運動には唯と思って時間のあるだけゴルフをやっています。あの皆様からもこれから其の剣に上達しました。ついで。益々又人びとは大ありますが私には不向ですから其れくらいはありません。では今日はこれで身体も心も大切に。

Kakuchiku Tamura

土曜日の朝ですが曇って涼しくなりました。
相変らず元氣で暮らして居りますから
安心して下さい。別にこれと申す変ったる
無く同じ様な日を繰返へして居ります。
一部の人が去ってからもうすでに一ヶ月餘
になり段々逢ふ日が近くなったとよ
ろこんだのも過り後の通知が無いので
がっかりして居ります。典ちゃん坊や
ん弘も丈夫ですか。そちらも随分
暑くなったでせう典子学校は何時から
休みになりますか。岡崎さんからお
たよりがありますが割合に近い所に
居られるのですが其後手紙も差上げ
て居りません。こちらも申上げた通り
今朝は涼しいのですが過ぎ去った一週
間は可成暑く過し讀書も出来ず
涼しい日かげをさがしてもむだな時間
をすごします。どうぞ身体を
呉々も大切に及ばぬ事に心いためず
来る日を待って下さい。では今日は
これで。

七月十五日

Kakuchika Tamura

大分暑くなりました。そちらも随分暑いでせう。近頃同室に居る人の処へ来た手紙では暑くて夜も十二時過迄ねむられぬとの事です。お察しします。クーラーを附けた人が澤山あるさうですね。うちでも附けましたか。
私は相変らずです。室で過し讀書も出来ませんので日中をさけて朝夕ごいんつをけいこします。先日は若い人々の芝居があり昨夜は今週の活動寫眞の夜です。現在の仕事の関係上筋肉労働には出ませんがなかなかひまもありません。今の所私共の唯一の希望は一日も早く共になれるやうとのみですが案外後れて居ります。子供達の學校は休みになりましたが、孔はどうです。益々悪くなりますか。言葉も大分おぼへたでせうね。
では身体を大切にして晴れやかに日々を送って下さい。子供達にもよろしく。五月十九日
和

Katsuhiko Tamura

三時頃から曇って降り出しさうに思はれた
空も夜に入っても降らずこの手紙書く
今雷と共に大つぶの雨が屋根にば
らばらあたって来ました。ほこりを
しづめ暑さとかんわしてよい雨です。
そちらも随分暑いさうでしのぎにく
いるでせう。クーラーを入れん所が
澤山あるさうですがどうしました。
私はおかげで元氣で暮して居ります。
あなたも子供達も大丈夫でせうね
睦ちゃんが送って呉れたきれいな
寫眞が一昨日着きました。誠にう
れしく感じました。よく禮と申傳
へて置いて下さい。學校は何時休
みになるのでせう。家族でキャンプ
も追々実現するのでせうか中々手間
掛ります。時には望みがあるのか無
いのかうたがはせられます。実にた
より無いるです。では今夜は
これで御氣嫌よう
五月二十五、 / Kakuchiku Tamura

五月九日附のお手紙を誠になつかしく拝見
致しました。相変らず元氣で恙が無く
御暮の由此上も無いよいたよりです。
典ちゃんも睦ちゃんも日々學校へかよつて居
るとみ、先日両人から大へんよい手紙をも
らひました。出来るだけ早く返事を出し度
いと存じて居ります。九日の母の日に彼等
が心をこめて手製のプレゼントおくったる
は私もよろこばしく存じました。弘の寫眞
を寫したさうですね樂しみにして待って居り
ます。何故皆んな寫さなかったのでせう。
私も幸と丈夫で日々を送って居ります。二三ヶ
前ゴルフクラブも他のものもしまひました。
別によい報知ではありませんが氣に掛
けるにも及ばぬと存じます。通知信は送
達すると存じます。
睦ちゃんからの書画はおきも受取りましたか
らよろしく申して置いて下さい。皆さんへ
よろしく　では今日はこれで次の
たよりまで　さようなら

五月二十九日　Katuchiku Tamura

DO NOT WRITE HERE!　NICHT HIER SCHREIBEN!　NON SCRIVETE QUI!　書クナ

御手紙なつかしく拝見致しました。元氣でお暮しの由何より
よいたよりで嬉ばしく存じます。お兄さんや竹森さん
の御家族も御変りありませんか。随分暑くなったで
せうね。こゝも暑くはなりましたがたへられぬ程ではあ
りません。幸丈夫で急はしく日々を送って居りますから
御安心下さい。一日も早く御目に掛り度いと願って居
りますがなかなか待たせるので待遠しくなります
子供達の学校も今月中旬迄だったさうですね
二人ともさぞ大きくなったでせう。柔道はよく氣
を附けてけがをせぬ様して下さい。運動も度を
過ごしては害になります。時によるとこの次の手紙は
ちがった消印があるかも知れません。別に案ずる
事はありません。弘の写真を待って居ります。
いたづらぼうずで困るでせう。
ゴルフクラブもしまってしまったのでもう遊べません
日中は忙しいので余りたいくつしませんが夜は雑
誌位を読んで時をすごします。では今日はこれで
萬事氣をつけて心を晴かにもっていて下さい

梅乃殿

Katsuchika Tamura

DO NOT WRITE HERE!　NICHT HIER SCHREIBEN!　NON SCRIVETE QUI!　書クナ

MY ADDRESS IS: Kakuchika Tamura
MEINE ADRESSE IST WIE FOLGT: ~~ISN~~-23-4-J-1012
IL MIO INDIRIZZO È: 3RD Internment Co. 19 0.2.
私ノ住所ハ Camp Livingston ~~Internment Camp~~
Box 20, General Post Office
~~New York, New York~~

W. D., P. M. G. Form No. 4-1
November 1, 1942

☆ 16—31605-1　U. S. GOVERNMENT PRINTING OFFICE : 1942

SANTA FE, NEW MEXICO

June 1943–May 1944

Original letters in Japanese from Katsuchika to Umeno

Mrs. Umeno Tamura
65-3-D
Rivers, Arizona

Katsuchika Tamura
Barrack 52
Santa Fe Detention Station
Santa Fe, New Mexico
June 8, 1945

昨夜こゝに到着致しました。元氣です。割合涼しく氣候も
よく眺めも大層ようございます。到着早々ですが落附か
ず只一筆こちらへ移ったる事と新しい所書だけを御通
知して置きます。大分近くなり手紙の往復も早く出来る
さうで何より嬉しいであります。家族が一共になるるん
近くなったのかどうか確な事も分りませんが早くさうなれば
よいとそれのみ祈って居ります。皆元氣でせうね
よろしく申して下さい。皆さんも呉々もではは今日はこれ
で御身大切に

勝周

六月八日

妻へ

DETAINED ALIEN
ENEMY MAIL
EXAMINED
BY 25-3
U.S.I. & N.S.

Mrs. Umeno Tamura
63-3-D
Rivers, Arizona

Kakuchika Tamura
Barrack 52
S. F. Detention Station
Santa Fe, N. M.
June 10, 1943

萬事都合よく落付き元氣で暮して居りますから安心して下さい。
朝夕は大層淋しく殊に今日は曇ったのでスエターがいります
都合が出来たら二十弗ばかり送って下さいませんか。まだ
リビングストンから金が来ません。
お変り無いでせうね。子供達はどうです。随分暑いで
せう。学校は休みになりましたか。
高い處から町がよく見えます。眺めもよく空氣も
きよくデンバーによくにた處です。山が二方を
かこんで京都を思ひ出させます。砂地で短靴
だと小石がよくはいります。では今日はこれで御身
大切に心晴やかに

六月十日
勝周

梅乃殿

DETAINED ALIEN
ENEMY MAIL
EXAMINED
BY 2-5-3
U. S. I & N. S.

Mr. Umeno Tamura
65 - 3 - D
Rivers, Arizona

Kakuchika Tamura
Barrack 52
S.F. Detention Station
Santa Fe, New Mexico

五月二十七日附の手紙がリビングストンをめぐって今日着きました。なつかしく皆元氣との何よりのたよりで嬉ばしく存じます

当方は萬事都合よく行って居ります

七千尺からの高地だそうで朝夕は大層涼しく皆が暑い思ひをして居る時私共はめぐまれて居ると云はねばなりません。昨夜大分新しい人々が来しばらくぶりであった人があります。では御氣嫌やう

勝周

六月十五日

梅乃殿

Mrs. Umeno Tamura
65-3-D
Rivers, Arizona

Kakuchika Tamura
Bzk. 52
S. F. Detention Station
Santa Fe, N. M.
June 18, 1943

御手紙なつかしく拝見し弘の写真を受取りました。大きくなりましたね。随分いたづらするでせう。手紙にあったのみで無くヒラに居ったと云ふ人に逢って其人も私ににて居ると申ますが私には私によりあなたにまだにて居るやうに思ひます。いづれにしても丈夫さうでよくふとって居るので何より嬉しいのです。典ちゃんや晴ちゃんも大きくなったでせう。あれらの写真もあれば、[illegible]と思ひます。[illegible]中の人がたくさん来ました。帰った人もありますが、私達の将来はさっぱり解りません。今となっては一日も早くハそりーキャンプに行ければそれが何よりだと思ひます。しばらくぶりで皆に逢ひ種々話がつきませんがやはりヒラの近所の人の話が一番なつかしく近頃にちかいようたよりでした。そちらも次から次、いろいろのことが起るのですね。子供についてもさぞ心配なさるでせう。では今回はこれで萬るに気をつけて。典ちゃんからの[illegible]がつきました。

六月十八日
勝周

梅乃殿

DETAINED ALIEN ENEMY MAIL EXAMINED BY 25-3 U.S.I. & N.S.

Mrs Umeno Tamura
65-3-D
Rivers, Arizona

Kakuchika Tamura
Brk 52
S.F. Detention Station
Santa Fe, New Mexico
July 2, 1943

DETAINED ALIEN ENEMY MAIL EXAMINED BY U.S.I. & N.S.

先般お手紙を受取りましたが何かと忙しくゆっくり讀む暇もありませんでしたが夕食もすみ一雨降って静かになりましたので繰返しなつかしく拝見しました。子供達も暑さにかかわらず元気で暮して居る由何よりと存じます。当方はおかげで涼しく夜も心地よくねられこの点は感謝して居ります。お願ひした二十弗は確かに受取りました通知が後れたのはある所が近頃迄私に知らして呉れなかったからです。無理でなかった様にと祈って居ります。今年の春そこから来た人に逢ひあれこれの出来事を聞かされ人間の世のあさましさにそぞろ心を淋しくしました。そちらへ帰る人もだんだんありますが誰が次か誰も知らず、ハミーキャンプの方も一向はかどらず、さてさてあての無い話です。では次のたよりまで心晴やかに日を送って下さい。

勝周

七月二日

妻へ

当地に到着してからすでに一ヶ月になりました。さすがに二三日暑うございましたが今日は午後うす雲って涼しくなりました。至極元気で暮して居りますから安心して下さい。日々大工さん達が忙しさうに鉄槌の音をさして食堂の建築を急いで居ります。来週は新しいテイブルで食事する様になると思ひます今のところは毎日ピクニックの様で愉快です。過日お友達の奥さんが逢ひに来た時弐位の子が別れるに望んで伯父さんバイくと云ったとって笑ひ話でした。子供達は丈夫でせうね典ちゃん睦ちゃんは夏期学校を始めましたか。子供さへすなほに育ってくれゝば何の楽でも無いのですが典夫さんも随分大きくなったでせうね。近頃ゴルフコースが出来たので時々遊びに行きます。時にフレンチキャンプに残した私のダブセットはどうしても手に入らないのでせうか。では暑さの折柄身体大切に暮して下さい。

七月六日午後

勝用

懐しき

妻、

七月二日夜附のお便りを懐かしく拝見しました
きびしい暑さにもかゝわらず元氣でお暮の由
誠に嬉ばしく存ります。とこに入ってからも汗
が流れるとのことさぞねづらいこととお察しします
此處は幸と高地なので日がおちてからは涼しく
野外での活動の夜などはスエターがいる位です
多少はセンター、歸る人もありますが大多数
はまだどうなるのやら解らず落付か無い
心で其々其々を送って居ります。野菜や
メロンは豊富のことと存ります当方でも野
菜はつくって居りますがメロン類はありません
朝はオレンヂやキャンタループを共へられ
ます。では今日はこれで　身体を呉々も
大切にして下さい。

暎用

七月九日

妻へ

Mrs. Umeno Tamura
65-3-D
Rivers, Arizona

Katsuchika Tamura
Barrack 52
Santa Fe, Detention Station
Santa Fe, New Mexico
July 14, 1943

本は七日附お手紙いつもながら懐かしく拝見致しました。
極暑にもかゝわらず皆々元氣でこれも佛様の御加
護と感謝の念にたへません。私も相変らず悪い所も無
く消光して居りますから安心して下さい。過日雨が少
し降ったさうですね。涼しさも暫くは續かなかったでせう。
水位充分であればと思ひますが多数の人ですから
隨分使ふのでせう。スペインの領事の話では十月末
頃迄には家族同棲も實現する様申して居りまし
た。今迄後れ勝ちで此度も信じてよいやら悪いや
ら解りませんが信じ度く思ひます。別に不平
は無いのですが別れ別れに居るのは誠にたへら
れぬのです。大分帰る人もあり帰った人に逢は
れたかも知れませんが私は一寸チャンスが無さそうです。
勿論帰る人と私共の間の差も認められませんがこれが世の
中だと思ひます。何れにしてもお互に注意して健康に
逢ふ日を樂しく待ちませう。では今日はこれで

七月十四日夜

妻へ

勝

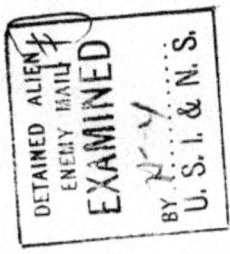

DETAINED ALIEN
ENEMY MAIL
EXAMINED
BY ...
U. S. I. & N. S.

Umeno Tamura
65-3-D
Rivers, Arizona

Kakuichiku Tamura
Barrack 52
S. F. Detention Station
Santa Fe, New Mexico
July 22, 1943

御手紙も受取り新聞も次から次へ来ますので
萬事都合よく運んで居ると安心して居
ります。私も幸ひ元気で皆さんの事や自分
の事やで忙しく其日其日を送って居ります。
加州のこの頃の空は美くしいのですが此處もすきとう
った空と青々とした山が三方めぐって居りますので
眺望はよく外で多く暮します。昨日は面會
の婦人が子供を連れて来て居ったので私ももう
あの位になったのでは無いかと想像してみました。
こうした時代のつねとして悲劇喜劇が起り
ますが心雄々しく総てに当たらねばなりません
センターへ帰った人々から通信が有ります
が何れもよいたよりで別に悲感する程でな
い様思はれます。ローワーへ帰った人には妹さん
の所より皆々もよろしくとたのんで置きました。
共ちゃん睦ちゃんも丈夫で夏期學校へ通
って居るのですね。随分大きくなったでせう
寫眞は高いですか。フレンチキャンプでの寫眞
は有りますが近頃のも見たいと思ひます
では今日はこれで御氣嫌やう。

七月二十二日

勝

妻、

DETAINED ALIEN ENEMY MAIL
EXAMINED
BY ....
U. S. I. & N. S.

Mrs. Umeno Tamura
65-3-D
Rivers, Arizona

Katsuchika Tamura
Bk 52
S.F. Detention Station
Santa Fe, N. M.
July 24, 1943

早いものでもう一週間もすると移ってから二ヶ月になり
ます。そちらの暑さにくらぶれば随分感謝せね
ばならぬのですが別れてをるので何となく物たり
なく落ちつかぬ日が續くだけです。學校を教へる
やうたのまれましたが今度はことわりました。ゴルフ
はコースが出来ましたので行きますが思った程上
達せず。讀書も圖書が充分無いのと眼の具合
が悪いので予期した程出来ません。食堂も新築
されてピンポンもなくなりました。昨夜は活動が
有り今夜は芝居がある筈です
あなたも子供達も元氣でせうね。水はまた充分
でありませんか。暑いのに困るでせう。クーラーか
ファンで[illegible]あるのですか。池田さんの娘さんの話
の様子ではたいていのバラックが何れかはもって
居るとのことでした。
皆さん、呉々もよろしく
今日はこれで

勝 (田)

七月二十四日

梅乃殿

DETAINED ALIEN ENEMY MAIL
EXAMINED
BY
U. S. I. & N. S.

Umeno Tamura
65-3-D
Rivers, Arizona

Katsuchika Tamura
Bk 52

今朝は美しく晴れた高原地殊色の影です。日中は
太陽がきびしいので午前中散歩をします。三方山にかこ
まれ「方は二の日」になつて居り時々は羊を追ふ子
供達の聲も後、物さびしい世の中とも思はれず
平和の氣がたゞよつて居ります。かつては同じ様
な平和の朝に起きてゴルフ場へ急いだこともあつたの
ですが今は再び同じ道を同じ氣分で走るか
あるか無いか全く解りません。多分はないと思ふ方
がよいのでせう。萬事は都合よく運んで居ります
これと申してよいたよりもありません。移る前は
こちらへ来たらもつとてきぱき運ぶと予期して来
たのですがその予期も今の所裏切られたかたちです。
追々には整理されるのでせうか先は何時になるかかいもく
わかりません。相変らず暑いのでしのぎにくいで
せう。子供達は丈夫で學校へ通つておりますか
きつと見ちがへる程大きく成つて居りませう。一日も早く
逢ひたいと念じて居ります。
では今朝はこれで 呉々も身心共にさわやかに
暮されん様

七月二十八日
勝田

妻へ

DETAINED ALIEN
ENEMY MAIL
EXAMINED
BY [illegible]
U. S. I. & N. S.

Mrs Umeno Tamura
65-3-D
Rivers, Arizona

Katsuchika Tamura
Brk 52
S.F. Detention Station
Santa Fe, N.M.
July 29, 1943

其後御氣嫌よく御暮しの事と存じます。
先週は子供達からファーザーヅデイプレゼントをもらひ誠によろこばしく思ひました。
近頃はさぞ暑いでせうね御察し致します
当方も種々の事が起りましたが萬事都合よく運び愉快に暮して居ります。
昨日も日がさして居るのに大水が流れて来たので驚きましたが結局山に降ったた夕立が音をたてゝ流れて来たのです
不思議なけんしようです。フタクトンの人々にも逢ひました。帰る人もありますが御承知の通り私は番がまわって来さうありません。今はこれで御身体御大切に

六月二十九日

梅乃殿

勝周

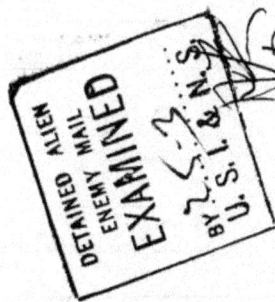

DETAINED ALIEN
ENEMY MAIL
EXAMINED
BY 2-5-3
U.S.I.&N.S.

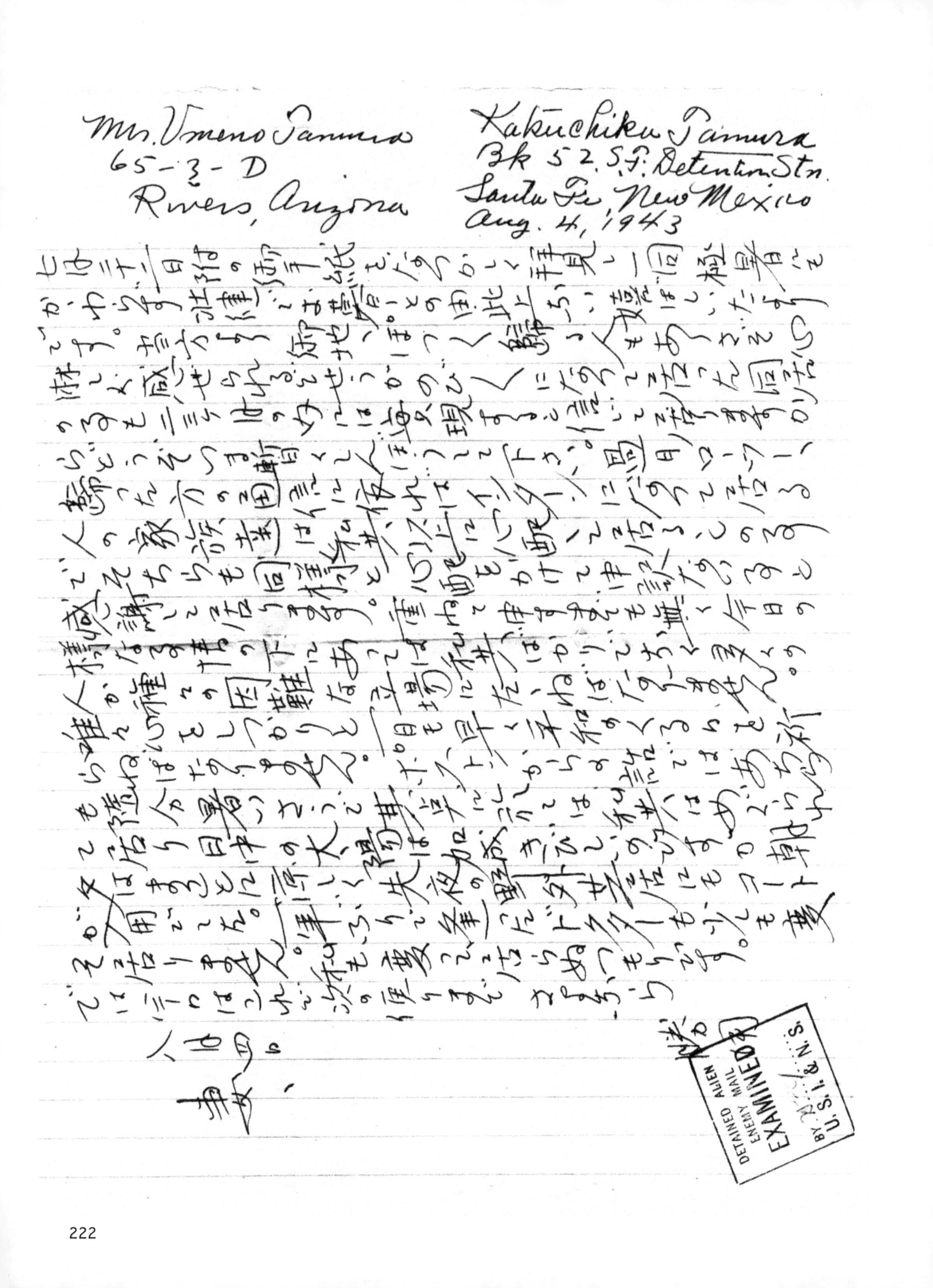

Mrs. Umeno Tamura
65-3-D
Rivers, Arizona

Kakuchiku Tamura
Bk 52 S.F. Detention Stn.
Santa Fe, New Mexico
Aug. 4, 1943

[illegible]

DETAINED ALIEN ENEMY MAIL
EXAMINED
BY [illegible]
U. S. I. & N. S.

Mrs. Umeno Tamura
65-3-D
Rivers, Arizona

Katsuchika Tamura
52. S.F. Detention Camp
Santa Fe New Mexico
Aug. 9. 1943

DETAINED ALIEN
ENEMY MAIL
EXAMINED
BY
U. S. I. & N. S.

八月に入ってからヨタヨリ雨がヨタメイちら〳〵まとんが気持のよい雨でうっとうしい空で長ふりするのでは無く一降りふるとまた雲切れがしてあをくてた空がみえて来ます。高い土地の常だと思ひます。相変らず差ちらく甘かん其日〳〵すぎて行くだけでお知らせも変化もありません。犬もセンターに残って居る人に比らふれは私達は隨分居気かも知れはせんかいくら心配しても楽でもどうすることも出来無いので時の来るのを待つより仕方がないとかんねんして居るのでせう。子供達は元気で学校通って居りますか。弘も大きくなって世話の焼けるでせう。美て下さる新聞や其處から評向する様ではほぼ察することが出来ます。人の話で野菜物はよく出来る様ですね。フレンチキャンプ地方から深い経験を持った多くの人が行って居る故でせう。メロンはどうですか。甘味がありますか。私達も時々食べます。コロラドのロッキーホードはメロンの有名の産地とりか私達の所へ来るのはそこからかどうか知りません。圖りよいものではありませんでした。皆さんよろしく。御無沙汰申して居ることもおわび申上げて置いて下さい。

勝周

八月九日

梅乃殿

Mrs. Umeno Tamura
65-3-D
Rivers, Arizona

Katsuchika Tamura 52
Santa Fe, Detention Station
Santa Fe, New Mexico
Aug 13, 1943

昨夜は芝居の催がありこうした所であり得ぬと思ふ位の出来ばへでした。静御前やお米になったおやまも上出来で大さわぎでした。野外でしたが九時頃からは涼し過ぎてオバーコートを引っかけた位でした。其処は相変らず暑く子供達もあせもで困るさうですね。水の充分ある事はせめてもとおもひます。

すでに帰った方々から聞かれたでせうが私共の生活には別に案ぜられる必要はありません。あなたがたがなやまれたと同様私も一日も早く一所に暮したいとは昨年六月からの願ひで過去一年間それのみを唯一の楽しみとして一日一日をすごして来ましたがまだ実現して居らぬので時には気もいら〳〵しますがいたずらにあせってもとかんねんして待って居ります。配給云々は別に苦にする程では無く私には必要以外に持物もありこれ以上ふやし度くありません。たゞ先日辞書を二冊注文したのでおこづかいが手うすになりさうです。別に急ぎませんが出来たら三十冊程送って戴ければよいと思ひます。これも配給についてお尋ねがあったので一寸書き添へただけで今日明日に必要とするのではありません。別に収入の無いのにこうしたおねがひも無理ではないかとも存じます

では今日はこれで、

八月十三日

勝

妻、

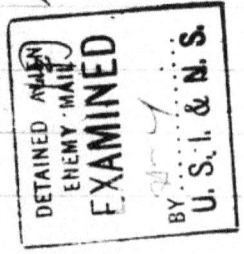

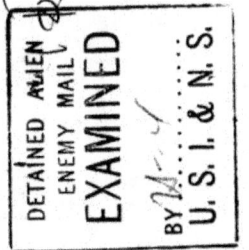

Mrs. Umeno Tamura
65-3-D
Rivers, Arizona

Kakuchika Tamura
B. 52. S.F. Detention Station
Santa Fe, N. M.
Aug. 17, 1943

昨夜は大雨で枕下の窓を開けて置いたので夜中
起きて閉めたくらいでしたが今朝は晴れて
心地よい日よりになりました。ゴルフや野球
にそれぞれ出て行きますが私は集会が
あるのでお席せねばなりません。集会々
はこりごりなのですが相変らず出てます
こんな仕事を頼まれてことわるにも
出来ずまわって居ります。此處の涼しさに
ひきかへて随分暑いさうでお察しします
皆んな元氣でお暮しですか。それはさう
と住友の一件はどうなったのです。あの儘
ですか。あのまゝなら今の所あのまゝにして
置けばよいと思ひますが先日こゝへ手紙
が来たのでお尋ねする次第です
では今日はこれで御機嫌よう

八月十七

梅乃殿

勝か 田

DETAINED ALIEN
ENEMY MAIL
EXAMINED
BY ....
U. S. I. & N. S.

Umeno Tamura
65-3-D
Rivers, Arizona

Katsuchika Tamura
Barrack 52
Santa Fe Detention Station
Santa Fe, New Mexico

暑さにもかからず元氣でお暮しの由まことによろこばしく存じます。私も幸恙なく大丈夫で日々を送って居ります。其處でも一部の人が十月末にはアーレーキへうつらねばならぬ様聞きますが兄さんや妙森さんはどうなるでせう。交換船が出た後、多少の家族はハミリーキャンプへ行く事と思ひますが此度は私達も其選に入り度いと祈って居ります。昨日ワシントンの人々と共に寫眞をとりました。出来たら早速送ります

では御氣嫌よう

八月二十六日

梅乃殿

勝周

DETAINED ALIEN
ENEMY MAIL
EXAMINED
BY U. S. I. & N. S.

Mrs. Umeno Tamura
65-3-D
Rivers, Arizona

Kakuchika Tamura
Bk 52
S.F. Detention Station
Santa Fe, New Mexico

八月三十日附のお手紙とはがき拝見しました。三人[illegible]
お[illegible]の中何よりと存じます。私も至極壮健にて日々を
送っていますから安心下さい。今夜は静に雨が
降って屋根にあたる音が淋しく聞こえてきます。隣の
人の本[illegible]を読んだりして淋しさを感じております。
お金もクラブも確かに受取りました。前回に送っ
た[illegible]品が無事に届いて[illegible]
思いました。

近々に家族キャンプの移動があるとも聞きますが
[illegible]になるかわかりませんが
一日も早く達者でお目にかかれる日の来るのを祈って
[illegible]

では御身大切に
八月三十日

梅乃殿

覚ち(か)(田)

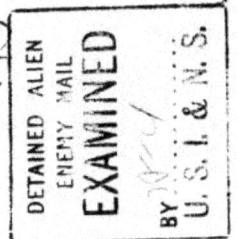

DETAINED ALIEN
ENEMY MAIL
EXAMINED
BY [illegible]
U. S. I. & N. S.

Umeno Tamura
65-3-D
Rivers, Arizona.

Katsuchika Tamura
Barrack 52
Santa Fe Detention Station
Santa Fe, New Mexico
Sept. 3, 1943

今朝は早く起きて朝食前に散歩しましたがすでに散歩して居る人体操をして居る人等それぞれ早起きの人々が運動をして居りました東側に山があるので日の出が平地より後れますが日が山の端に掛った時は実に美しい影です。交換船もいよいよ港を出たと云ふので私共の友達も海上の人となって長い航海の途についたでせう。小供達も丈夫で正しく云はって行きますか。私は相変らず元気です。次週は通信が一通だけと命ぜられましたが決して案じて下さいますな。今日はこれで この次まで さようなら

勝か田

九月三日

梅乃殿

DETAINED ALIEN
ENEMY MAIL
EXAMINED
BY U. S. I. & N. S.

Umeno Tamura
65-3-D
Rivers, Arizona

Katsuchika Tamura
Barrack S2
Santa Fe Detention Station
Santa Fe, New Mexico
Sept. 10, 1943

朝夕はむしろ寒いと申しても大げさで無いやうに有りました。野外での催しものも夜は寒過ぎます。そちらは相変らず暑いでせう何時頃から涼しくなるのですか至極元気で暮して居ります。其處に五家族がハミリーキャンプへ行くやう通知があったさうですか私達の番はまだまゐりませんかそれのみが一番よいニュースと待ちに待って居ります。写真が出来ましたから送ります。太陽がつよかったので目つきが面おかしく写って居りますがこれよりまだのんきに暮して居ります。皆元気でせうね。身体を充分注意して下さい

では御気嫌よう

勝周

九月十日

妻へ

DETAINED ALIEN
ENEMY MAIL
EXAMINED
BY [illegible]
U.S.I.&N.S.

皆丈夫で暮して居られますか。こうした時代に遭遇して
個人的罪は無くとも避けられぬ難を負はされ単調
な生活にあきられる事とお察しします。お國の御父
さんがなくなられた事も誠に残念な事です。申す
迄も無く皆の事を案じて居られた事と思ふと
言ひ表はす言葉もありません。お母さんも御心痛
の事とは存じますがせめて平和の日が来て皆が逢ふ
事の出来る日まで御壮健で居られるやう心から祈って
居ります。兄さんへも私からのおくやみをよろしく申上
げて置いて下さい。私は幸と至極丈夫で日を送って
居りますから安心して下さい。子供(達)もすなほ
に育って居りますか。では次の便りまで御気
嫌よう 九月十六日

慕しい

妻、

勝が用

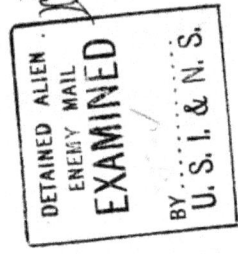

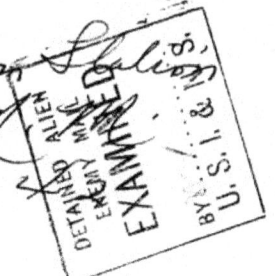

Umeno Tamura
65-8-D
Rivers, Arizona

Katsuhiko Tamura
Bk 52
S.F. Detention Station
Santa Fe, N.M.
Sept 23, 19

DETAINED ALIEN
ENEMY MAIL
EXAMINED
BY
U.S.I. & N.S.

其後お変り無くお暮しの事と確信して居ります
昨日身体験査がありましたが至極健康です
から安心して下さい。近頃はよいたよりはいつも
家族の方から来るやうですがよつたより
はありませんか。週々そちらから来た方の
話ではクリスタルシチーへ行く家族の中に
はいつて居ると云々と申して居りましたかもし
そうだとしたらどんなによろこばしいでせう。
日夜祈るはほかに無く一日も早く皆の無事
なかほが見たいとそれのみです。写真は
送って置きましたからついたると存じます。
では次のたよりまで さようなら

九月二十三日
梅乃殿
勝田

Umeno Tamura
66-3-D
Rivers, Arizona

Katsusuke Tamura
Brk 52
Santa Fe Detention Station
Santa Fe, N.M.
Oct 2, 1943

DETAINED ALIEN
ENEMY MAIL
EXAMINED
BY 5-3
U.S.I. & N.S.

九月二十七日附のお手紙を拝見し恙無くお暮しの由
安心致しました。典ちゃんも睦ちゃんも學校へ
通學始めたさうで何よりです。何があっても修學
を怠ってはなりません。近頃の弘はどんなですか
相変らずいたづらで困りますか。そちらも大分
涼しくなった様ですね。当地も朝夕は寒い
位とは云へ、日中は秋日和で実によい氣候で山々の
眺めも美しゅうございます。すでに十月で
すが此れと云ふよいたよりもありません。先日
写真を送りましたらどうした間違かとう
返ってかへって来ました。再び送って置きました
今頃はお受取りの事と存じます。岡崎
さんからおたよりありますか。あの後生
れたあかちゃんは男の子でしたか。では又

十月二日
勝田
妻へ

Umeno Tamura
65-3-D
Rivers, Arizona

Kakuichi Tamura
Brk 52
Santa Fe Detention Stn.
Santa Fe N.M.
Oct. 9, 194

DETAINED ALIEN
ENEMY MAIL
EXAMINED
BY
U. S. I. & N. S.

寫眞を受取った由の御手紙を受取り一同元氣でお暮しの由何よりと嬉しく存じます私も至極壮健で消光致して居りますから安心して下さい。山の高い所は雪でおはれて白くなって居りましたが昨日の暖い日でまた消へてしまいました。秋で木の葉が黄色になりだし淋しい冬と思はれおります。早く冬にならぬ前に一共に暮らせるの出来るやうそれのみ祈って居りが私の向く範囲ではこと申すよい知らせもちかく莫然とした生活ではこれでさようなら

十月九日

勝田

梅乃殿

Umeno Tamura
65-3-D
Rivers, Arizona

Kakuichika Tamura
Blk 52
Santa Fe Detention Station
Santa Fe, N.M.

御氣嫌よい事と存じます。轉住に轉住が重って
さぞ動搖して居られると思ひますが何うすも
忍耐して善處して下さると安心して居ります。
時に加州住友銀行の整理委員から八ケましく
申して来ますがどうしませう 利子共二百七十弗
位になって居ると思ひます 證書が送って呉れれ
ば都合が出来れば片付けて置けば何かの役に
立つ事があるかも知れません。
冬分にふるとよく曇って小雨が降ったりします
が朝にふるとからりと晴れて氣持ちよい日
和にあります。多人数で落付いて讀書も
出来ませんがごルフや外のあそびで元氣で
其日々を送って居ります では次ま

十月十二日
妻へ
勝

DETAINED ALIEN ENEMY MAIL EXAMINED
BY ぶー7
U. S. I. & N. S.

Umeno Tamura
65-3-D
Rivers Arizona

Katsuhiko Tamura
Barrack 52
Santa Fe Detention Station
Santa Fe, N. M.
Oct. 20, 1943

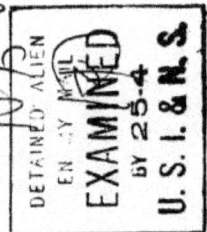

小包を受取ったとの御手紙と受取った子供達より
こんだうで何よりです。大分寒い朝もあって
今朝はバラック入口の用水にうす氷がはって居り
ました。遠望にある青はかった木々も黄色に変
って秋を想はせます。お別れしてすでに二た
秋を迎へ、いろいろ御目に触れるはっきりしたものも
知らず心もめいるときもあって秋を一しほ
感ぜずには居られません。貴あなたも同じ
思ひになやんで居られることと察します。
どうぞ子供達のため心晴れやかに暮して
下さい。私は何と思っても丈夫そうにうって
居るでせう。では今日はこれで

勝彦

十月二十日

梅乃殿

DETAINED ALIEN
ENEMY MAIL
EXAMINED
BY 25-4
U. S. I. & N. S.

Umeno Tamura
65-3-D
Rivers, Arizona

Katsuchika Tamura
52
Santa Fe Detention Station
Santa Fe, N.M.

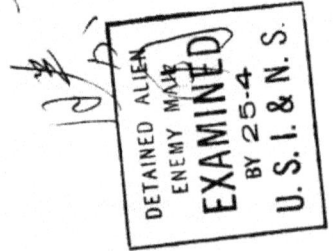

皆丈夫でお暮しですか 私も至極元氣で暮して居
ますから安心して下さい。三日程前大分寒く
手もかゆいとかさくになりましたが今では此風
もやんで空も一点の雲なく晴れて居りますから
日中は暖いよい方になると思ひます。近頃
はここでも大分野菜をつくってよい品が出来る様
なりました。大根なども随分ふとって漬物やたい
こんおろしにして食卓に上ります。トパズへ
一時面会に行った人の話ではセンターも近頃大分
住みよくなったさうで其處も同様だと思ひます
昨年ストーブが入らないで英夫さんや弘の手
が氷の様であったとの事などを想い出し今
年はそんな事は無いだらうと思ひます。
竹森さんや兄さんの家族方へ呉々もよろしく

十月二十二日

妻

勝[illegible]

Umeno Tamura
65-3-D
Rivers, Arizona

Kakuchika Tamura
Brk 52 Santa Fe Detention Station
Santa Fe, N.M.
Oct 25, 1943

十廿十九日附の飛行郵便での御手紙を受取り萬事承知致し
ました。当所よりセンターを一時訪問する方も大分あり私も
願ってと思はぬではありませんでしたが第一費用が相当かかり
ます第二には途中運輸機関が陸は混むさうで容
易でないさうです第三で最も私の氣に掛るのは御目
にかかってもしばしで又相別れねばならぬ事です。
フレンチキャンプであの夜お別れして以来朝暮心とはな
れぬのはあなたの事です何時も早く一共になりたいのは日
夜祈って居るのですが不幸にも今日まで其運に至らず
一共に暮した日より別れて暮した日の方がながくなった
悲しいくらいになって居ります。けれど思ひは日月の長短で
計るものではないと幸福で樂しかった過ぎし日を想ひ
忍耐して待てば再びあふ時が来ると確心して居り
ます。で出来ればこんど逢ふ時は再び別れる事のない
様と一時的訪問で又別れねばならぬ事を思ふと私
にはたへられぬ様おもはれます。銀行の方はお金さへ
都合がつけば私から証書をたしかに返して呉れるかどう
か問合はせて見ます。さうしたお金が御許にあらうと
は予期して居りませんが兎に角御相談した譯で別に
よい方法が無ければ今しばらくあの儘にして置くより
仕方ありません。それから御参考迄申上ますが訪問
が許可になっても順番があって一人だけ[illegible]に行くのは
六ヶ敷いと存じます。では何事も忍耐して時の来るのを
待って下さい。

一九四三、十月二十四日

勝周

妻へ

DETAINED ALIEN
ENEMY MAIL
EXAMINED
BY 25-4
U. S. I. & N. S.

Umeno Tamura
65-11-A
RIVERS, ARIZONA

Katsuchika Tamura
Brk 52, S.F. Detention Station
Santa Fe, N. M.
Nov. 1, 1943

昨朝今朝と霜が降って食堂へ行くにも外套が必要ですが
日中は暖で外で運動が出来ます。すでに十月に入り十日は
暦を切り捨て残る所二枚になり云ひ知れぬ思ひに
胸がいっぱいになります。典ちゃんと睦ちゃんの手紙に
よれば新しいバラックに移ったさうで種々忙しかったでせう。
申す迄も無くフレンチキャンプ立退後数知れぬ御心
労で手紙等には書けぬるも多々あったろうと御察
しします。こうした時想出すのは芭蕉の事です。或年の秋、
彼は門人千里を伴って東海道を旅したことがあったさうですが
二人にとって何よりの楽しみは憧れの富士の偉容に接する事
でしたところが其日は折悪しく雨が降って一面模糊として期待
は裏切られました。千里は残念がって雨を怨むことしきり
でしたが芭蕉は「霧しぐれ富士を見ぬ日ぞおもしろき」と
誦んで一向悪天候にとらはれることは無く却てあるがまゝの相
をあるがまゝに見る楽しみに自我を没入して居ったさうです
勿論私共は凡人で中々芭蕉の様な心きようにはなれま
せんが出来る丈今の境遇をいたづらにかこつことなく
試練の貴い機会と達観したいものです。センター訪
問もどうした理由か一時中止の状態になって居ります
えさんや小森さん、呉さんもよろしく。岡崎さんから
たよりがありますか。

勝周

十一月一日

梅乃殿

DETAINED ALIEN
ENEMY MAIL
EXAMINED
BY 25-3
U.S.I.&N.S.

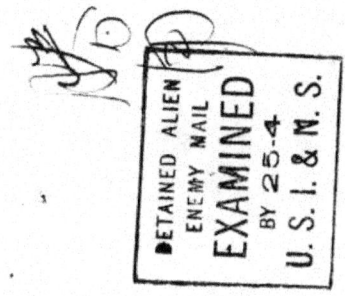

Umeno Tamura
65-11-A
Rivers, Arizona

Katsuchika Tamura
B.52, S.F. Detention Station
Santa Fe, N.M.
Nov. 10, 1943

二三日ゆるやかな天氣が續いて愉快な日を送って居
ます。当地の氣候は近頃どうですか。御手紙で
心組みも承知し住友銀行へは手紙を出して置
きました。何とか申して来るでせう。時に其処にも
歯科医が居るのでせうがあなたの歯は其後よろ
ブんありませんか。早く入れる様願ひたら其、
運びに至らず残念でした。私もビスマークに居
った時親知らずが一本かけ出し其仲つめ方が
よくなく此処へ来てから根だけになってしまひ
ましたので一昨々日ぬいてもらいました。勿論注
射してぬいたのでぬくときは左程でありませんで
したが無理して身をいためたので注射の薬が
きかなくなると一寸氣持が悪ふございました。
今もまだあごがいたいのですが氣持はさっ
ぱりして元氣になりました。子供の件は歯で
くるしんだるもありましたが三十二本そろっ
た歯をはじめてぬくので少し氣にも為り
ました。あなたにも子供にも思ひ歯のトラブル
無い様念じて居ります。子供達はすな
ほに育って居りますか
では御氣嫌やう

十一月十日
勝周
梅乃殿

DETAINED ALIEN
ENEMY MAIL
EXAMINED
BY 25-4
U. S. I. & N. S.

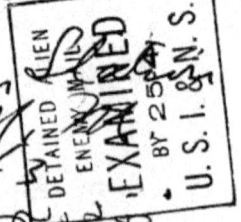

Umeno Tamura
65-11-A
Rivers, Arizona

Katsuchika Tamura
B2K52
S.F. Detention Station
Santa Fe, N.M.
Nov. 18 '44

DETAINED ALIEN ENEMY MAIL
EXAMINED
BY 2504
U.S.I. & N.S.

お妻あ〜りませんか 新らしい住家にもなれましたか
子供達は丈夫ですか 寒くなりますからかぜを引
かさぬ様注意して下さい。氣候の変り目か此処
でも大分風邪がはやって私達のバラックからも近頃
三人ばかり病院へ行きました。私は幸ひ元氣で
病氣しませんが充分氣は附けて居ります。
過去十日程よい天氣が續いて毎日ほとんど
屋外で暮せます。昨日はサンタフェーのほん
とうのゴルフ場へ行きました。練習する割
合に少しも上達しませんがまあ〳〵運動にと
思って續けて居ます。讀書や其他もう少し
有益なる事に時をつかいたいのですがバラック生
活では氣が落ち附かずとかく無駄なるに
時を費して居る様で自分ながら何か云ひ知
れず氣に掛ります。えきさんや竹森さん、
も御無沙汰して居りますがよろしく御申上
げて置いて下さい。では今日はこれで御
氣嫌よう

十一月十八日
勝周
妻へ

Umeno Tamura
65-11-A
Rivers, Arizona

Katsuchika Tamura
Brk 52
Santa Fe, Detention Stn.
Santa Fe, New Mexico
Nov. 23, 1943

お寒くありませんか。長く天氣が續き輕かぜ引きが大分出ます。私は幸ひ至極元氣です。住友銀行から返事が来ましたから同封して送ります。静子さんに讀んでもらって出来たらそちらから直接銀行へ私からとはっきり書いて送って下さい。尚証書二枚は必ずあなたの方へ送ってもらう樣にして下さい。私からも銀行へはさうするから証書をそちらへ送る樣申し送って置きます。ではこれで。

十一月二十三日

勝周

梅乃殿

DETAINED ALIEN
ENEMY MAIL
EXAMINED
BY 25-4
U. S. I. & N. S.

Umeno Tamura
65-11-A
RIVERS, ARIZONA

Katsutsuka Tamura
Brks 52 S.F. Detention Station
Santa Fe, New Mexico
Nov. 30, 1943

DETAINED ALIEN ENEMY MAIL
EXAMINED
BY 254
U.S.I.&N.S.

感謝祭の日にしたため下さった御手紙をなつかしく拝見
致しました。お正月にはイースターには感謝祭
クリスマスにはと期待しなどのもいつも裏切られて
今日に及んでしまいました。帰る人達と何の相違
も認めませんがこうした事情下にあっては、あり得
可きるとただ忍耐して時の来るのを待って居
ります。若し銀行、金を送ったならば記事を
受取ったら知らして下さい。フレンチキャンプにある荷物
に就いては今暫く其儘がよいと思ひます。クリス
タルの家族キャンプには今後は本人の家族が行く
るはないやうです。従ってツールレーキが他の新ら
しい場所と思ひますからもう少し目鼻のつく
迄待った方がよいと考へます。ツールレーキへ
行くのは自分は苦にしませんが子供をつれて
の旅行を楽せぬ譯には行きません。持物
はすでに多過ぎて冬物は全然必用ありません
お金もいる時よお願いします。今は元気です
では御返事まで

十一月三十日 勝田

妻

Mrs. Umeno Tamura
65-11-A, Rivers, Arizona

Katsuchika Tamura
Blk 52
S.F. Detention Station
Santa Fe, N.M.
Dec. 4, 1943

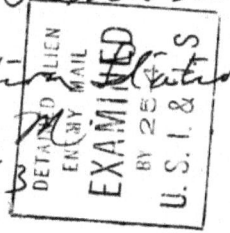

DETAINED ALIEN ENEMY MAIL EXAMINED BY 25 U.S.I. & S

一昨日は大雪が降って山も里も一面銀世界と変りまし
たが今日はよい天氣でうすぐらに朝食に行くのに
コバルト色の空にキラキラする星と黒く浮んだ山
影と実に美しい景色でした。相変らず至極
元氣で暮して居ります。英ちゃん睦ちゃんからの
クリスマスカードも着きました。住友からは証書領
収書目、署名する様申して来ました。昨日送り返して
置きましたからあちらで受取次第証書をそちらへ送る
と申して来ました。ツールレイク行きの事は今の所ただ可能
性があると云ふだけでそれ以上のことは申されません
クリスマスも正月も再び別々に迎へねばならぬと
思ふと云ひ知れぬ淋しさを感じます。過去消極
的に運命とすべてを受けて居ったのがあやまりで
あったかも知れません。皆の健康を心の底から
祈って居ります。

十二月四日

梅乃殿

勝田

Mrs. Umeno Tamura
65-11-17
Rivers, Arizona

Kakuichiku Tamura
Brk 52, S.F. Detention Station
Santa Fe, New Mexico
Dec. 8, 1943

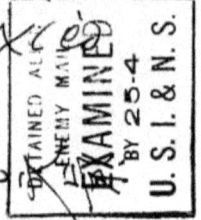

DETAINED ALIEN ENEMY MAIL
EXAMINED
BY 25-4
U. S. I. & N. S.

寒さが加って来ましたがお変りありませんか。子供達も元
でせうか。私は相変らず元気です。寒い日もありますが今迄
は割合に天気都合もよく昨日も午後はゴルフに行きました。
家族同居問題も来月は目鼻が附く様申して居ります
ツールレーキに家族の居る人々は近々全部あちらへ行く様
申して居ります。あなた方もツールレーキへ移ればヨリ早く
様にも聞きますが親しい方々に別れるより子供達の
ためにどうかと案じて居ります。そちらではさう云ふ話
はありませんか。昨日は此度の交換船で来たと云ふ
緑茶をもらひました。そちらへも行きましたか。
一ヶ月程軽いかぜが流行りましたが幸ひ今は下火に
なり私はかからずすみました。今後もこの冬中
かぜは引き度く無いものです。あなたはじめ子供達
充分注意して下さい。では御気嫌やう

勝田

十二月八日
妻へ

Mrs. Umeno Tamura
65-11-A
Rivers, Arizona

Kakuchika Tamura
B.52 S.F. Detention Station
Santa Fe, N.M.
Dec. 10, 1943

DETAINED ALIEN ENEMY MAIL
EXAMINED
BY 25.3
U. S. I. & N. S.

昨日は終日雪が降りましたが今日は晴れて太陽が銀世界に輝いて居ります。数日こうした日が續けば地上の雪もとけて戸外で運動が出来ますがそれ迄は短い散歩位で室内で暮さねばなりません。

クリスマスのパッケージが着きました。種々予期しなかった品物を送って下さって心からよろこばしく感じました。子供の様に待切れず睦ちゃんの毛糸の犬や暖かさうなフェター、ゴルフボール等を手にとってよろこびました。細長い箱だけは開けずにクリスマス迄待つ事にしました。典ちゃんにも睦ちゃんにもよく申して置いて下さい。私からもほんのしるしだけ送って置きました。典ちゃんの本も注文したのでしたが品切で来なかった為め急に手許にあったあしたもので間に合せました。機会があったら何かうめあはせに送りますからよく申しておいて下さい。住友銀行からはあなたに証書と共に送った手紙の写が来ましたから萬事都合よく解決したると思ひます。

では今日はこれで　十二月十日

勝田

梅乃殿

Umeno Tamura
65-11-A
Rivers, Arizona

Katsuchiko Tamura
Brk 52 S.G. Detention Station
Santa Fe, N. M.
Dec 24, 1943

皆変りありませんか私もおかげと至極丈夫で暮して居ります。
一昨々日から大雪でどこもここも銀世界です　朝は随分寒いです
ですが今日は幸ひ日が出て気が晴れ晴れとします。典ちゃんと
睦ちゃんから手紙をもらひました二人とも元気なやうで何より
です或るセンターではドクターの不足もあるさうですどうぞ
呉々も健康に注意して下さる様。園田さんからクリスマス
カードをもらひました返事を出して居ります。あちらも
今随分寒いことでせう。当所からも大分出る人もあり
家族のある人は皆いらいらして居ります。センターのインターン
されてる家族の者も同じだと思ひます。同居問題も来春
でなければ目鼻は附かぬと思ひます。度々繰返すやうで
ありますがどうぞ心を晴れやかに持って私共のみを考へず
一般的世界の不幸を想ひ一日も早く平和が来る事を
祈って下さい。ワシントンの大部分の人もそれぞれ家族へ帰った
ので時には何故私だけと悲しみにたえぬ事もありますが
また左より以上不幸の人の身を思へばまた思ひ返して
いたずらにかこつよりは心を平静に持って来る時
を待つより仕方ないとあきらめます。皆の善
ないのを心から祈り乍ら

十二月二十四日
妻

勝田

Umeno Tamura
65-11-A
Rivers, Arizona

Katsuchika Tamura 53
Santa Fe Detention Station
Santa Fe, N.M.
Dec. 29- 1943

DETAINED ALIEN ENEMY MAIL EXAMINED BY 25-4 U.S.I.&N.S.

皆変りありませんか 私は相変らず至極元気ですから御安心
下さい。送って下さったクリスマスのプレゼントをクリスマス、三日前にひ
らくのはなんとなく気がとがめたので当日が来るとはれた気分で
開いて子供の様にあれこれ見てよろこびました。スエターは糸
を切って着て見ると暖温くて丁度よく合ひます。裏を
見ても一向店のしるしがありませんしあちらこちらへかへして見
てはじめてあなたが編んだなと気が附きました。誠に
着心地よく何よりのもので毎日感謝して着て居ります。
有難う御座いました子供達にもよろしく申て置いて
下さい。ゴルフボールも沢山に有りました当分買はんで
すみます。ネクタイも役にたちます。お茶はつきましたか
今日又ペン軸一本弘のおもちゃとキャンディを送って置き
ました。私が馬や牛をこしらへて居りましたら同じ位
の年の子供を持って居る人が三つにも近い子供は
そんなおもちゃでは満足しませんよと云って居りました
知らぬ内に大きくもあり智恵も進んで私の考へて
居る様なベビーではないかも知れません。
近頃はよく雪が降ります。つららも差渡し二寸近
くもあるのがあります。晴れた日は寒くない景色で冬と
云っても暗い心になる様なことはありません。恐らくそこの
皆が考へて居るよりよほど気楽な生活を送って居
るのですから安心して下さい。これが本年のしまいの
たよりだと思ひます。では御機嫌よく新年を
迎へられるやう。

勝田

梅乃殿

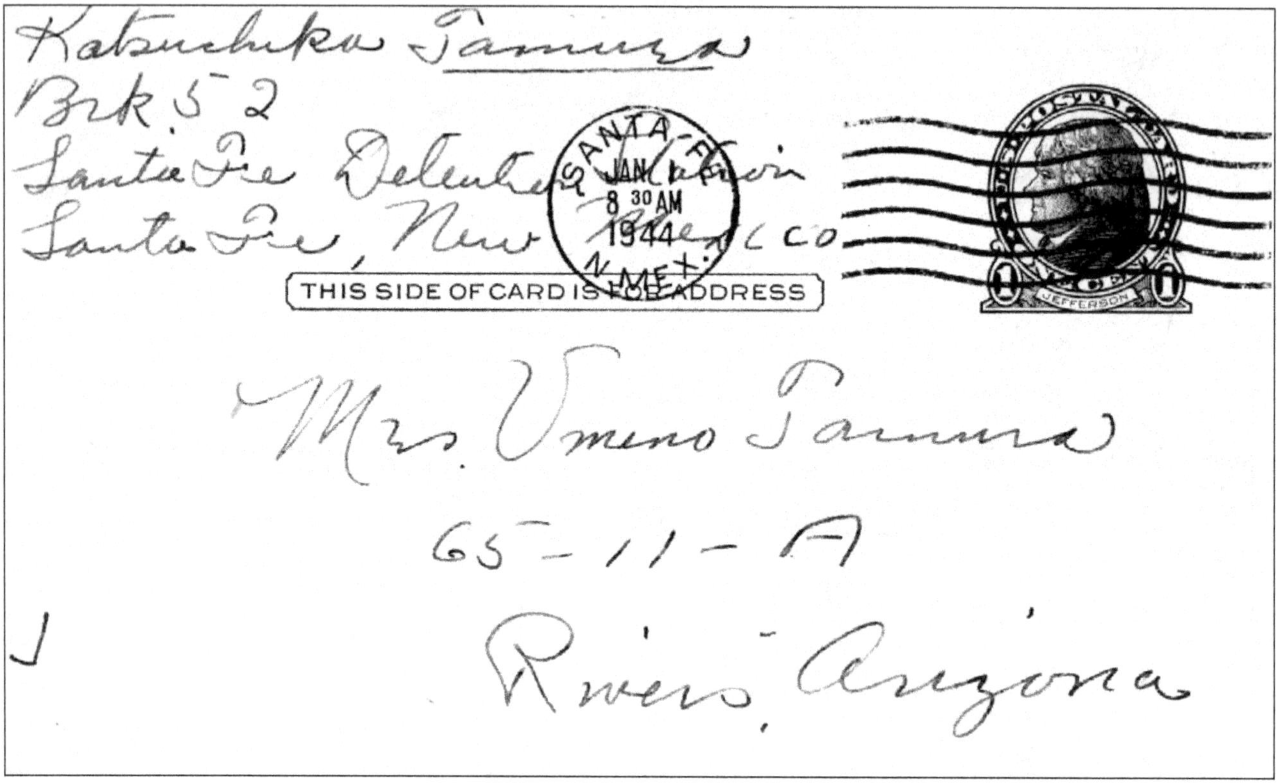

Katsuchika Tamura
Brk. 5 2
Santa Fe Detention Station
Santa Fe, New Mexico

SANTA FE
JAN 1
8 30 AM
1944
N. MEX.

THIS SIDE OF CARD IS FOR ADDRESS

JEFFERSON

Mrs. Umeno Tamura
65-11-A
Rivers, Arizona

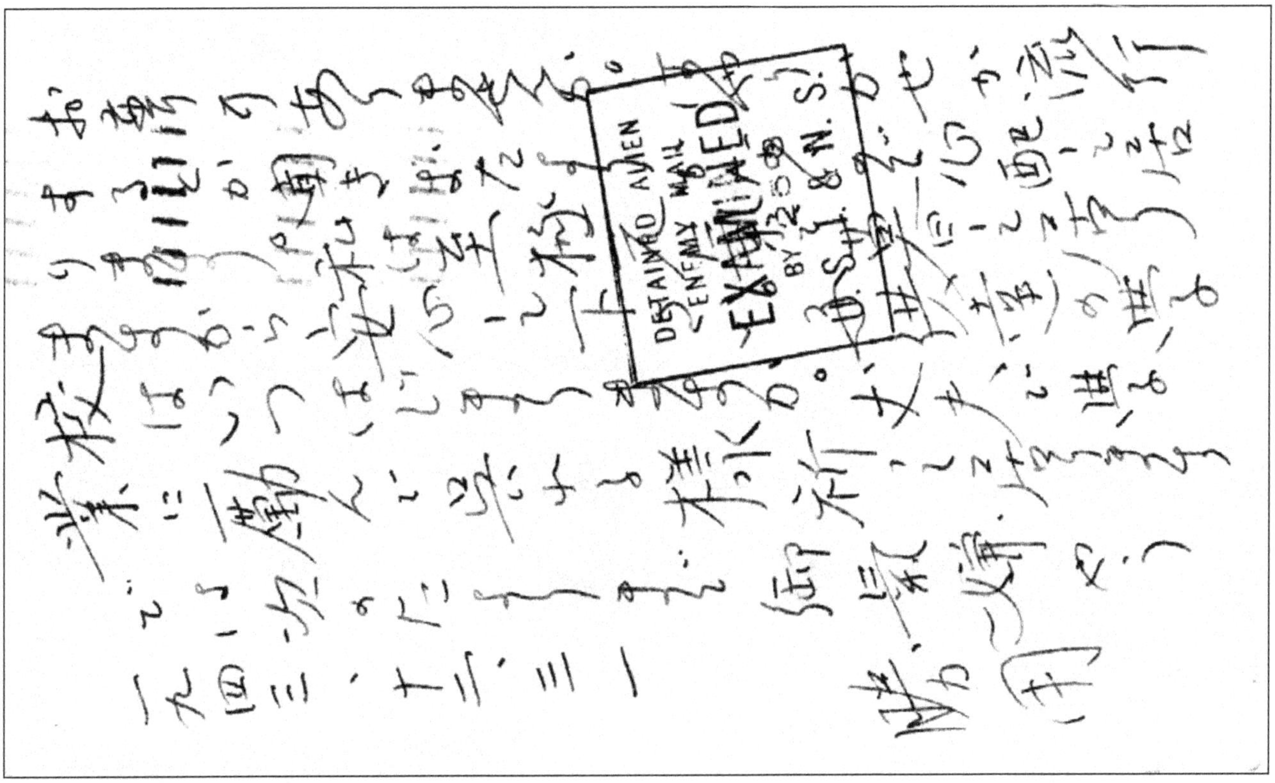

Postcard, both sides, to Umeno from Katsuchika.

Umeno Tamura
65-11-17
Rivers, Arizona

Katsuchika Tamura
Bk 52
S.F. Detention Station
Santa Fe, N. M.
Jan 6, 1944

DETAINED ALIEN ENEMY MAIL
EXAMINED
BY 26-4
U. S. I. & N. S.

年末・おたよりを二週受取りお変り無く新年を
迎へられたるとよろこんで居ります 私も淋しいながら
お別れして二度目の正月を迎へました。至極元気で
すから安心して下さい。もちとピーナットアーモンドが
昨日到着しました。おいしく戴きました。交換
所で醤油が来ましたので蒼附物がおいしくなり
ました。一共になれるのは最善を盡して居り
ます。私にはそれ以外希むことが何もありませんので
あなたの心持もよく解り決して心にそむく様な
るはありません。急ぎませんが其内に三本
程送って下さる様お願いして置きます。
御無沙汰して居る方々へ呉々もよろしく
では今日はこれで 御気嫌やう
勝田

一月六日

梅乃 殿

Umeno Tamura
65-11-A
Rivers, Arizona

Katsuchika Tamura
Blk 52
S.F. Detention
Santa Fe, [illegible]

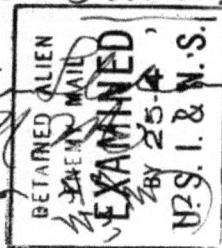

DETAINED ALIEN
ENEMY MAIL
EXAMINED
BY 25-4
U.S. I. & N.S.

相變らずよい天氣が續いて居ります。この冬もさう悪いことはありません。私も至極元氣で暮して居りますから安心して下さい。先日はサンデエゴから寒鰤(ブリ)を注文してさしみや煮魚にしてたべました。出る人が大分ありますので動搖(ドウヨウ)して居りますが心堅固に落ちついて時の來るのを待ちたいと思ひます。

先日は質問がありましたので家族同居を私の第一希望としてありのまゝを申述べて置きました。何れにしてもあなた方が息災で暮して居るので私には何よりの慰安です。

皆さんによろしく

ではまたの日まで

一月十九、

勝田

妻へ

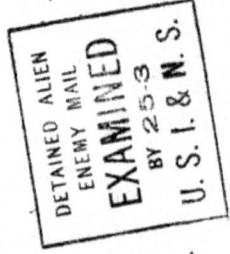

Umeno Tamura
65-11-D
RIVERS, ARIZONA

Katsuchika Tamura
B.52. S.F. Detention Station
Santa Fe N.M.
Jan 11, 1944

今日はどんよりと曇って居りますが割合に暖い御座
ります。相変らず至極元気で居りますから安心して
下さい。子供達の学校もはじまった事と存じます
二人とも元気で通学して居りますか。弘もよい
言葉悪い言葉併せて学ぶ事と思ひます。誰
の子供も通る道でやむを得ぬと思ひます。
家族同接問題もぼつぼつは片附いて行くらしい
ですがはかばかしくは運んで居りません。時に
は家族へ帰る人をうらやむやうな場合も
ありますがいたづらにいらいらしてもいかぬと
思ひなほして時の来るのを待たうと忍耐して
居ります。そちらでも種々苦労があるでせうが
健康に注意して子供の教育に専心して下さい。
では今日はこれで次のたよりまで　御気嫌
やう
一月十一日
妻へ
勝周

DETAINED ALIEN
ENEMY MAIL
EXAMINED
BY 25-3
U. S. I. & N. S.

Umeno Tamura
65-11-17
Rivers, Arizona

Katsuduka Tamura
52 SO. Detention Stn.
Santa Fe, N.M.

一月の日和としては稀なよい天氣で太陽が
氣持よくさして居ります。ゴルフコースは相変らず
雪が一面で三月頃迄は遊べさうもありません。
小包を土曜に受取りました。ありがとう
御座いました。毛糸の靴下はよく出来て
居ますしサイズも丁度よくあいます。
この用紙も早速役に立ちます。小
数の人がクリスマスシテイへ行く通知を
受けましたが私には何の通知もありません
でした。弘も元氣になつたさうですし典ちやん
瑛ちやんも丈夫で通學して居るさうで此上
もなくよろこばしく存じます。
では次のたよりまで さようなら

一月十七日 勝か[illegible]

梅乃殿

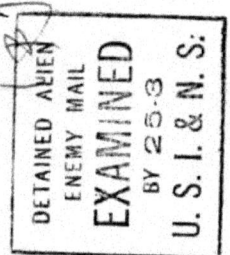

DETAINED ALIEN
ENEMY MAIL
EXAMINED
BY 25-3
U. S. I. & N. S.

Umeno Tamura
65-11-17
Rivers, Arizona

Katsushika Tamura
B.52 S.F. Detention
Santa Fe, N.M.

DETAINED ALIEN
ENEMY MAIL
EXAMINED
BY 25-4
U. S. D. & N. S.

今日は日曜で大雪のあとよく晴れ
ワクの窓からさしこんで居ります。近頃
で恙無くお暮しの由寔に感謝して居ります。
そちらからすでにクリスタルシテーへ移られた家
族もあり何かと心に動揺を感ぜられる事
と存じますが何れ近い内にそれぞれ決定
するでせうから今しばらく心堅固に待って
下さる様おねがひします。私も出て行く人を
送る度毎に自分が送られる人の内にはい
って居ったらばどんなによろこばしいことであ
らうとつくづく思ひます。ワシントンからの
人も一人へり二人へり今では私一人で何故か解
りませんが現在のやうなる状態下にあるはさわ
がずあちらからの決定を待つより外はあ
りません。唯一つ私共に幸福なるはあな
た方も私も至極元気でこれは深く感謝
せねばならぬ点と存じます。では今朝
はこれで 呉々も御気嫌よう
一月三十一日 勝
梅乃殿

Umeno Tamura
65-11-17
Rivers, Arizona

Katsuhiko Tamura
Brk. 52
Santa Fe, Detention Station
Santa Fe N. M.
Jan. 26, 1944

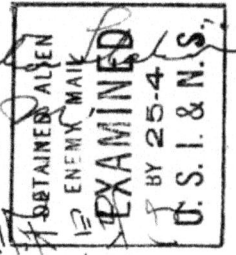

OBTAINED ALIEN ENEMY MAIL
EXAMINED
BY 25-4
U. S. I. & N. S.

雪が昨夜から降續いて居ります。氣温は
割合に高いので戸外で運動が出来ぬ位
で苦にはなりません。お變りありませんか。
私は至極元氣ですからお安心下さい。
スタクトンの方々も一人へり二人へり残り
少くなくなりました。私のも早く決定
しさうで中々はかが行かず未だ何れとも
決定して居りません。何となく氣が落ち
附かずやるせない思ひにたへません。
急ぎはしないのですがお金をお願ひした
手紙を受取られましたか。時によると
当局で忘れて居るのもあるすのでおたづ
ねします。兄さんの所もよ寂しいのでせうね。

一月二十六日
勝田

妻へ

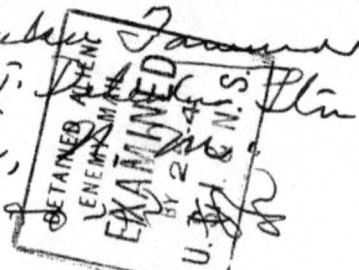

Umeno Tamura
65-11-17
Rivers, Arizona

Katsuichi Tamura
B,5 2 S.J. [illegible]
Santa Fe, N. Mex.

DETAINED ALIEN ENEMY MAIL
EXAMINED
BY 2-4
U.S.I.&N.S.

お金を有難うたしかに受取りました。これ
で当分充分です。またお願ひするまでは送
はお送り下さるに及びません。お尋ねのツール
レーキとクスリタルに就いては氣候から言へ
ばツールレーキの方がよいやう[illegible]及びます
私としてはあなた方の旅行を案じて居り
ますから日本行ハ取消してもとうと帰
れば好都合だと其様願って居りますが
思ふ様決定するかどうかは今の處
絶對に解りません 何れにでもきまれば
それに従って最善を盡すよりほか
ありません いづれにしてもいま動くと
危険ですからどうか心ほがらかに思
討して下さる様呉々もお願ひします。
身体は至極丈夫です。あなた方も
同様と聞き何よりと安心して居ります
では今朝はこれで

勝田

二月五日朝

梅乃殿

Umeno Tamura
65-11-17
Rivers, Arizona

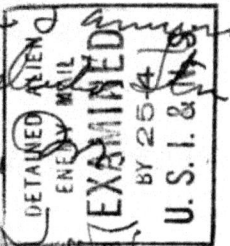

Katsuchika Tamura
352 S. [illegible]
Santa Fe N. M.

DETAINED ALIEN ENEMY MAIL
EXAMINED
BY 2544
U.S.I. & N.S.

其後お変りありませんか私も至極元気
ですから御安心下さい。十日程よい天気が續
き温くもあり春の様でしたが今日は雲っ
て雪模様です。一日一日何の音沙汰も
無くすぎて行くので氣が氣でありませんが
どうする事も出来ません。尤も廣く思
ひを及ばせば自分ばかりの不幸をか
こつ譯には行きませんが矢張り人間
であれこれ案ぜぬ譯には行きません
そちらでも同様で殊に小さい子供が
あるので種々心配する事とお察しします。
こんど岡崎さん、手紙を書く時私から
もよろしく申上げて下さい。又え竹森
さん手嶋さんもお変りありませんか
では今日はこれで呉々も御元氣で

二月九日
勝周
妻、

Umeno Tamura
65-11-A
Rivers, Arizona

Katsuchiku Tamura
352 S.F. Detention Stn
Santa Fe, N.M.

三月四日附のお手紙をありがたく拝見しました
お気嫌よくお暮しの由何よりと存じます
私も幸ひ至極元気です。其後ちゃんの
音沙汰もありません。三ヶ所の何れかで
せうか先方できめるので私にはどうする
事も出来ません。過日クリスタルシテイー、
行った人のたよりでは大層よい所の様
申して居ります。尤もあちらの夏を
知らぬからで暑さは随分きびしいそう
です。当地も暖い日が多くなりました
ので戸外で運動も出来大分楽に
なりました。当地も暖くなったそうです
が気候の変り目ですから充分注意
して下さい。ではまたのたよりまでさようなら

三月十一日
梅乃
勝周殿

DETAINED ALIEN ENEMY MAIL
EXAMINED
BY 25-3
U. S. I. & N. S.

Umeno Tamura
65-11-…
Rivers, Ariz.

DETAINED ALIEN
ENEMY MAIL
EXAMINED
BY 25-4
U.S. I. & N. S.

Katsuchika Tamura
Brk 52 S.F. Detention Stn.
Santa Fe, N.M.

其後お変りありませんか私は無事
至極元氣で暮して居りますから安心して
下さい。今日ツールレーキ行きのサインを
しました。確定した日は解りませんが
何れあちらへ移るやうになると思ひます
あなた方が先に行くのではないかと思ひ
ますそちらから通知があるでせうか
其積りでいて下さい。案ずるよりは小さい
子供を連れての旅行ですからこうした際で
すから何もしのんで最善を盡して下さい
兄さんや竹森さんとも別れねばならぬし
子供達も友達と一時失ふので悲しむ
可哀さうですがどうする事も出来ぬ事
態ですからどうぞよく承知して下さい
では今日はこれで
二月十六日
勝周
妻女へ

Umeno Tamura
65-11-A
RIVERS, ARIZONA

Katsuchika Tamura
352 S.T. Del
Santa Fe, N.

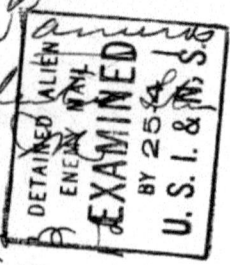

お変りありませんが私にとって一番幸福な
皆が大丈夫であることです。健康が吾々の幸福の
第一義であることは云ふ迄もありません。私もお
かげと元気です。先日申上たのはまだ決定
して居りませんがほぼきまると思ひます。あなた
方が先に移動して後に私共が行くやうになると
思ひます。聞いただけではよく解りませんが氣
候の点などはクリスタルシチーよりよいと思ひ
ますから子供にも都合よいと思ひます。只あ
なた方の長い旅行を案じますが余り氣
苦労せず最善を盡して下さい。そちらでは
まださう云ふ話はありませんがスタクトン地方では
田舎の方が二人程行きます。両方ともそこに
家族がおられますが何れ一共に行くのだと
思ひます。もし案外早くて何時出発するか
手紙で知らして下さる間がありませんでしたら
あちらへ着いてから知らして下されば宜しいです。
では今日はこれで

さよなら
勝周

二月二十三日
妻へ

Umeno Sawamura
68-11-A
Rivers, Arizona

Katsuichi Sawamura
B.52 S.
Santa Fe

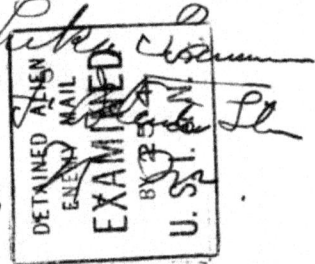

DETAINED ALIEN
ENEMY MAIL
EXAMINED
BY 254
U. S. I. & N.

私の方には甚だ別に何の知らせもありません。若しそちらで皆が行くやうでしたらつとめて行った方がよいのではないかと思ひます。私の方でも出来る丈の事はして居りますが何分一寸したるに時間がかかりますのでこの上後れるより何とかして行った方がよいかと思ひます。容易でないことはよくよ察しますから先々願って置いた通り實現すればこの上もないと希って居ります。其後お変りないのでせう。私も相変らず至極元気でおります。天候もこの数日春やかで其実申分ありません。困難に見えることでもぶつかって見ると案外であることがしばしばありますから過度の心労はなさらぬ様とも願ひます。

三月一日

勝彌

梅乃殿

Umeno Tamura
65-11-17
Rivers, Arizona

Katsuchika Tamura
B.52 S.F.
Santa Fe

DETAINED ALIEN ENEMY MAIL EXAMINED BY 25-4 U.S. I. & N.S.

夜明け前から雪になってまだ降り續けて居ります
寒さは左程でなく相変らず元氣で暮して居り
ます。ただ氣に掛るのは先々の願書を出して置
いた件に就いてまだ何の返事もないのです
一日も早く決定してお目に掛る機會の来る様
日夜祈って居りますがどうなるのか一向解ら
ないので深い雲か霧の中にはいって居る様な
氣がしております。あなたも同様だと思ひ
ます。子供達は皆丈夫ですか。もし私が
一時歸宅をゆるされない場合でも若し
ほかの人も出發してしまってたら出来たら
一寸ん行かれたらよいのではないかと思ひます。
荷造りさへ誰か男のひとかして呉れたら
途中はなんとかなるのではないかと思ひます。
私も出来る丈そちらへ歸ってリーレーキへ
行く様つとめて居りますがその為めに後
れるより早く落付く處へ行った方がよいと思って
ます。 三月三日 朝
勝
田
妻へ

Umeno Tamura
65-11-A
Rivers, Arizona

Katsuchuka Tamura
852 S.F. Detention Stn
Santa Fe, N.M.
March 5, 1944

DETAINED ALIEN ENEMY MAIL
EXAMINED
BY 9253
N.S. & W.S.

昨日は私にとって忘れる事の出来ぬ日でした。
午後戸外からバラックへ帰って来たら、ベッドの上に書留
の小包が到着して居ると云ふ通知の紙片があったので
何を送ってもらったのかと不思議に思ひ乍ら一刻も早
く見たいので土曜の午後の閉める前の事務所へ走せ附け
ました。事務員が小包の山から私のを取上げるのを見る
と案外小さい包なので内容が何かさっぱり想像
がつきませんでした。検査を要するので事務員が包を
開くのをじっと見つめていた私の胸には期待に伴ふよろ
こびが一ぱいでした。ケースが出て来てはじめて時計で
はないかと云ふ感にうたれましたがケースを開ひて
實に立派なブルヴァリストウオチ見た時は遍ゝ
びっくりしてしばし言葉も出ませんでした。こんな
よい時計が青空から下った様に来るとは全く予
期しなかった所でまとめ難いよろこびの思ひを
どうこゝに表はしてよいかくるしみます。どうぞ
たらぬ所はお察し下さい。二月二十六日したゝめた
お手紙はなつかしく拝見しました。皆元気だ
さうで何よりと存じます。私も変りありません
其後これと申して進んだ話は少しもありません

三月五日午後　勝田

妻へ

Umeno Tamura
65-11-17
Rivers, Arizona

DETAINED ALIEN ENEMY MAIL
EXAMINED
BY 25-4
U. S. I. & N. S.

Katsuchika Tamura
BRK # 52
SANTA FE DETENTION STATION
SANTA FE, NEW MEXICO
March 11, 1944

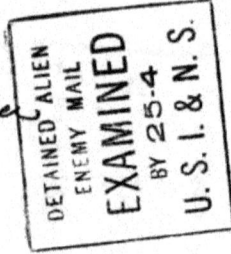

暖い春日和が續いて居ります。農園の方もぼつぼつ始めました。あちこちにある花畑もきれいに手入してありますがまだ霜をおそれてか苗木は植付けてありません。三月六日附のお便りをなつかしく拝見しました。皆が恙がない由何よりも感謝して居ります。私も幸至極元気で居ります其後何の通知も受けて居りません何れにしても一日も早くお目に掛れる様それのみ祈って居ります。ビスマーク以来一共に暮して居られた方々が出て行かれると云ひ知れぬ淋しさを感じます。手嶋さん竹林さん兄さん、よろしく。手紙を書く時は山崎さんへも呉々もよろしく申上げて下さい。では今んはこれで次まで

三月十一日　勝用

妻、

Umeno Tamura
65-11-17
Rivers, Arizona

Kakuchika Tamura
52 S.F. Detention Stn.
Santa Fe, N. Mex.

お変りありませんか。私も至極元気です
から御安心下さい。一昨々日は大風が吹いて
砂ほこりで昨朝は大掃除、朝中かゝり
ました。種々うわさはありますが私共へ
正式の発表は何もありません。そちらで
ツールレーキへ移動のはつきりした事は
解りませんか。先日出して置いた願書に
も何の解答もありません。急にそちらへ
帰られる様んなつたらどんなによろこば
しいでせう。家族と同居する人々
も次から次へ片附いて行くのであとまで
残されて居る私も気が気でありません
貴そちらも同様と存じます。而しどう
する事も出来ません今暫く心堅固に待つ
て下さい。子供達へよろしく
　　　　　　　　　　勝力用
三月十六日
梅乃殿

Umeno Tamura
65-11-17
Rivers, Arizona

Katsusuke Tamura
52 S.F. Detention Stn.
Santa Fe, N. M.
March 21, 1944

春が来たと云ふる事こゝでも春日和が續いて居つたのですが昨日雪が降つて今日はまた冬が歸って来た様です。勿論長くは續かぬと思ひますから晴れさへすれば暖かになると思ひます。四日の土曜日には腕時計を受取り思ひ掛けぬるに驚きましたこの十八日の土曜日には睦ちゃんの日本着をきた寫眞を受取り誠によろこばしく感じました。よく寫って居ますし随分大きくなったので深い感慨にたへません。何かと不自由の内にも子供達に趣味、教養を怠らぬのは本当に必要なことだと思ひます。皆んな恙が無いると推察して安心して居ります私も至極壮健で一日も早く歸宅の命令のあるのを待って居ります。

では次のたよりまで。

三月二十一日

梅乃殿

勝助

DETAINED ALIEN
ENEMY MAIL
EXAMINED
BY 25-3
U. S. I. & N. S.

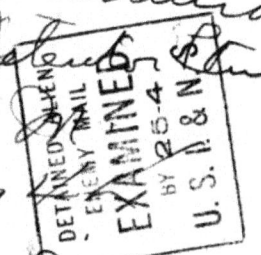

Umeno Tamura
65-11-A
Rivers, Arizona

Katsuchika Tamura
352 S.F. Detention Stn
Santa Fe, N. M.
March 28 19

DETAINED ALIEN
ENEMY MAIL
EXAMINED
BY 25-4
U. S. I. & N. S.

どうした訳か手紙が後れたので残念に思ひました
早速増田さんの奥さんへお悔の電報を
打って置きました。増田さんはよい人で私
も種々御世話になりました ほんとうにお
気の毒でした 御遺族の方へ呉々もよろしく
申上げて下さい。

其後これと申してはっきりした通知はあり
ません。いらいらしながらも時の来るのを
待つより仕方ないとかんねんして居ります
そちらで皆が壮健で無事に暮して居
ると云ふ事が何よりの慰あんです
取急いで今日はこれで

三月二十八日　　勝か田

妻へ

Umeno Tamura
65-11-17
Rivers, Arizona

Kakuchika Tamura
3.52 S.F. Detention Stn
Santa Fe, N.M.
April 2, 1944

昨日毎週二回ある活動を見て帰る時は星が輝いて居りました。
が今朝未明に起きた時は雪が降って居りました而しこの
手紙を書く今は再び快晴となって心地よい日が予想され
ます。数日来暖かった故か地上の雪は消えて行くのに
葉の無い木々は真白で實によい景色です。高地
なので春雨とでも云ふところが雪になるのでせう。
三月二十九日附のお手紙と写真をなつかしく拝見しました。
私も同様な心持でこんなに後れるならもっとクリスマス
シチー行を願へばよかったと思ひます。氣もいらく
しますがまたかう見て年を取った人氣の毒な家
庭の子持の人などがまだ片附ずに居るので早く
歸った人に比ぶれば不幸ですがこれらの人より
自分も健康であるしあなた方も丈夫で暮して
居られるので餘り不平も云へぬとこらへて居ります。
何かと心労なさるでせうがどうぞ動ようせず心晴
れやかにいま暫く待って下さい。随分風儀が悪いやう
噂くるもありますが子供達への[illegible]きょうはどん
なすでせうか　四月二日

勝田

梅乃殿

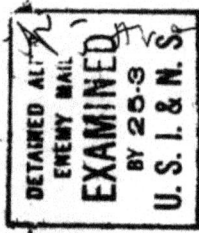

Katsushika Tamura
352 Detention Stn.
Santa Fe, N. M.
April 9, 1944

Umeno Tamura
65-11-A
Rivers, Arizona

お別れして以来二度目の四月八日を迎へて弘もすでにまる三つになったわけと驚きました。あれの生れる頃はこうした事にならうとは夢にも思って居りませんでしたのに。想出深い事です。先月そちらへ帰れる様な通知がありましたから近い内に帰れると思ひます。この上もないよろこばしい事です。一ヶ月位待たされる人もありますがどうぞ一日も早くと祈って居ります。近頃は気候もよく至極元気で暮して居りますから安心して下さい。子供達の手紙によれば皆丈夫さうで何よりです。元さんや竹森さん手嶋さんもお変りなくいると推察して居ります。どうぞよろしく申上げて下さい。

では今日はこれで　さようなら

勝田

四月九日

妻へ

Umeno Tamura
65-11-17
Rivers, Arizona

Katsuchika Tamura
B.52 Detention Station
Santa Fe, New Mexico
April 14, 1944

四月八日附のおたよりをなつかしく拜見致しました。
お案じ下さったさうですが幸ひ至極元氣で風邪
一つ引かず暮して居りますからどうぞ安心して下さい。
そちらも一同丈夫で消光して居られる由この上も
無いよろこんで居ります　前便で申上まし
た通り其處へ歸へすと發表がありましたから
時間の問題で二ケ年餘待った希望が達せられ
る日が近づいた訳です。私にとってこんなところには
いるのはあきあきです。そちらへはまだ何の通知も
ありませんか。時によると通知があってから一ケ月
もかゝる人があります。センターの方が早くして
呉れると早いとか云ふ人もあります。出來たら
そちらでも早くして呉れる様たのんで居て下さい。
では萬事に氣を附けて愉快に逢ふ日を
待って下さい。

勝田

四月十四日
妻へ

Umeno Tamura
65-11-17
Rivers, Arizona

Katsuchika Tamura
52 Detention Station
Santa Fe, N.M.
April 19, 1944

お変りありませんか私は相変らず至極元氣で暮し
て居りますから御安心下さい。近頃は春の花曇とでも
云ふのでせうかよく曇って雨になるかと思ふと雪に変って
しまひます。尤もそれもあめゆき程度で大しては積り
ません。寒さも左程でありません。過ぎた日曜に
は今年はじめてのベースボールもありました。現
在の私は出発の日を一日も早かれとそれのみ祈って
居ります。二ケ年餘にもなるのですから飛んでも行
きたいような心持はよく御推察下さることと
思ひます。責任ある仕事もみな人にゆづって
ひたすら命令のある日を待って居ります。
何れにしてももう暫くと思ひますからそちらでも
皆々健康によく注意して心堅固に待
って下さい。では今日はこれでさよなら

勝周

四月十九日

梅乃殿

DETAINED ALIEN
ENEMY MAIL
EXAMINED
BY 25-3
U. S. I. & N. S.

Umeno Tamura の
65-11-17
Rivers, Arizona

Katsuhiko Tamura
P. 52 Detention Station
Santa Fe, N.M.
April 27, 1944

DETAINED ALIEN
ENEMY MAIL
EXAMINED
BY 25-4
U.S. I. & N.S.

至極元氣で暮して居りますから安心して下さい。一日千秋の思ひで待って居りますがまだ確定した發表はありません。私ばかりではありませんが待遠しいであります。どうして早く歸って呉れないのでせう。子供達は皆丈夫ですが夢にまで逢ることをみて少しも氣が落ち付かず心をこめての仕事はまるで氣がしません。[illegible]も近頃はよく風が吹くので思ふ様になく只一日でも早く歸って呉れたらとそれのみ祈って居ります。勝田では

今はこれで

四月二十七日

妻、

Umeno Tamura
65-11-A, Rivers, Arizona

Kakuchika Tamura
B.52. Detention Stn.
Santa Fe, N.M.
May 1, 19

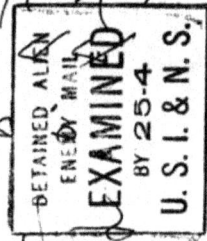

相変らず元氣で出發の通知を今日か明日と待って居ります。今はすでに五月にはいり当所に来て以来一ヶ年近くなりますなんと月日が早くたって行くことでせう。

皆々丈夫で暮して居られますか。こちらも気候が大分暖く成りましたがそちらはすでに暑い位でせうか。得られるかどうか解りませんがぜひ入用のものがありましたらつとめて見ますから知らして下さい。

其處の新聞も次から次へ送って下さいますから様子はよく解ります。

では今日はこれで皆さん達へよろしく
勝田

五月一日
梅乃殿

Kokushika Tamura
B.52 Detention Stn.
Santa Fe, N.M.
May 5, 1944

Umeno Tamura
65-11-17
Rivers, Arizona

DETAINED ALIEN
ENEMY MAIL
EXAMINED
BY 2.5.3
U. S. I. & N. S.

今朝は稀なよい天気で小高いところから
四方の眺めもとくに美しく健康で生ある
身をつくづく感謝せずには居られません
そちらでも一同恙無くお暮のこと
と確信して居ります。まだ出發の
日は發表されて居りませんが近いう
ちだと信じて居りますからどうぞ
しばらく忍耐して待って下さい
様おたのみします
では簡單ですが無事で居ります
お知らせまで
勝か周
五月五日
妻へ

TULE LAKE, CALIFORNIA

OCTOBER 1945–FEBRUARY 1946

Original letters in Japanese from Katsuchika to Umeno

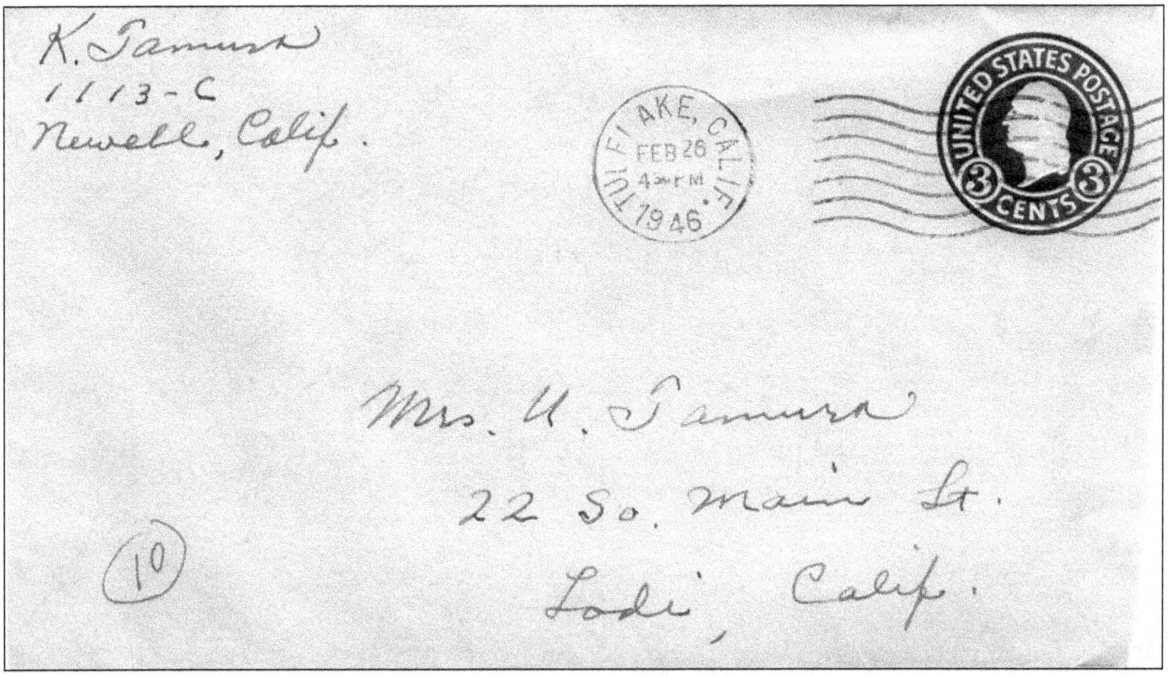

今日はすでに七日です其後天氣都合はよく寒い日はありません
でした。私の風邪もすっかりなほりました。
汽車の旅行はどうでしたか。いろく案じましたがあの翌日の朝は
そちらへ無事着かれたると安心しました。どんな様子ですか
随分忙しいのでせう。子供達はどうですか弘と修はどんな
です。二人が居るのでさうした所の生活も容易で無いでせう
何にしても氣を樂に持って最善を盡して下さい。
松雄さん夫妻にも手紙を出して置きましたが呉々もよろしく
申上げておいて下さい。
ブラックマネージャーの山本夫妻は五日朝出ました。其他
ほかには出た人はありません。隣りの藤井さんが昨夜結婚
して山本さんのバラックへ住むさうです。残った本田さんと云ふ
若い人も近く出るさうですから隣はがらあきになると思ひます
急に淋しくなって夜はひとしほきがめいります。本をよんだり
ラジオを聞いたりして十時頃まですごしてねます。
あの翌日三共エイエイをもらひに行きましたら「今日のの代り
にきのふ二つあげました」と云って呉れませんでした。こゝに
あるのは近日の内に送ります。荷物は全部着きま
したか。
私の事に就いてはまだ何と云ふ通知もありません。朝夕
出て行く人達もこの三日程バスのストライキか何かで日
延べになって居ます。山崎さんもまだ帰って来た
やうな様子はありません。
種々変化はするのでせうが弘の我儘を充分気をつけ
て下さい。
では今日はこれで。そちらの様子を知らして下さい。

勝田

梅乃殿

今は夜の九時過ぎですが隣りの若い人達が出たあとに誰れかが
移って来てトンカン音をたてたりにぎやかな話ごゑが聞えます
過りひっそりして居るよりよいかも知れませんがやかましすぎ
るのもよいものではありません
昨日はゴルフに行ってコンクリートの溝の中へボールを
落し取ろうとする汁足をすべらして水の中へおち
こみ腰から下はずぶぬれとなって帰って来ました。ひどい故
か気持が悪くなりましたが今日はよくなりました。どぶ
ねずみのやうにぬれてバッグをかたに一て帰って来
るすがたは過り見よいものではありませんでした。
今日から兵隊は引きあげて移民局の役人になり
ました。これで三日毎夕雷が鳴り雨が降りますが
朝は晴れて日中は暖かです あの後まだ朝も霜
がありませんのでスタックが少し咲き出しました。
ミセス光吉も数日の内にそちらへ行くさうです
睦子と弘のコートはクリーナーから来ましたが私の
ハットはまだ来ません もう四十日になります。食事
はメスへ行きますが鐘がよく聞きとれぬので困り
ます。三は学校へ通って居りますか。弘はどうです。

10/10/45

十月十日

梅乃殿

勝由

其後どう。忙しいのでせうね。妹さん一家は？
三日程夕立があってあったのに今朝はよく
晴れたので霧が深くかゝって桑港を想はせる様な朝です
私の方には別にこれと申して変ったことはありません。昨朝佐呆さん
が来て十五日の午後此處をたってコーダイへ行くと申して居り
ました。
先日サクラメントの佐藤さんに逢ったので種々話しましたが
私共のケースは時の問題で心配はない様申して居られました。
佐藤さんの話のみで無く私も種々の方面からうはさを総合して
見ますとさう思ひますから、ダクトン方面の人にたのむことはまだ
はじめてなかったらもう少し待ったらどうかとおもひます。もっと
早かったらそんなでもないのですがすでにすべてが終局した
のに今さら頼のむと事情を知らぬ人には変に思はれる
かも知れません。私としてはもう少し待ってどうしてもさうした
証明が無ければならぬ時によく事情を述べて頼んだ
方がよいやうに考へます。知っての通り水野さん住田さん等
早くから手続した人にもまだ一人とも通知がありません。
あなた方がそちらに居る以上一日も早く出たいと思ひますが
今の所どうすることも出来ませんからもう暫くがまんする
より仕方ないと思ひます。松雄さんも多忙でせうし今の所
すべてがはっきりして居りませんから話しても話しにく
いと存じます。
こうした事情ですからあなたもさう思ったらしばらく
すべてを見合せて居って下さい。

では

勝田

十月十二日

梅乃殿

10/12

土曜日、午後山崎さんがたづねて来られローダイや
コンチキャンプまで行きあなたにも逢ったと云って
頼まれた土産を持って来て呉れました。めずらしく
思ひ掛けないもので、その上大へんよろこばしいことでした。
宗さんの話ではよく解りませんがぶどうのシーズン中
はずいぶん忙しいのでせう。弘と修が居るまで骨の
折れる事と想像して居ります。今朝モセス光吉
が立ちました。其處へ行くのだと思ひます。御餞別
をあげて置きました。ほかにはまた家族の出た人はありません。
今日アンダーウェヤーも着きました。この秋はあれ一枚で充分
だと思ひます。何れもっと寒くなれば、いまある厚いのを
着ますから。まだ氣候はあの後づっと暖かです。今夜は
日が暮れてから雨が降り出しました。庭のスタックも青々
して二三は紫の花が咲き出しました。天氣さへよければ
半日はゴルフに行くので、書面は左程でありませんが夜は
淋しくて困ります。共ちゃん睦ちゃんはどうして居り
ますか。幸福さうですか。弘は丁度智恵のつく時で
いつも悪いことを学びますから充分氣を附けてやって下さい。
其後耳はどうですか。少しはよくなりましたか。身体を過ぐ無
理せぬ様して下さい。
当方でも一日も早く出られるやう出来るだけつとめて
居ります。宗さんの話では松雄さんが二三日内にフタネトンへ
行って下さるやうに言って居りましたが。私からも手紙で行く
まへにさうして戴いてあればそれで結構です。どんな
結果でしたらう。

おやすみ

勝田

十一月十五日

梅乃殿

晴れては居ましたが雲行が悪いと思った天候が遂に昼頃から雨になりました。何となくもの憂い日です。皆んな元気で晴れやかに暮して居るでせうか　それが何よりの願ひです。

既に新聞で御承知になったことと存じますが此処も他センター同様来年一月一日迄に閉鎖されることになりました。今でも毎日出る人がありますが今後ますます殖るでせう。

去る十九日正午頃、妻、シヤワーへ行く道でミセス、松本が驚いた顔付で「田村さんパロールになって居る人達に又インターンの命令が来ましたよ。辻さん片山さん入谷(?)さんなど皆んな受取ったさうです。あなたには来ませんか」との言葉でやれやれまた面どうなるとブラックマネージャーの所へ行って見たらば、はたして私にも来て居りました。只簡単にパロールを取消してインターンにすると云ふ丈だけで此処に出張して居る移民局の名で来ました。よく問合せて見ますと名目が違ったと云ふだけで今迄と同じでいま直ぐ他に移すと云ふのではないやうです。知っての通りWRAに預けると云ふのでパロールにしたのですからWRAの解散が明らかになった以上こうして置かぬと都合悪いのだと思ひます。何れにしてもこうはっきりきまれば私も出来る丈早く運動して早く出たいと思ひます。吉見さんのでも奏(?)えのでも手に入らないと私の方から出す願書も出来ません。メス、オペレーションの方へ頼んで置いた証明書も呉れましたがよく働いたと書いてあって役に立ちさうありません。困ったものです。　こうしたる情(?)ですから

思った程容易で無く時日を要するかも知れませんが
最善を盡したらどうにかなると信じます。
ブラック８のワーデンをして居た楠見さん（田中の
おじいさんと一緒に居る人）が近く出るので ワーデンをやらぬ
かとすゝめられましたから明日からやる事にしました。
堀之の仕事をもらう話もあったのですが堀之はまだ何時
出るかはっきりしませんし御承知の通り仕事が無いと
又メス、働く様今度はいやでも引込まれますから
ワーデンでもして居ったらかってよくはないかと思ってです
あなた方が去ってから今日迄三週間程割合に天氣が
よかったのでゴルフばよく遊びました。而しこれから雨が
降ったり雪や寒さで遠り、戸外へは出られなくなるだろう
と思ひます。碁の相手でももう少しあるかと思ひましたが
皆それぞれ思ひ思ひの仕事や遊びがあるので一向誰れ
も来ません 山崎さんも落付かぬ様です。無理のない事
です。では今日はこれで

勝田

十月廿一日　日曜日

梅乃殿

手一っぱいだと云って居られます。等(ヒトシ)さんが来春ハイスクール
を卒業するさうで其後でなければこちらへ来るかどうかはっきら
しないさうで何れにしても来年の七八月頃迄はシカゴに居る
るにきめて居るさうです。織本さん夫婦さんはやはりシーブック
に働いて居るさうで マーイさんはめがねのドクターにちゃん
きまりです。近田さんはシカゴのWRAに働いて居るさうです。
子供達は皆元気で幸福に暮して居りますか 弘はけんか
はしませんか。
松男さん 妹さん、呉々もよろしく

では

勝田

十月二十四日

梅乃殿

皆アモンヅを受取りました。からのまゝコーストしたのは始めてゞすが、そう味のよいものでたのしみにして居ります。

別に変ったこともありませんが時の問題で皆出るやうになると申して居ります

ガーデンの仕事は月曜から居ります 午後の四時から十二時迄と云ふのですが別に仕事はありません。一週間五日働いて二日休みです 私のは土曜日曜が休みです。五日の内一日位エキストラの仕事があります 日中勤務の人は小学校の前に立って小供の帰る時自動車を注意したりするのですが夜の番の者はハイスクールである活動夜などにネッテに行くのです 昨夜は早速私の番に当って知っての通りの大黒帽をかぶって立番に行きました。影画は日本物で「ぼっちゃん」と云ふ題でした。自分では中々行かないのですが役目で行って見て来ました。ジムの中でも帽をかぶって居るので知った人に逢ふとてれくさい気がします。遇らよくにやるので誰れかと思ひましたなどと布哇連中から冷かされました。

近頃はキャンテーンに煙草が多く来て何んでも買へます シガレットでも澤山来て居るので箱で買へます もう煙草に不自由する事はないと思ひますが キャンテーンが閉るとなると随分不便だと思はれます。私の帽子はまだ来ません。閉る店には来るでせうと云って居ります。今の所何一つ入用のものはありません

今日竹森さんから手紙が来ました。相変らず同じ仕事を夫婦でやって居るさうです。物價が高いので月三百五十弗で

三週間位より天気が續くと又暫く気候が悪くなるのが此処の
天気模様だと思はれます。あらしがあって後四五日前迄朝
は霜がありましたが日中は暖くよい日和が續きましたが雲は低く
風は吹き時々雨があるのが今日この頃です
まだ働く人が多いのですが子供の世話や食事の手つだいやら忙しいで
せうね どうぞ無理せず身体を充分注意して下さい。
其後耳の工合はどうですか。
松本さんは早く出たからよいのでせうけれど佐々木さんは後れ
たので駄目でした 今からは一時出所は六ヶ敷いので何れ其後
佐々木さんも出切に出るのでせう
山崎の宗さんは今朝自分丈たって行きました。焼け
た後に出来た家が少さいさうで先へ行って家をたて増して
家族を呼ぶのださうです。 朝の四時半に出たので私は見
送に行きませんでした
隣の田辺さんは手術のためまた病院へ行きました。吉川
ドクターも先日手術を受けられたさうです。 あのブラク
には其後出た人はありません。あなたが居ると せんたく
ばやシャワーで色々話を聞いてきてくれたのですがこの節は
他のひとの様子は全然解りません
今日五十四の中野さんが来ました ミセスを先へ出すと
話して居られました。 私もこの頃はあなたがたが早く
出たのでほんとうによいことをしたと思って居ます。
では今日はこれで

勝田

十月二十九日

梅乃殿

難波さんにことづけられた手紙をたしかに受取りました。
現在の所私に関しては先日発表になった方針書を送った通りで何時頃か確定はして居りませんが何れ「ヒヤリング」があると存じます。申上げた通り十中八九点はよいと思ひます。出来る丈のことはして置いた方がよいと思ひます。

別紙の人々は個人的の交際と云ふよりは公共のことで知あったのですから、どの美点証明して呉れるか知りませんが、出来れば身分証明（Chracter witness）と云ふものが欲しいのです。若しそれが不可能の場合は、公共の事業（Community activities – officcal or unofficial, such as Community Chest, Red Cross, USO etc）どの位私がスタクトンの人々と協力（cooperated）して尽したかの事実を証明してもらへばよいのです。

綾雄さんとか其他の市民権あって[illegible]した様な人に証明してもらうのもよいと思ひます。

あなたからも一應願書を Ennis 宛出して置いた方がよいでせう。

十月三十一日

勝田

梅乃殿

去る三十日布哇行の家族の人達が三百二十人程たちました。この次は第二回日本行ですが予定の七日が延びて来る十六日に船が出ることになって居ます この度は五千人から乗船出来ると云ふので当所からも随分行くだらうと思ひます。中津井さん吉田庄九郎さんなども仕度して居ます。辻さんも行き度いらしいですが ミセスが赤ちゃんが出来て居るらしいので 病室のある船でないと乗せないとか云って この次にすると云って居られます。段々閉鎖期に近づくので 出る人日本行の人などで何処へ行っても荷造に忙しいのです。 私共にはまだ音沙汰ありません 先日の話ではじきと申して居りましたが 又何時の事か一向解らなくなりました。このふうではクリスマスやお正月に出られるかすらも疑はれます。
×人も人がないので一部分はヴランテヤーでやって居ります 私も其内にヘルプに行かねばならぬと思ひます。いづれにしても後に残ると何かとうるさいるです。キャンティーンも十月末日で閉めましたが 今度は個人経営で日用品を売ることになって居りますから其方は不便ありません。
其処は近頃いくらか人がへったのですか。まだ多数の人にお飯を喰べさすのでしたら中々容易でないでせう。種々不便ですか。修は丈夫で育って行きますか。もう S M A も無くなったでせうね。子供達も元気ですね では呉々も健康に注意して下さい。

勝田

十月三日

梅乃殿

其後皆元氣で暮して居りますか。岡崎さん方もお變り無いですかよろしく申上げて下さい。少しはひまになりましたか。

廣いやうで狹いのが世間だと云ひますが此處でも知あいの人でむしろ遠い所に居って知らぬと思った人があちら方の出たるを皆知って居るのには驚きました。有馬さんや藤田さんは私近出たやうに聞いたと云って居られました。若い人達

昨日午後中津井さんのミセスが一寸見えました。若い人達の関係上帰国を願ったのださうですが自費で帰りたいがと相談に来られたのです。家族のある人達は荷物やお金に制限があると云ふので心配して居るのです。どの位の程度持って行けるかまだ發表して居りませんが何れにしてもこれらの人々は心配すだと思ひます。深江木さんもさうした関係上一たんスタクトンへ帰ると申して居られます。

畑中さん方は二日の午後あちら方と同じ時間の汽車でロスアンゼルスへ帰りました。ミセス福永は今日午後出ます。福永さんの息子方は多分日本行でせう。ミセスだけこちらへ残るさうです。お氣の毒ですがこのさいやむを得ぬのでせう。

土曜日は快晴でしたが今日は朝から雨です前々から心掛けて居てまだはたしてないので今日は村野さんや吉田さんをおたづねしたいと思って居ります。

ではけふはこれで身体を大切にして下さい。

勝田

十二月五日

梅乃殿

ミスター スペンスの書いて呉れた証明書を受取りました。大層よく書いて呉れたので非常によいと思ひます。氏のしんせつを深く感謝して居ります。松男さんの活字打にもよく御礼を申上げておいて下さい。

早速昨朝 WRAのローヤーの所へ行き約束の願書を書いてもらおうとしましたらローヤーの言ふには先日ヒヤリングを申込んだのだから今からワシントンへ送ってもヒヤリングの節提出した方がよいだらうとの事でローヤーの意見に従ひました。尚あれ一つにたよらないで出来たら他の人のももらっておいた方がよいと存じます。あちらの方からもミスター氏宛事情をうったへて手紙を出しておいたらよいと考へます。

今日で雪空が一週間も續いて居ります。降續く訳でも無いのですが地上のがとけぬうちに後から降るので今朝は三寸位積って居りました。周囲の山々も真白です。昨朝九時に堀さんがユタへ行きました。校村さん達は後に残って居ります。

先日書くのを忘れましたが竹森さんの手紙に手嶋の治美(じき)さんは大平洋方面に出征して居るのださうです。手嶋さんの御夫妻も治美さんの早く帰って来るのを願って居るさうです。

昨日サクラメントの佐藤さん来られ今日は一共に有馬さん(桑港)の所へ遊びに行くことにして居ります。

子供達はの?。弘はいたづらはおちって居りませんか。ベビーも元気ですね。

勝周

では御機嫌よう

十月十日朝

梅乃殿

一同元氣ですか。岡崎さん所一家もお變りありませんね。相變らずの天氣です御承知の様に大しても積りませんが雪が降ったり止んだりして風は南か北が常に吹いて居ります。私共に関してはまだ何の話もありません。布哇の家族持と獨身者が近い内出發します。布哇の人々は布哇、獨身の人々は日本行です。このブラックからは井原さんと白井さんで日本行は安井さん田中おじいさん(かまぼこ)を貰て3人)福永さんの三人兄弟等です。まだ久恒さんへ行きませんがあの方も大ぶ行くのでせう。備田さんや水野さんもまだ何の通知もありません何れ一共にするのでせう。
昨日廣美さんが見られて睦ちゃんが君枝さんへキャンディを送ったと云って礼を云って居られました。寒いので過り外へ出られませんから本を讀んだり碁をうったりして居ます尤も碁の方はよい相手が無いので原内さと時々さします。
先日送ったSMAと其他は受取ったのでせう。昨日キャンディを少し送って置きました。そちらにいくらでもあるでせうが子供には送ってもらふとまた別な味がするでせう。
今年は風邪は引き度く無いと気を注意して居りますからそれだけは安心して下さい。あちた方も気を注意して下さい。では

勝田

十二月十八日朝

梅乃殿

春日附の手紙を受取りました。萬事都合よく運んで何よりと存じます。松男さんへも呉々もよろしくお礼を申上げてをいて下さい。

まだ正式には發表しませんが可成確實に私共も近い内に自由になる由でよろこんで居ります。或はヒヤリングも無しですむのでは無いかと思ひます。多分クリスマス前には歸れると存じます。

子供の世話、其ん處が忙しい事の上に種々奔走するは最初であったろうと思ひますが出來る丈けする事をして置いたので安心です。

中野さんの家族もすでにロスアンゼルスへ歸られたさうです。中野さんの云はれるには六校、教材資金として借した二千は其後寄附にしてしまったさうです。キャンテンも後十日程で閉めるので商品を原價の三分の一位で賣って居りますがさてこれと云って必要な品もあまりないので買ひません。割戻金も四、五、六は記目は呉れて居りますが構らへぬのですぐ後は會費位が返って來る位だと思ひます

では正式に發表がありましたらまたすぐ知らせますが今日はこれで

十月二十日

勝男

梅乃殿

其後元氣で暮して居りますか　典ちゃんと睦ちゃんは學校や
友達で幸福ちやうに思はれますが弘と修はどうです。修は大きく
なったでせうね。今でもおとなしいベビーですか。
毎日不愉快な風が吹いてあきあきします。むしろ雪でも
降って静かにしてくれゝばよいと願って居ます。時に去年
はありませんでしたが今年は感謝祭にターキーが来ました
二〇〆、だけで十四五来たさうで皆に多さんあり
ました。二十三日の早朝は第二便の日本行の人達を送
り出しました。当所からは四百何人位で今朝のラジオ
の放送ではすでにシャトルから出ぱんした由です。其後
松野さん夫婦がスースンへ行きました。息子さん丈
一人残って居ります。エセ又、福永も一旦オークランド
へ出たのですが息子三人が日本へ行くので詰向として
来て居られます。娘さんを一共にオークランドへ連れ
て行き度いのださうですが今の處まだそれが出来ない
さうです。松本さんも歸って来て家族を連れてまた出まし
た。昨日村野さん、見舞に行きました。大分よくなっ
たさうですが病氣であった故か年を取ったのには驚き
ました。山崎さん、も行きました　エセ又は出る人を
送って行ったと家に居りませんでした。また宗さんが迎に来る
運びにはなって居ないやうでした。
私達に関してはまだ何んの發表もありません。布哇行があった
り第二便の日本行があったりまた忙しいのでせう。
身体を大切にして下さい。

十一月二十五日

勝田

梅乃殿

12/6/45

今日は朝から少し雲切れがして太陽が時々出ますが風は相変らず吹いて居て戸外には必要以外出られません。来る十六日に出る日本行の人達の荷物が毎日高校の講堂に運ばれて検査されて居ます。検査は別に六ヶ敷いやうではありませんが全部出した品物をまた入れなほすので容易で無いやうです。木の箱は重いからと云ふので大分大きな袋にして居ます 清野さんや小川さん等は随分困るでせう。

藤村先生がシカゴから「法輪」と云ふ今度創刊した新聞を送って呉れました。中西部仏教会の附属開教師となられたさうです。多分そちらでは日本新聞を読むので外部のことは私より詳しいかも知れません。何れにしても先生があちらで活動して居られることはよろこばしいことです。

黒い靴の裏が大分悪くなったので キャンプ内の修繕所のあとに個人經営でやって居る人の所へ持って行きましたら三弗五十仙位かゝると申しました。あれも過ぎよい靴では無し そんなにかゝるのならむしろ新しいのを買った方がよかったと思ひました。個人經営なので相当もうけるのかも知れません。

佐々木吾助さんから手紙が来ました。今ソロリンに居るらしいです。移民局に保証人を立てるので随分あちこち運動したらしいです。今はあの規則が無くなったのでもうあの運動はありません。

深三木さんも荷造りをすったらしいので数日内に出所するのではないかと思ひます。土井さんは今日午後サクラメント方面に行くらしいです では次まで

勝田

十二月六日

梅乃殿

12/10/45

元氣で暮して居ますか。子供達はとうです。
私はおかげで恙ありません。
先週は一夜病院の番人に送られました。若いミセスで
氣が狂ったとかで自分の子供を殺したのです。まだ一人十ヶ
月と云ふ可愛い女の子が幸ひ大したけがもちく助かって
居るので同情にたへませんでした。不安定なので過り
心配した結果だと思はれ無理の無いすると考へられます。
この度の日本行もはじめの五千人とかがまた千五百人位
にへらされたので大分次の船を待たねばならぬ人が出
来ました。清野さんや小川さんのやうに店主人が
あちらに居る人もこの便では行けぬさうです。荷物は
出して高校の講堂に入れてあるのでまたよう分けるの
で大仕事だと思ひます。
昨日は私の休日だったのでメス、ヘヴランチヤーとして働き
ました鍋や金を洗はされました。午後は一時頃から
四時頃まで休みましたから左程えらくはありませんで
した。
今朝は昨夜中降った雪が五寸位積って居ましたが
幸ひ風も無く温度は割合暖かです。
其内に勝さんの所へ手紙を書き度いと思ひますから
住所をわかって居ったら知らして下さい。
では今日はこれで次便まで

十二月十日
勝用

梅乃殿

12/13/45

寒い位で別に変ったるはありません。
深木さん御夫婦が昨日午後スタクトンへ向けて出まし
た。マンロウストリートに在る元の教會へ一時落付くのだそう
です。中尾さん（アリスのママさん）へベビーが生れました。
クリスマス迄には帰れると予期して楽しみにして居りま
したが未だに確たる通知が無いのではっきりしたるすは
解らなくなりました。御存知の様に此處では全然
クリスマスプレゼントは得られませんから御金を同封
して二十弗送りますからこれであなたと共ちゃん
睦ちゃん弘、修五人と岡崎さんの子供達三人へ
適当なプレゼントを求めて私からとして贈るやうに
して置いて下さい。
私の方は今の處何にもいりません。朝だけは家へ
もらって来て自分でコーヒーをわかしてのみます。
シュガーが少ないじゃーにほとんど一ぱいになって居ます。
近頃になってグレープフルーツをよく呉れます。晝と
夕はメスへ行って喰べます。メスの働く人も大分
少くなりましたがジランチャーや何かでどうやら前と
変り無くやって行きます。個人經営のキャンテーンで
新聞雑誌やブレッド、フルーツ、ピーナツバター等
賣って居りますから不便はありません。修に野菜
や卵を喰べさして居ますか。
では今日はこれでお金を受取ったら一寸知らして置いて
下さい。

十二月十三日
勝田
梅乃殿

12/15/45

松男さんが来られるとは全く予期しなかったので驚きました。
丁度土曜日・朝で仕事が休みでしたから メスに手つだいに行って居たので最初来て下さった時は家に居りませんでした。十時頃一寸帰りましたら隣の田辺さんがローダイから来た方がこれを置いて行ったと紙包を呉れました。ブラック二九に夕方迄居るからと言傳はありましたが誰れとも名を聞いて居いて呉れなかったのでどちらかといぶかりましたが兎に角二九へ行って見やうと丁度雪降の眞最中でしたがおたずねして見た所 またあいにく誰れも居られませんでした。表にナアエのカーがあったので或は松男さんではないかと思ひましたが近所に居られる様子もなかったので残念乍ら帰らねばなりませんでした。
午後晝食後じき松男さんの方から来て下さって一時間ばかり話し何かとうかがって大層安心しました。
クリスマスのプレゼントはここにそれ迄居るやうでしたら開くまいとカレンダーの上にかざって居ります。二パウンドのバタは松男さんが下さったのと存じ今朝早速食べましたがさすがほんものはおいしゆう御座いました。大きなストライプバスも下さいましたから片身だけ私が食べて片身は有馬さんへあげました所 非常によろこばれてあげた甲斐があったと思って居ります。よいホイスキーを大ふよばれました。
有馬さんも日本へ帰られると一寸パンも食べられませんしこの魚は買ふと云ふて手に入らないのでよろこばれるのも無理ないです。御飯もメスのではこんなおいしいお魚と一共に喰べるのにもったいないと わざく家でたいて居られました。
私は夕方御飯だけもらって来ておさしみにしてたべました。今夕もまだあります。丁度この十日程雪がとけぬ上、上へと降るので随分積って居ります。魚も雪でパックして置くので幾日でももっと思ひます。
私の方に關しては松田さんに話して居いた通りでまたはっきりした通知はありませんがこの週間には何とかきまるだらうと信じて居ります。
國籍離脱者もヒヤリングがあって出られるやうになるやうです。
難波さんがローダイへ行くと云はれるのでこの手紙をお願します。では次便迄）

勝田

十二月十五日

梅乃殿

昨日小包を受取りました。開けてプレゼントが一ぱい
あったので驚きました。こんなに澤山もらうとは全
然予期して居りませんでしたから。誠によろこば
しく幸福です。松田さんの持って来たのと共で十一
あります。全部カウンターの上にならべてクリスマス
の朝を樂しみに待って居ます。いち〱ふって見た
ので中によいものがあるのも想像しましたが今開い
ては話に外れたやうな氣がするので当日迄は手を
つけぬ事にしました。

松田さんの来た朝大分雪が降り其後寒いのと
次々に降るので道は白いコンクリートでひいた様
になって居ます。昨朝は一番寒く鉄柵も眞白ち、
スクリーンのやうにちり電線は白い糸でぱったやう
でした。去年こんなでしたら子供達がさぞよろこ
んだでせうに。

和英の其他なんの音沙汰もありません。水野
さん住田さん達も同じです。この分ではどうしても
来春になるでせう。

忙しいだらうとはよく想像して居りました。せめて
心配せず氣だけでも樂に持ってもう暫くがまん
して下さい。子供達が幸福であるので何よりです。
此處も来る二十八日の船で五十人から歸るので其人達
がたつ迄はごた〱します。

では又

十二月二十日

勝岡

梅乃殿

クリスマスを楽しく迎へられたる事と推察します
私も一人で送ってもらったプレゼントを開き皆の心盡しを
嬉しく感謝しました。おいしいものが澤山で楽しみにして居
ます。

過日書留で現金を送りましたが受取りましたか。私の
写真と同時に送ったですから受取られたる事と存じますが
十七日附のあなたの手紙には写真を受取ったとはあり
ましたが書留のことが無いのでどうしたるかと案じて居
ります。

帰国される一部の人達が昨日出発しました。残りは明日
此處をたちます。明日の中には中津井さんと吉田さんが
行きます。このブラックからは田中さん小川さん清野さ
ん達です。こゝもいよく淋しくなります。

竹森さんへはお礼状を出して置きます。

クリスタルの山岸さんから来た手紙に依るとヒヤリング
はすんださうですがまだ其結果は解らぬさうです
又今此處も来春早々始めるのだとは思ひますが
まだ確たる日附は発表して居りません。

身体も丈夫ですし何の不平もありませんが天氣工合
が悪いので一日室内にとじこめられて居るのでたいくつです。

この手紙を受取次第典ちゃんにでもリーダース ダイゼスト
(Reader's Digest - January, 1946) 一月
分を買って送って下さい。

では今日はこれで

勝田

十二月二十六日

梅乃殿

今日でとうとう本年も最終の日となりました皆もすこやかで新らしい年を迎へるをよろこびにたへません
私も相変らず元気です。
お金も受取れた由で安心しました。
過日の手紙でお願ひした リーダース、ダイゼストと
申す誌雑はユーのキャンテーンで買ひましたから
まだ送って居らなかったらいりません。手数だ
とは思ひましたがユーの賣店はあてにならぬので
お願ひしたのです。
日本行が出たあと随分淋しくなりました。メス
も半数位は閉鎖されました。
クリスマス後割合に暖かくゴルフにも時々
行けます。昨年も今頃はよい日和が四五日
あったとおぼえて居ます。
萱(かや)さんから年賀状が来ました。グレンデール
アリゾナとしてありました。私からも出して置きまし
た。
では今日はこれで

A Happy New Year

勝田

十二月卅一日

梅乃殿

元氣で新しい年を迎へたることを感謝して居ります
天氣都合も申分無く終日ゴルフを遊びました。
此度は三十日に全部料理して渡してあったのでお互に便利でした。ブラックにあったお金でターキーを買ひ、杉村さんが錆ずしを作りあんぱんもあって御馳走が澤山ありました。
来る四日から私共のメスは閉鎖され八区は十一区に七区は十二区の食堂に行くことになりました。私は端から端迄行かねばなりません。
一昨々日三十日の午後四時半頃高校の講堂から火が出て二時間ばかりにあの大きな講堂全部焼落ちてしまひました。幸ひ風が無かったので講堂だけでくひとめて附属の建物は助かりました。原因は種々うはさしますがこの新聞が出ないと当局で何んときめて居るか解りません。今迄当所は火災が無かったのですがとうとうしまひに大火ですであのよい建物をおしいことでした。
当所も大分淋しくなりましたがまだ七千位は居るさうです。自由の人はどうしても今月中には出ねばならぬのでこれから毎日出所の人で忙しくなると思ひます。私達の中でもある人にはぼつぼつ出所自由の通知が来るらしいですからもう間も無いことと思ひます。勿論今月中に全部片附かねばRAは手を引いても司法省がしばらくは經營して行くのかも知れません。待遠しいことですが時の来るのを待つより仕方ありません。
ではお機嫌やう

一月二日朝

勝甲

梅乃殿

其後皆元氣ですか？、ベビーは？——よく雨が降る
さうですね。 私は相變らず恙ありません
昨夜から悪い風が吹きまた特に寒いので室にかゝりきり
です 十二月一ぱいでガーデンの仕事はやめさせられまし
た。人が少くなつたので必要無くなつたのです。遊ん
で居るより何か仕事すると思ひますが働人を求めて居
る所は皆えらい仕事の所ばかりです。それに私の方
も近所ではちいかと思ふのでどちらにしてよいか解
りません。 もう十人位の人達には通知が来ました
住田さんへも五日に出所してよいと云ふ通知があつた
さうです。 私のはあの方達より大ぶ後れて手續
したのですから少し後れるのでせう。
天氣工合が悪いと遊んで居るのも樂ではありません
土曜日の夕刻寺川ドクターが病院で死去せられ
ました 実に同情にたへません
藤村先生から新年の手紙を同封して置きます
では今日はこれで
どうぞからだをきを附けて下さい。

勝田

一月七日

梅乃殿

まだ待って居ます。私には何の音沙汰もありません
佳田さんは昨日サクラメントへ歸りました。離脱者
のヒヤリングは始まって居ます隣りの原田さんはすぐ
にすみました。結果はまだ解りません。昨日サクラメント
の佐藤さんが来られましたが一世の人のヒヤリングは二十日
過ぎになるさうです。私のはヒヤリングを受ける手順
になって居りませんから無しに出られるのだらうと思ひ
ますが中々ゆっくりです。私と同じ事情の人
でもまだ来ない人もありますから案ずるには及ばぬ
と思ひますが待遠しいのは待遠しいと思ひます。
誕生日の祝を有難く受けました。此日におぼえて居てもらった
と思ふとなによりもの嬉びでした。昨年はあなたの誕生日
にはあした時で祝ふ事も出来ず今年は一共に祝ひ
度いと思ひます。
ブラックに人が少ないので寺川さんのお葬式は手だい
させられました。時節柄会葬者は割合少なかった
けれどクリスチャン式で嚴に行はれました。私が司會
したのです。家族の方々は明日午後ロスアンゼルスへ歸
ります。未亡人の御両親があちらに居られるさうです。
まだセロリのパッキングに行く人達があるのですが
冬でも働く人が居るとすると食事の世話が中々
たいへんなのでせうね。典ちゃん睦ちゃんの手紙では
子供達はたいそう樂しさうで何よりです
では今日はこれで

一月十二日

梅乃殿

勝田

一月二十八日附の手紙を拝見して種々心痛して居られ私も前々から
お察し日夜案じて居りますがどうする事も出来ぬ状態
です。十二月廿日迄は誰れもアリーにちっともわからなかったのでお互に
あきらめもありましたが前便で申上ました通り十二月二十九日
土曜日に少し通知があり一週間後一月五日土曜日に住田さん
や戸嶋さんに通知があったので少し宛来る事と予期して居
りました所其後三週間ちゃんの音沙汰もありません。井山さん
の様にワシントンへ問合せれば今考慮中だから何れ行く
通知を待てと申して来るだけです。私も始めは心棒して待
って気分でしたが近頃は悲しみも通り過ぎて馬鹿々々しさを感
じます。

あなた方の早く出たるは随分容易ならぬ苦労でしたら
うが全般から見てかえってよかった様に思って居ります。
先日中頃迄には自由の人は良人がインターニーでもリナオンレーで
も全部出されました。佐藤さん 浜田さん等の夫人も皆出ました
このブラックでは瀧口さんが自由で ミセス リナオンレーです
から瀧口さんだけ男の子一人連れて早く出て居られます。
こうした関係であなた方の出た後は常にさびしくして日本行
の人達もあり子供達にもあなたにも決して心よい所で無く
私も幾度かまあ あなた方がそちらに落付いて居るので
それだけは安心だと心の奴で繰返へしたるがあります。
私のケースにしましても結局あなたが先に出てスタクトン方面
に骨を折ったのが効果を示して居るのだと存じます。先日申上
げた通り一世の人の ヒヤリングボードは一月二十二日に始めて二十六日
には帰ってしまひました。私外数人にはヒヤリングはありませんでした
それは結局ミセス フォードや ミセス ブラウンの手紙が効を
奏して居るのでは無いかと想像します。あれをして居らなかった

ら私にもきっとヒヤリングがあった譯です。勿論ヒヤリングをした
人でも皆止まることが出来るとは考へますが結果が知れる迄なんだ
か心配せねばなりません。中野さんや水野さんのミセス達に来た
手紙とあなた宛の手紙には相違がありますからそれだけ
よいと見なければなりません。こうしたるもあなたが早く出
て運動したからでそうで無かったら中々めんどうであったと
信じて居ります。知っての通りあの人達も非常にこんな意と
云ふ譯でないのですからあなたでも行って親しく逢って居らなかった
ら手紙を書いて呉れるのもむずかしいのであったらうと思
って居ります。

お互に種々つらいこともありますがせめて子供二人でも幸福で
あったらせめてものなぐさめです。一日千秋の思ひは私も同
じですが何と思ってもどうすることも出来ぬ状態です。どうぞ
心静かにもうしばらく待って下さい。それが私の切な希ひ
です。

では今日はこれで次便迄

さよなら

勝田

二月一日

梅乃殿

お機嫌よくお暮しのことを心から祈って居ります
子供の世話や又私のことを案じて種々心配し心を労さぬ
でせうが、我々の力でどうすることも出来ぬことですから出来る
丈晴れやかに日々を送られるやう望んで居ります
私は相変らず元気で居りますから其点は安心して下さい
WRAの居る女に荷物は出すやう話があったので昨日
終日かかって荷造りしました三箱あります。一箱はまだ
使へると思った瀬戸物類とブランケット本等をつめ。次のは私の
トランクを木の箱に入れ、フレイトで送ることにし もう一箱は
ゴルフクラブと大工道具類を入れました。まだ取りに来ませんが
数日の内には出して呉れると思ひます。一ヶ月もかかるのでしたら
まだ先の話しですがもし私が帰るより先きに着きましたら
受取って置いて下さい。

今週中にはブロック十一、移らねばなりません。人数が少く
なったので便宜上中央のブロックに移されるのです。今頃になって
本当にめんどうなるのですがどうすることも出来ません。幸荷
造りだけすんだのでベットと身のまはりのものを移せばよいので
す。

日本行の船がまた二十日に出るさうです。辻さんもこの船で行く
やう予期して居ったのですが二三日前にベビーが生れたのでまた
乗船出来ぬさうで気の毒なことです

暖かい日もありましたが寒い日は去年より寒さが極しいやう
思はれ雪が数日続きまだ冬の真中のやうな気がします

では次便まで さようなら

勝田

二月十一日

梅乃殿

お変りありませんか。私は相変らず元気です
まだ正式には何の発表もありませんがこの度は私共のケースは三月初め
全部片附くさうですから其頃迄にはきっと帰れます　誰れにも何故
か想像のつかぬ理由でこんなに後れ随分色々苦労があり人知れ
ずなやまれたるとお察しいますが承知の如く私達にはどうと
るすべもなく明日が明日と半年近くもたってしまひました
話に依れば帰国者や離脱者の処理にせわしく当センターのインターニー
のケースは先月二十日当所でヒヤリングがあった頃から手をつけたの
ださうです　WRAを来月十五日迄には住民を全部外部へ
出すことに決定しましたからこの度はそれ以上後れる事はあり
ません。離脱者の内で送還知らせを受けて居る者は男は
サンタフェに家族並びに女子はクリスタルシティー、近々行くことにな
って居ります。
十七日の日曜日に八区から十区へ移転しました。空屋にちった後
ストーブを取はずしてしまったので自分達で運んで附けたので大事
でした。たとへ一二週間ねるにしてもまるでねずみの巣のやう
な所にはねられないので掃除したり何かで二日位はそればかりに
掛ってしまひました。引越も自動車でするので自分のだけし
よいのでは無く皆んなでヘルプしあったのでストーブを附けたり荷
物を運ぶ丈で終日かゝりました。
2/21/46
去年から度々つめてもらってだめであった歯がいよいよかけて
しまったので痛みはしませんでしたがぬいてもらいました。
其後あなたの手はどうですか。

二月十九日附の手紙を受取りました。皆元気で暮して居る由この上も
無いです。
今日ユタの堀さんから手紙をもらひました。堀さんは先〻加州へ行った時其
處へ寄ったさうですね。杉村さんの大きい男の子と娘さんがまだ此處に
居るので心配して居るやうです。
荷物が着いたさうですね。サクラメント ロダイ方面は個人で契約を運搬
して居るので早かったかと思ひます。先〻一台トラックが顚覆したさうで
大部そんをした人があるさうです。
横井さんの若夫婦も自由になりました。
私達にはまだ何とも申して来ません實に困ったものです
徳男さんの御夫妻へはよろしく申上げて置いて下さい。
風さへ吹かなければ此處にも春らしい日が時々あるやうになり
ました。
辻さん一男の子が生れました。そのため先〻の船に乗る事が
出来ず一時クリスタルシテーへ行くのださうです
相変らず毎〻働きには行って居ります。水野さんも先〻迄病院
のボイラー焚きに行って居りましたが今はボイラー焚きだけ全部
白人になりました。
予定より長引いたのでWRAも食糧の買込に困難なのかあの頃
より食物は悪くなりました而しめずらしく今頃になってターキー
がよく来ます
では今日はこれで健康に充分注意して下さい
二月二十五日
勝由
梅乃殿

⑩ 2/25/46